Cases on Information Systems Service Management

Rahul K. Patel
Illinois Institute of Technology, Chicago, USA

IGI Global
Scientific Publishing
Publishing Tomorrow's Research Today

Vice President of Editorial Melissa Wagner
Director of Acquisitions Mikaela Felty
Director of Book Development Jocelynn Hessler
Production Manager Mike Brehm
Cover Design Jose Rosado

Published in the United States of America by
IGI Global Scientific Publishing
701 East Chocolate Avenue
Hershey, PA, 17033, USA
Tel: 717-533-8845
Fax: 717-533-7115
Website: https://www.igi-global.com E-mail: cust@igi-global.com

Library of Congress Cataloging-in-Publication Data

LCCN: 2025009707 (CIP Data Pending)
ISBN13: 9798337323527
Isbn13Softcover: 9798337323534
EISBN13: 9798337323541

British Cataloguing in Publication Data
A Cataloguing in Publication record for this book is available from the British Library.

Table of Contents

Detailed Table of Contents

preventive measures. This part stresses investing in R&D, collaborating, complying, and ensuring decision-making is informed by data running through the supply chain.

Information security has become a cornerstone of modern IT service management, driven by the increasing reliance on digital infrastructure and the ever-evolving landscape of cyber threats. IT security is essential to protect sensitive data, ensure operational continuity, and build trust among stakeholders. As organizations adopt complex IT environments, the need for a systematic approach to managing information security within IT services has never been greater. IT Service Information Security Management outlines strategies for safeguarding the confidentiality, integrity, and availability of IT services while aligning with organizational goals and compliance requirements. Key topics include implementing proactive security measures, conducting risk assessments, managing vulnerabilities, and orchestrating incident response processes. Many case studies and examples are included to provide practical insights into overcoming challenges and adopting best practices in IT service information security management.

Software projects are one of the most critical elements that determine the success of businesses in today's technological world. However, the management of these projects is quite complex and includes many uncertainties. Along with uncertainties and complexities, effective management of risks and accurate cost estimation are necessary for the successful completion of projects. Therefore, risk management and cost calculation are among the basic elements of strategic decision-making processes in software projects. In this study, the types of risks encountered in software projects, risk management strategies and cost calculation methods are discussed. In this study, considering all these situations, the relationship between risk management and cost calculation processes is examined and various suggestions are presented for the effective implementation of these processes. The purpose of this study is to emphasize the importance of risk and cost management processes in software projects and to reveal the role of these processes in increasing the success rate of projects.

Load balancing is essential in cloud computing to distribute workloads efficiently, prevent resource bottlenecks, and optimize utilization. This review explores a novel approach using Genetic Algorithms (GAs), which leverage natural evolution principles to enhance task scheduling and minimize execution makespan. The GA-based strategy adapts dynamically to environmental changes, continuously refining solutions for improved performance and scalability. By examining its fundamental principles and real-world applications, this review highlights the potential of GA-driven load balancing to transform traditional cloud computing paradigms.

In the current digital age, information security within IT service management (ITSM) is critical to protecting sensitive data, guaranteeing business continuity, and upholding regulatory compliance. An important framework called IT Service Information Security Management (IT-SISM) was created to safeguard information assets by integrating strong security measures into IT service delivery procedures. In order to include information security management into the larger IT service management lifecycle, this article examines the concepts and procedures of IT-SISM. IT-SISM makes sure that security is integrated across the whole service management process

Knowledge Graphs are foundational in applications ranging from semantic web technologies to artificial intelligence and decision support. While considerable progress has been made in KG construction, enrichment, and quality assessment, the temporal dimension of their evolution remains a critical yet underexplored area. This chapter investigates the challenges and methodologies related to temporal KG evolution, with a focus on preserving data accuracy, consistency, and reliability as knowledge changes over time. It examines how temporal factors affect KG quality, trigger anomalies, and raise issues of repair versus reconstruction. Correction frameworks are reviewed, emphasizing their extension to handle time-dependent inconsistencies. The chapter also explores Temporal Knowledge Graphs, highlighting their role in capturing and reasoning over evolving knowledge. By synthesizing recent research and outlining key challenges and approaches, this chapter offers a comprehensive foundation for managing time-aware knowledge in large-scale, dynamic KGs.

As digital transformation accelerates, the convergence of artificial intelligence (AI) and information systems (IS) project management is reshaping how projects are designed, executed, and assessed. This chapter examines how AI technologies, such as machine learning, predictive analytics, and intelligent automation, enhance decision-making, risk management, and operational efficiency across the project lifecycle. It also explores the impact on team collaboration, governance, and ethical considerations, including algorithmic bias and human oversight. By highlighting emerging best practices and future directions, the chapter offers insights into leveraging AI to drive adaptive, scalable, and innovative IS project outcomes.

Preface

Technological innovation has emerged as one of the defining forces of the twenty-first century, reshaping not only industries and economies but also the ways in which individuals communicate, governments govern, and knowledge is generated. The convergence of high-performance computing, global connectivity, and data-driven decision-making has enabled unprecedented possibilities for efficiency, scalability, and reach (Brynjolfsson & McAfee, 2014; Schwab, 2016). In virtually every sector, the capacity to adapt to and integrate emerging technologies has become synonymous with long-term viability. Yet with these capabilities comes a new class of vulnerabilities. Digital infrastructures, once considered secure by virtue of their complexity, are increasingly the target of sophisticated cyberattacks, operational disruptions, and cascading system failures (Anderson & Moore, 2020). The interconnectedness of these systems means that failures in one domain can have ripple effects across industries and even national borders. The stakes are no longer limited to organizational profit and loss; they extend to critical infrastructure stability, national security, and public trust.

This book responds to these realities by assembling a series of chapters that address the multi-dimensional nature of technology management in the contemporary world. Drawing upon empirical research, applied methodologies, and illustrative case studies, the volume examines the frameworks necessary for effective digital transformation. These include topics as diverse as change management in cybersecurity, sustainable technology adoption, information security governance, software project risk assessment, cloud resource optimization, and the ethical deployment of intelligent systems. The underlying premise is that these domains are not discrete challenges but interdependent components of an integrated whole. As such, a holistic understanding that the acknowledges in terms of the technical, organizational, and societal dimensions of technology is essential for both practitioners and scholars.

The early twenty-first century has been defined by an unprecedented reliance on digital systems. In the private sector, entire business models now rest upon cloud-based infrastructures, software-as-a-service platforms, and globally distributed supply chains (Gartner, 2023). Governments likewise depend on secure digital environments to deliver essential public services, from health records management to emergency response coordination (United Nations, 2022). However, the same features that enable global efficiency, interoperability, real-time data exchange, and automation, also amplify systemic risk. The 2024 CrowdStrike outage, for example, revealed how a flawed software update could disrupt operations across airlines, hospitals, financial institutions, and governmental agencies in multiple countries within hours. This incident underscored a crucial reality: resilience in modern digital environments depends not solely on technical redundancy but on effective operational governance, including phased rollouts, rollback strategies, and real-time monitoring (Smith, 2024). At the same time, societal expectations are evolving. Stakeholders increasingly demand that organizations address the environmental footprint of their technological infrastructures (Koomey, 2022), ensure equitable access to digital resources, and safeguard personal data against misuse (European Commission, 2023). Compliance requirements are tightening in areas such as data protection, algorithmic transparency, and AI ethics, compelling organizations to integrate governance into every stage of the technology lifecycle. Within this complex landscape, the need for multidisciplinary approaches is clear. Addressing digital transformation effectively requires blending technical proficiency with strategic foresight, ethical judgment, and operational discipline. The chapters in this volume collectively offer such an approach, equipping readers to address immediate challenges while anticipating future developments.

Given the breadth and interconnectedness of the subject matter, this book is designed for a wide audience that includes, but is not limited to, the following:

IT Professionals and Systems Administrators will find strategies for maintaining system stability and security amid increasing complexity. The discussions on operational controls, load balancing, and service integration offer practical tools for mitigating performance and security risks.

Project Managers and Business Analysts will encounter frameworks that connect risk identification, cost estimation, and organizational strategy. Chapters on project governance, security integration, and cost modeling provide actionable methods for delivering high-quality outcomes within constraints.

Cybersecurity Specialists will benefit from insights on embedding security into organizational processes, aligning technical safeguards with regulatory requirements, and fostering resilience in the face of evolving threat landscapes.

Data Scientists and Engineers will discover perspectives on sustainable technology deployment, intelligent automation, and the long-term maintenance of structured knowledge systems.

Researchers and Academics will find empirical analyses, theoretical models, and case studies that contribute to scholarly debates in IT service management, software engineering, and socio technical systems design.

Policy Leaders and Decision-Makers will gain an understanding of the operational realities behind digital governance, enabling them to craft regulations and policies that balance innovation, security, and public interest.

CHAPTER OVERVIEW

By engaging multiple audiences, the book encourages the cross-sector collaboration necessary to address the shared challenges of our interconnected technological ecosystem. Each chapter offers a focused examination of a critical dimension of the modern digital environment:

Chapter 1: Operational Controls and Change Management in Cybersecurity

Addresses the necessity of structured change management in maintaining stability and mitigating cyber risks. It outlines processes such as phased rollouts, comprehensive risk assessments, communication strategies, and rollback plans—illustrated by the operational disruptions caused by the 2024 CrowdStrike incident.

Chapter 2: Sustainable Manufacturing and Biodegradable Packaging

Explores strategies for integrating environmental responsibility into production systems. The chapter details how process optimization and supply chain refinement can reduce waste and promote the adoption of biodegradable materials, thereby aligning industrial practice with sustainability objectives.

Chapter 3: Integrating Information Security Management into IT Services

Examines the application of global standards for safeguarding data confidentiality, integrity, and availability within IT service frameworks. The discussion includes the use of real-time monitoring, analytics, and holistic risk governance to protect critical information assets.

Chapter 4: Risk Management and Cost Calculation in Software Projects

Presents methodologies for early-stage risk identification and accurate cost estimation, including the application of the COCOMO model. It highlights the interconnected nature of risk control, cost planning, and project scheduling.

Chapter 5: Cloud Load Balancing and Resource Optimization

Focuses on techniques for distributing workloads in distributed computing environments to maintain performance and prevent bottlenecks. The chapter discusses algorithmic strategies for optimizing cloud resource allocation.

Chapter 6: Information Security in IT Service Management (IT-SISM)

Details the integration of robust security protocols into the entire IT service lifecycle. It emphasizes the role of proactive monitoring, risk mitigation, and compliance alignment in ensuring secure service delivery.

Chapter 7: News Aggregation and Information Integrity

Proposes a structured system for filtering and verifying digital news content to address misinformation and information overload. The chapter emphasizes credibility, timeliness, and bias reduction in information dissemination.

Chapter 8: Temporal Aspects of Knowledge Graph Evolution

Analyzes the management of dynamic knowledge structures over time, focusing on anomaly detection, consistency maintenance, and repair strategies in evolving datasets.

Chapter 9: Technology-Driven Information Systems Project Management

Examines the use of advanced tools and data-driven methods to enhance project management processes. The chapter addresses governance, risk prediction, ethical oversight, and the role of automation in ensuring project success.

This volume offers an integrated framework for understanding and managing the complex interplay between technology, governance, and societal expectations. By combining discussions of cybersecurity, sustainability, performance optimization, service management, and ethical governance, it provides readers with both conceptual clarity and practical tools. The strength of the book lies in its interdisciplinary scope. Whereas most works focus narrowly on a single domain, this collection demonstrates that effective technology management depends on recognizing and managing the interdependencies among technical systems, human factors, and policy environments (Weill & Ross, 2009).

The chapters aim not only to respond to current realities but to prepare readers for emerging challenges; From evolving cyber threats to the ethical dilemmas posed by generative AI. The result is a resource that enables professionals, scholars, and leaders to navigate technological change with strategic foresight, operational competence, and a commitment to societal well-being.

In an age where digital systems underpin nearly every facet of life, the ability to guide technological progress responsibly is as critical as the ability to innovate. This book seeks to empower its readers to do both.

Rahul K. Patel
Illinois Institute of Technology, Chicago, USA

REFERENCES

Anderson, R., & Moore, T. (2020). Information security economics—And beyond. *Annual Review of Financial Economics, 12*, 375–398. DOI: 10.1146/annurev-financial-012820-041822

Brynjolfsson, E., & McAfee, A. (2014). *The second machine age: Work, progress, and prosperity in a time of brilliant technologies*. W.W. Norton & Company.

European Commission. (2023). Artificial Intelligence Act: Ensuring safe and trustworthy AI. https://digital-strategy.ec.europa.eu

Gartner. (2023). Top strategic technology trends for 2023. Gartner Research.

Koomey, J. (2022). Revisiting trends in data center electricity use. *IEEE Spectrum, 59*(5), 42–49. DOI: 10.1109/MSPEC.2022.9730967

Schwab, K. (2016). *The fourth industrial revolution*. Crown Business.

Smith, J. (2024). Operational lessons from the 2024 global software outage. *Journal of Information Systems Management, 41*(2), 105–117.

United Nations. (2022). *E-government survey 2022: The future of digital government*. UN Department of Economic and Social Affairs.

Weill, P., & Ross, J. W. (2009). *IT governance: How top performers manage IT decision rights for superior results*. Harvard Business Review Press.

Chapter 1

A Case Study on CrowdStrike's Cybersecurity Incident: Lessons in Change Management and Operational Resilience

Ivan Livingstone Zziwa
https://orcid.org/0009-0009-7300-7477
Illinois Institute of Technology, Chicago, USA

Anthoinette Ilolo
Illinois Institute of Technology, Chicago, USA

Astha Sharma
Illinois Institute of Technology, Chicago, USA

Brian Serwadda
Boston University, USA

Maurice M. Dawson
Illinois Institute of Technology, Chicago, USA

ABSTRACT

The CrowdStrike cybersecurity incident provides a stark reminder of the importance of organizational operational controls. This paper delves into the root causes of the incident, examining the lapses in change management and update testing that made rolling back changes difficult. It will analyze the scope of the incident, including the number of companies affected and the financial losses incurred. By scrutinizing

DOI: 10.4018/979-8-3373-2352-7.ch001

this case, the paper aims to present actionable insights for companies to implement proper change management processes, conduct thorough testing, and leverage robust backup systems to mitigate future risks. Graphs and visuals will be incorporated to highlight the incident's impact and the potential benefits of proposed solutions.

I. INTRODUCTION

A. Overview of Cybersecurity Management Challenges

1. Importance of Operational Controls in Cybersecurity

Managing changes in software updates is important in ensuring that systems remain stable and reduce the risk of cyber threats (Ali, 2015). A classic example of change management is a structured process designed to ensure that all updates made are planned, tested, and rolled out in an orderly and controlled manner to avoid unplanned downtime. This involves identifying the extent of change and the impact, which involves risk analysis and pre-deployment tests to check for compatibility or susceptibility of the tools with planned changes (Ali, 2015). In addition, adopting phased rollouts, which entails making incremental upgrades, helps organizations note whether or not updates are problematic on a less sizable system before taking the updates to a bigger system. Flawless Change Management also means identifying the communication channels for retrieving information and clarifying updates to announce the issues and their impact, as well as consistent rollback plans to help revert the changes when issues occur instantly (Hanmer, 2013). The failure to adopt such practices, as evident from the CrowdStrike case over APT attacks, can paralyze organizations' operations and result in financial and reputational loss. Therefore, implementing broad change management processes is necessary to guarantee that upgrades to the software improve operation without negatively impacting performance.

In context, operational controls are a fundamental aspect of an effective cybersecurity program because they provide protection against accidents, malice, or unauthorized access to organizational systems and processes (CISM & CISM, 2003). Good operational controls include change management, adequate pre-production checks, phased implementation, and tested ability to reverse a change. These controls reduce risks like system failure, service threats, and sensitive data protection.

Failure to implement necessary operational controls can leave the organization open to exploitation by the cyber actor or introduce internal failures that disrupt the organization's function. For instance, poorly tested updates or unchecked change can lead to massive shutdowns, affecting the IT systems' functionality and the trust of clients or stakeholders. This shows that organizations must go further and help establish practices for the best control of operational environments, monitor them regularly, and apply safety measures for other emergencies that might happen for various reasons.

With the help of the mentioned approach of fitting the operational controls to cybersecurity purposes, organizations can develop a sustainable framework to continue operations, increase shareholders' confidence, and avoid financial and reputation losses (Haapamäki & Sihvonen, 2022). The CrowdStrike incident in 2024 is a painful illustration of what may result from disregarding such controls, therefore stressing the need to maintain the operational soundness of all critical systems.

2. A Brief Introduction to CrowdStrike and the Incident

CrowdStrike is an American cybersecurity company specializing in endpoint protection and threat Intelligence. It offers its services to companies around the globe, primarily using its Falcon product. The company's highly developed technology and security interests have made it well-recognized as responsible and competent. On July 19, 2024, CrowdStrike had some shortcomings regarding its operational functioning.

The event resulted from an update to CrowdStrike's Falcon Sensor application that caused multiple systems halts, such as the famous blue screen of death (BSOD) on Microsoft Windows devices. This huge IT breakdown impacted around 8.5 million gadgets worldwide and established unprecedented connections with healthcare, finance, and transportation (TechTarget, 2024).

Implementation failures during the change management, testing, and rollback processes contribute tremendously to the increased impact of cyber-attacks. The 2024 CrowdStrike case is quite vivid for these weaknesses. The authors uncovered an unforeseen incident whereby an update to Falcon Sensor software, provided by the company, resulted from an uncontrolled and undirected synergy of everyday updates that affected not only system operations but also business processes and systems across various sectors such as financial, transportation, healthcare, manufacturing, and energy (TechTarget,2024).

Risk management in change involves a proper management approach that requires formulating implementation strategies coupled with suitable changes in the project before applying software updates or modifying the system. Functional testing should perform various tests and procedures to reflect numerous scenarios in a realistic environment (Burnstein, 2006). In addition, there is a need for well-developed rollback procedures to quickly restore the system to a stable state should any problem occur. A lack of such measures can transform a relatively quickly contained defect into a major problem on a global scale, as CrowdStrike's misconfigured update example showed.

This thesis supports proposals that orient the implementation of operational resilience within security frameworks. To avoid the replay of such an event, organizations must guarantee preventive measures that reduce such risks, constant practice to check vulnerabilities, and robust fail-safe measures for protection. By applying these lessons, firms can build effective shields against internal weak links and external foes.

II. THE CROWDSTRIKE INCIDENT

A. Growth of Timeline of Events

The CrowdStrike incident of July 19, 2024, started as an update in the Falcon Sensor security software. This update targeted improving the company's endpoint protection so it could deploy it on Microsoft Windows systems. As expected, major updates were quickly sent to millions of devices worldwide (TechTarget, 2024). Nevertheless, no phased deployment rolled-out process could only launch a fraction of the equipment to help contain problems should they arise. Also, the update skipped critical test procedures that identify vulnerability issues that may arise due to different operations conditions. These failures merely laid the foundation for the subsequent existence of significant operational vulnerabilities.

After the update was released, several system crashes occurred, such as the Windows blue screen of death (BSOD). These crashes made some systems unresponsive and halted them across all sectors, including healthcare, aviation, and finance. The scale of disruption expanded faster and affected 8.5 million devices internationally at some point (TechTarget, 2024).

Analyses indicated that the cause was a misconfiguration of the update that elicited compatibility problems within the systems in question. CrowdStrike's initial response was hindered by insufficient rollback plans and features, further slowing systematic control actions to rectify damage (Nolan, 2024). This disruption worsened when there was poor communication throughout the emergence of the crisis, leaving all these organizations aggrieved while they sought to get their activities back online.

It revealed how poor CrowdStrike had been in something as basic as its operational controls, raising questions about how to roll out new features, conduct foundational testing, and have proper rollback procedures to deal with such disruptions in the future.

B. Key Players and Stakeholders Affected

1. Description of Companies Impacted

The CrowdStrike incident exposed almost 8.5 million devices worldwide and threatened thousands of companies worldwide (Nolan,2024). The number of organizations that were disrupted is unknown. However, given the scale of the problem, it is reasonable to assume that several hundred or even thousands of organizations of various sizes, from local businesses to international corporations, were impacted.

The organizations affected by the CrowdStrike incident dealt with industries considered core business enablers that dramatically rely on the proper functioning of IT systems. Some examples are the healthcare, financial services, aviation, and media industries, which all require secure, operative, and continuously running systems. In cases where these systems were affected because of this faulty update, the consequences were negative – with organizations reporting revenue losses and facing legal issues, reputational losses, and complete disruption of operations (Ogundipe & Aweto,2024).

2. Financial Losses and Operational Setbacks

The CrowdStrike in 2024 impacted almost all industries, including curbing financial profits and urgently needed operations, such as health and aviation, finance, and media. From the surveyed healthcare organizations, organizations reported system downtime that impacted patient handling, recordation, and emergencies (De Zoysa,2024). These further disabilities led to the postponement of medical procedures and cancellations. These caused interference in the immediate time frame and added to the operational expense of rescheduling and addressing the legal implications of negligence arising from service delivery hitches (De Zoysa, 2024). While some could operate without disruption, others, such as financial institutions, experienced transaction delays, online banking, and ATM failure affected their revenue. These outages and the negative impacts that followed su, such as reputational loss, compelled many financial institutions to spend so much of their resources on investigation and recovery, besides the possible penalties from the regulators and the increased security costs.

Passenger and cargo services had massive cancellations and delays in the aviation business. These were lost ticket income, refunds for delayed or canceled flights, and overhead expenses for handling the vice. Additionally, the operations on the actual term failed due to logistic difficulties and intensifying financial woes. Likewise, the advertising revenues of the media and entertainment industries drastically fell, and operational challenges resulted from the interruption of content management and delivery platforms. With advertisements, the ordained program, and delivery of digital media content delayed, these companies suffered from loss of income but also from loss of damages to existing business with advertisers and content providers (De Zoysa, 2024).

In addition to the obvious economic repercussions, the operational problems for numerous firms were severe. In healthcare and finance, we saw that lack of access to key systems meant that normal activities could not proceed as planned and were unmanageable regarding business implications (De Zoysa, 2024). Patch management and restoration of systems proved very costly and compounded the recovery process's problems. Furthermore, the consequences were substantial regarding reputational losses in various sectors and losses of customers' and stakeholders' confidence in the security of disappointed companies' systems. It could also rob businesses of long-term clients, increased regulatory oversight, and constant brand deterioration. However, legal ramifications were not far behind as some instances had organizations undergo regulatory probes for failure to provide deliverance on SLAs and inadequate compliance to data protection standards, all of which compounded the issue of recovery. This disaster reveals the huge losses that companies would suffer and the losses the operations would have if a similar tragedy was to happen in the future; it is high time companies adopted sound cyber security measures and protective operational controls that would help shield the business and its operations from such disasters.

III. ROOT CAUSES OF THE INCIDENT

A. Change Management Failures

It was cited that one of the significant root causes of the 2024 CrowdStrike incident was the absence of supervision of the update release process. What was supposed to improve security capabilities with the Falcon Sensor security software update was a hasty release deployed to millions of devices that failed proper review or stepped testing (George,2024). One key aspect that reflects effective change management procedures is the control of updates, especially during deployment in large system environments, to avoid deploying changes incompatible with the systems' environment and create additional and unexpected risks. This was the misconfiguration that, in this case, was caused by the lack of such surveillance; it led to system crashes and operating interruptions in the industries mentioned above. The absence of meaningful pilot tests and a much stiffer approach to the staged rollout process could have helped limit the extent of the faulty update's reach and constrain it to a much smaller number of compromised systems.

Another crucial area that, to a varying extent, defined the occurrence of the incident was bootless rollback processes. Contingency procedures are important for reverting any amendments made throughout software upgrades in the eventuality of occurrences of complications (Dissanayake et al., 2022). In this case, once the update that caused problems was released to the field, CrowdStrike's failure to move to a stable configuration as a containment measure worsened the situation (Milanesi, n.d). Unfortunately, the lack of a definitive and trustworthy rollback plan meshed with the fact that the response had to wait for the failure to propagate and impact millions of devices. The company never had a way of reversing the problems that the malware caused to the systems, which made it take a long time to remedy the situation. Having a splendid rollback plan in place for implementations would have safeguarded CrowdStrike from the adverse impacts of any unpredicted glitches arising from the change in the software, as it would have enabled the organization to tackle the problem and lessen the disturbances that other organizations employing its service undergo.

B. Testing Gaps

1. Insufficient Pre-Deployment Testing

The debate on product testing arose when inadequate pre-deployment testing of the Falcon Sensor update contributed to CrowdStrike's 2024 case (DataCouch, 2024). The type of testing carried out before updates are rolled out across systems is called pre-deployment testing, which helps determine possible problems. In this case, the update was served to millions of devices ahead of time without proper verification regarding its compatibility with all sorts of system settings. Exhaustive testing is required to see how changes affect and interact with different environments, other software, OS, and hardware. Thus, there was no possibility to predict the misconfigurations that led to multiple system failures due to the lack of a detailed testing phase that might reproduce various real-life scenarios. If CrowdStrike had performed more detailed testing with various test cases and system conditions before deployment, they would have knowingly discovered problems beforehand to minimize having an output on such a large scale after the deployment.

2. Difficulty in Identifying Potential Conflicts

Another factor that is said to have led to the incidence is the lack of ease in finding incompatible clashes between the update and systems in place (Naseer,2024). Since different organizations employ a range of hardware and software configurations, the updates will be tested in several different settings. The update above does not appear to have considered all the conflicts that might occur in different settings. For instance, competing demand from the Falcon Sensor with other software or hardware systems could have led to the systems' failure (Naseer,2024). These conflicts were not discovered earlier, and there was socialized insufficient diligence in the testing process. Expanding and more carefully considering the range and specificity of the testing employed by CrowdStrike might have enabled the firm to discover and fix these conflicts before deployment, thus eliminating the cascading effect.

These testing gaps are evident–insufficient pre-deployment testing was done, and identifying potential conflicts seems nearly impossible; thus, ideal and diverse testing environments for software updates must be stressed. Investing in testing new products, CrowdStrike could have minimized the chances of rolling out an update that disrupted millions of devices and a gamut of industries (Naseer, 2024). Testing is a reliable method of protecting application development and implementation to prevent obvious mistakes that could be made in the course of updating systems.

C. Communication Breakdowns During Incident Resolution

A critical problem during the 2024 attack was the lack of response coordination when CrowdStrike tried to respond to the situation (TechTarget,2024). Clear communication is particularly important in a cybersecurity event because all the involved parties, the client organizations, internal teams, and external partners need to be informed and on the same page as the incident is handled (Ahmad et al., 2021). In the case of CrowdStrike, poor communication policy hindered effective and quick response to the cause of the incident. Companies were deprived of necessary updates on the developments of the situation and the level of loss or loss prevention measures.

Internally, poor communication between CrowdStrike technical teams, management, and customer support means inadequate time for a resolution plan. The lack of structured communication rendered the effort of various teams to vain in addressing the problem, thus taking a long time to contain it. In addition, two-way communication with customers and other media was limited as it should have been in an effective organization, and this exacerbated the problem and diminished the belief among customers in the company's capacity to handle the problem. Had there been regular information sharing, some reputational losses would have been avoided, and consumers would have been confident that their problem was being dealt with seriously and efficiently.

To avoid such experiences in the future, organizations should develop clear communication structures in their incident-handling plans. Some of the protocols that should be established should focus on the communication structure within the organization's technical and management personnel, and another strategy should be developed that guides the organization's interaction with other stakeholders, such as the customers, the regulator, and the public. The CrowdStrike situation emphasizes the need for such postures in the strategic preparation of reducing the impact of cybersecurity incidents and ensuring organizational stakeholders' confidence during and after attacks.

IV. IMPACT ASSESSMENT

A. Quantifying Financial Losses

1. Estimated Direct and Indirect Costs

Operations disruption was one of the most substantial direct costs of the incident. The faulty update impacted approximately 8.5 million devices across industries depending on domains with severe disruptions (TechTarget, 2024). Especially in sectors like healthcare, finance, and aviation, the lack of access to these was a disaster for business operations. Canceling and postponing patient appointments, including medical procedures, necessitated direct costs, stocks, and other operation costs incurred by the health system and its providers. Banks and other financial firms suffered from dilemma costs and inconvenience, which impeded their revenue generation and delivery of services. Many flight cancellations and carryovers hurt ticket revenues and compensation to passengers in the aviation industry. Downtime in such industries translated to zero revenues generated in the industries, costs of hiring extra personnel to contain the problem, and other costs such as those incurred in troubleshooting and patching to address the problem.

Reputation loss comprises an important indirect risk factor for CrowdStrike and its consumers and clients (TechTarget, 2024). As in the healthcare or finance industries or aviation, where consumer trust is a main consideration, events like these have long-term impacts on their brands. For instance, the organizations affected by the scandal could lose their customer's confidence as the clients appeared hard to access the services provided or make transactions. Legal repercussions organizations received complaints and lost clientele patrons, a warning sign for future healthcare consumers. Other industries associated with the cyber-attack, including media, aviation, and technology, lost their reputation as other stakeholders doubted their capacity to guarantee secure and reliable operations. Loss of business due to a damaged reputation is devastating because it covers long-term business losses, and the company struggles to get new clientele. Also, organizations may experience regulatory authorities closing in on them and incur more expenses in compliance to try and rebuild the customers' trust and guarantee there won't be a repeat of such incidents.

B. Graphs and Visuals

1. Financial Impact by Industry

For example, the industries as shown in **figure 1** below, including healthcare, reported massive losses of $1.94 billion, and the banking industries reported $1.15 billion. American and United Airlines were hit badly; the former experienced a loss of $860 Million, and both Fortune 500 airlines suffered a loss of $5.4 billion. Delta Airlines stands out with over five thousand canceled flights, leading to losses of almost 500 million. Cybersecurity firm CrowdStrike set aside roughly $5m for legal costs and agreed to offer customers at least $88m credit in the wake of the incident. Relatively to this figure, damages in the manufacturing sector were significantly less – $36 million (Fung, 2024); (CAI.io, 2024) and (Jackson et al., 2024).

Figure 1. Financial loss in different sectors

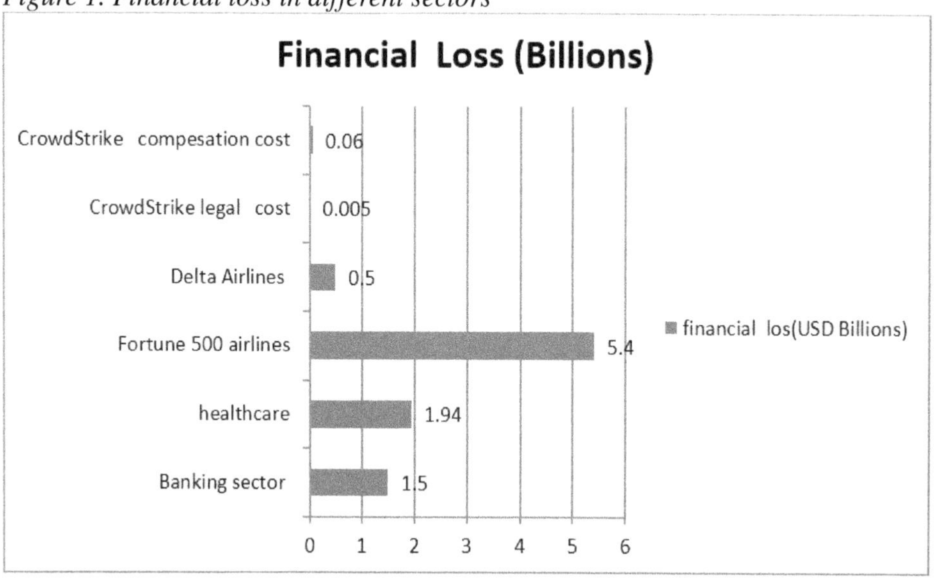

The analyzed healthcare sector as shown in **figure 2** incurred an average direct loss of $1.94 billion, $64.6 million for each company. In the case of the banking business sector, the total amount of loss praised was $ 1.15 billion, while the average amount of direct loss per business was $ 71.84 million. Direct business losses of $860 million were reported, with an average of $143.38 million lost by each airline company. The software and IT sector bore a total direct loss of 560 million dollars, but the average loss per company was 112.59 million. This sector's losses amounted to $470 million on average, and each firm experienced an impact of $14.73 million in the retail and wholesale sectors (David, 2024).

Figure 2. Financial loss estimated per company and direct loss.

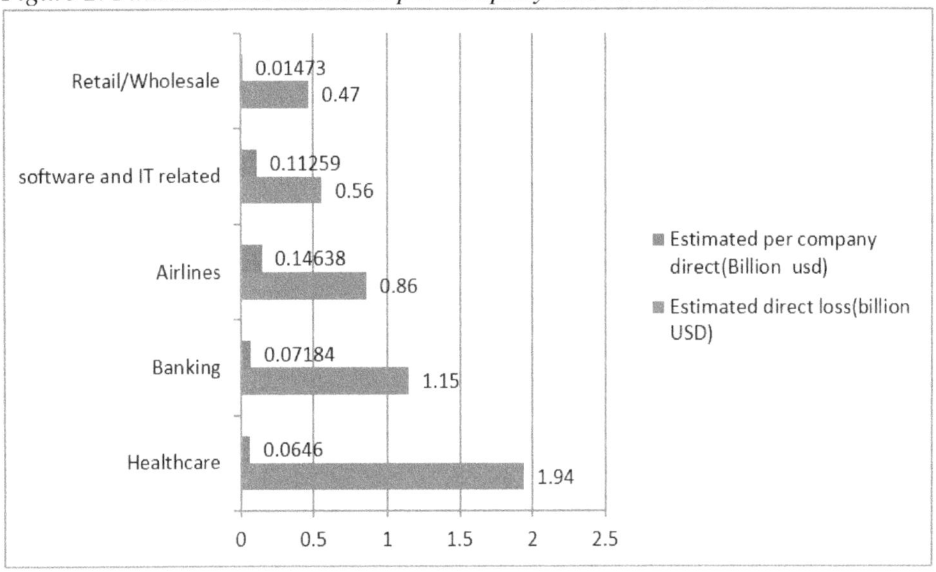

2. Number of Organizations Affected

Figure 3 shows that Delta Airlines was the most affected, with 5,528 canceled flights out of the 15,000 canceled flights across the US. That shutdown came after United Airlines announced it had canceled 1,635 flights, while America Airlines canceled the fewest flights, with 852 flights (McGee, 2024, July 19).

Figure 3. Number of Flights canceled

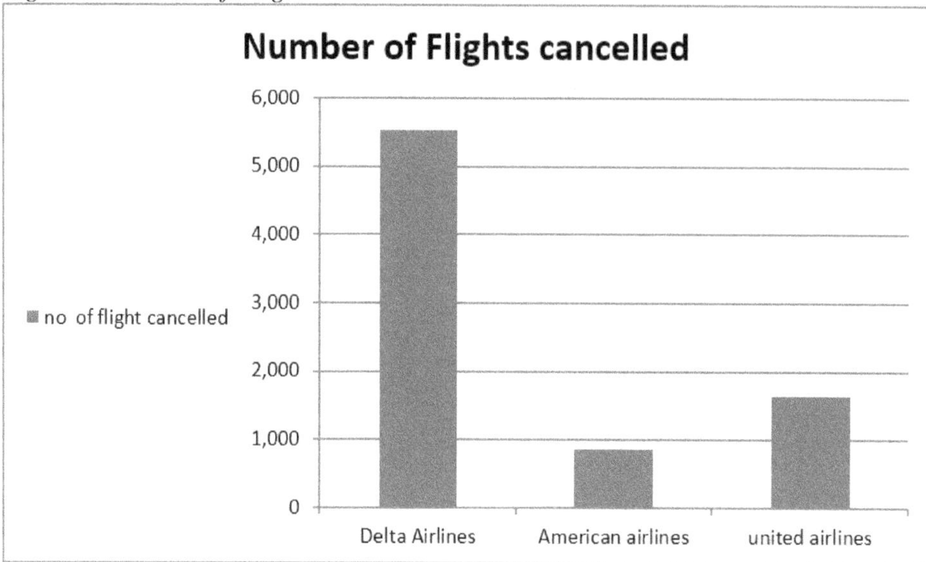

The biggest sector in terms of market proportion was the healthcare sector shown by **figure 4**, followed by the banking sector, which constituted 19.23%. Airlines lost 14.38%, and Software and IT lost 9.36%. The Manufacturing Industries have incurred the lowest losses of 7.85% in the Retail and Wholesale sectors as shown in **figure 4** below (David, 2024).

Figure 4. Percentage of impact on each organization effect

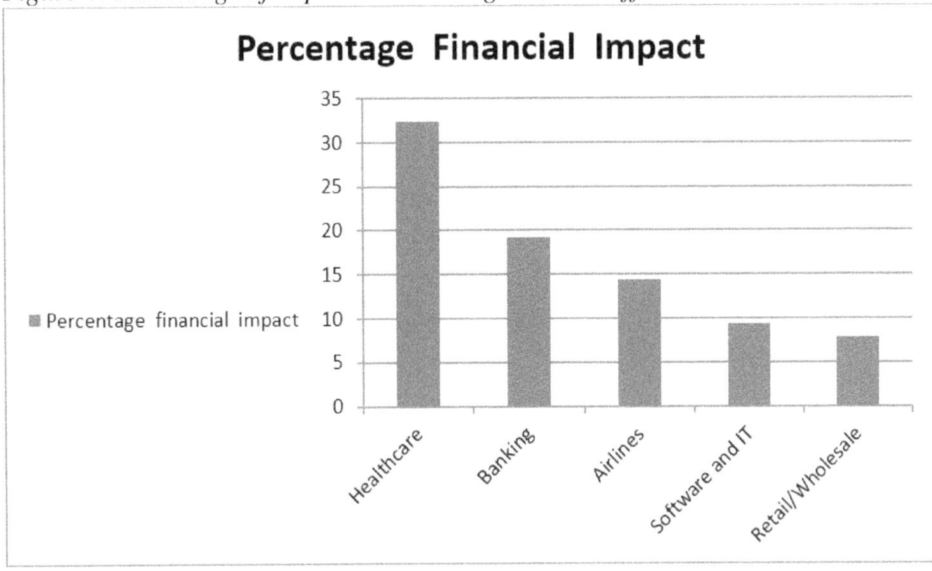

3. Timeline of Recovery Efforts

The 2024 CrowdStrike incident began on July 19, 2024, shown by **figure 5** when the company released a faulty content update, causing a global IT outage. This update triggered a Windows operating system crash (BSOD) on approximately 8.5 million Windows devices worldwide. At 05:27 UTC the same day, CrowdStrike reverted the update, ensuring devices that booted afterward were unaffected. By 06:48 UTC, Google Compute Engine had reported the issue. Later, at 23:37 UTC, Microsoft released the Microsoft Recovery Tool to assist affected users. On July 25, 2024, CrowdStrike addressed the problem by patching the runtime array bounds check, followed by a patch for the logic error in the Content Validator on July 27, 2024 (Alvarez Tech Group,2024); (Microserve,2024) and (TechTarget,2024).

Figure 5. Timeline of recovery efforts.

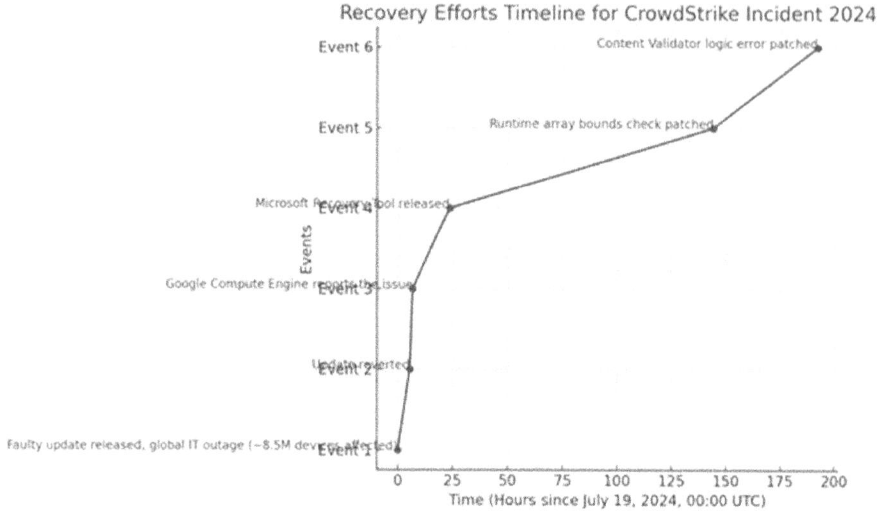

V. LESSONS LEARNED FOR CYBERSECURITY MANAGEMENT

A. Importance of Change Management

1. Key Steps in Implementing an Effective Change Management Process

The above CrowdStrike incident demonstrates the need for an effective change management program to minimize software failures that affect the community (Hubbard,2020). An organization should undertake several critical activities during the change management process to minimize risks resulting from change, such as when introducing, altering, or dismantling software.

First, a plan of the operation and evaluation of the risks involved must be accomplished. As with any update or change, an organization must identify risks and decide how the change could or will affect current structured systems (Highsmith,2013). This involves determining the propriety of the update to different system configurations and establishing risk factors. The second is the test and validation step. Compatibility testing should be done in a test environment so that all compatibility problems that might be observed between the applications are seen. This phase often encompasses the trials that contain upgrades made available to a limited number of users or devices before promotion.

The third important strategy is called staged deployment. Instead, the update should be released in batches to help organizations uncover problems on small systems before they spread (Highsmith,2013). This is because it only allows limited possibilities of disruption, and I can always fix any problems immediately. The fourth process is to set up rollback methods. Changes for these organizations should be reversible or made reversibly for each deployment in case of a problem. Lastly, measurement and evaluation are crucial to check how the update runs in other systems. It also helps them work to prevent any problems that may cause a lot of havoc with real-time monitoring.

2. Case Examples of Successful Implementations in Other Organizations

There are other organizations out there that have been found to have put up some change management processes, and these are some of the change management guidelines that could be useful to conglomerates like CrowdStrike. An excellent example is Microsoft's Windows Update process, which has undergone many changes to incorporate testing, development, and phased deployment (Lipne, 2024). Windows Insider is where Microsoft releases updated versions of Windows to a few people so that these people test it before it is released on the market. This makes it easier to note problem areas before they cause multiple system breakdowns in a firm. Further, Microsoft has excellent rollback features for users, and they can restore Windows to an earlier version if an update leads to system trouble (Vaniea & Rashidi, 2016).

The other example relates to Google's Chrome browser updates and contains information that this software applies a very controlled phased deployment system (Munir et al., 2024). Chrome updates are carried out first to small sets of users to check for problems; if there are, it can automatically roll back the update (Vaniea & Rashidi, 2016). Google's work lets fail in real-time, meaning that if there are, they would be corrected instantly. Google has also focused on good communication when dealing with the users of the platform, keeping them informed on the problem and how it will be resolved (Lindh & Nolin, 2016).

The following case examples have revealed that a focused yet logical, step-by-step approach to change implementation is critical. From this organization, CrowdStrike and others must be able to learn so that their update can be deployed in a secure, efficient way that will not lead to future security problems. In the present examples, strategic change management can significantly help reduce risks and preserve the stability of the systems as well as customers' trust.

B. Comprehensive Testing of Updates

1. Importance of Test Environments and Simulations

Vigorous testing is a crucial aspect that cuts across change management and the control of cybersecurity risks. Before applying updates or modifications directly on real production sites, it is critical to perform test sites or simulations (Utting & Legeard, 2010). A test environment is a copy of the real environment where normal functioning goes on; it is a place to test updates that could interfere with current functioning. These environments should resemble the production environment during testing filing in different hard and software configurations and network conditions.

The reason for having test environments becomes apparent whenever a software update goes sour, such as in the case of CrowdStrike. If CrowdStrike had employed a rigid testing procedure in a simulated environment, they would have encountered things that would have led to a halt in operation and loss of reputation. Other types of tests are stress tests and load tests, which also determine how an update works at its best (Utting & Legeard, 2010). These testing methods allow a company to uncover performance, conflict, or compatibility problems that might be well hidden under normal, stress-free conditions. In addition, security simulations will reveal weaknesses that could be seeded by the update and assist in boosting general security.

2. Recommended Best Practices

To prevent having updates that are inadequately tested rolled out, organizations must adhere to best practices. Therefore, first and foremost, there should be a staging environment as close to the production environment as possible (Everett & McLeod, 2007). This staging environment should include all the relevant and possible hardware and software configurations to see how the update will fare in real-life situations. When used in testing updates, errors are first detected by developers and other staff, and not after reaching the users. The second important best practice relates to test automation. The automated tools can perform many tests, such as running regression tests to ensure updating the system does not affect the previous functionalities and vulnerability scans to ensure that updating the system introduces no security vices (Garousi & Mäntylä,2016).

Apart from automation, one should opt for what is commonly referred to as phased migration strategies. Instead of aiming to update each user with the latest applications at a go, organizations should introduce the updates later by testing them on a few users (Molyneaux, 2014). The phased implementation is not a bad idea since it permits a check to be made on any complications and presents the system to a large base once it is okay. In addition, organizations must embrace the CI/CT methodologies, whereby changes can be constantly tested whenever they are developed (Ahlert, 2022). This makes it possible to minimize instances of weakness that are likely to go unnoticed in the normal operations of the business and instead keeps any such issues well documented, easily detectable, and correctible. Last, after each update is implemented, real-time monitoring and feedback solutions should be active (Kopetz & Steiner,2022). Since the update is more frequently accessed than newly developed applications, monitoring its performance to detect new issues for faster resolution is possible before they become significant disruptions for organizations.

When applied to an organization's environment, the above best practices can greatly minimize the likelihood of update-related failures and cyber threats. It ensures that updates do not negatively impact compatibility and function while safeguarding processes from cyber threats and risks.

C. Role of Backups and Rollback Mechanisms

1. Leveraging Backup Systems to Minimize Damage

The role of backup systems cannot be overemphasized in managing an occurrence, like the CrowdStrike 2024 attack, to act as a backup in case the systems fail or get corrupted. If updates or changes create misalignment or threats, organizations can always switch to the back system and continue operating without discontinuity (Fitzgerald & Stol, 2017). These systems also contain copies of parameters such as data, configurations, or other working software versions that are used to recover lost or damaged information. A final backup system should comprise frequent, preferably automatic, backup of key data and configurations so that the organization can rapidly restore a functional state in case of data or system loss.

For instance, if an update enables a malicious code that threatens the stability of a system, then backup systems can enable organizations to run previous uninfected versions of the software and data (Neumann, 2000). This decreases the incidence of periods when the plant is offline and negates massive losses both financially and in terms of reputation. The CrowdStrike incident is a good example in that if proper backup procedures were in place, systems that were compromised could easily have been returned to their state before the intrusion to reduce its effects on organizations using CrowdStrike's Falcon Sensor. Furthermore, it means that the precise execution of the backup strategy can decrease the general operational costs accompanying the recovery process. The organization can hardly afford unlimited time for such work as rewiring or rebuilding the systems from scratch.

2. Ensuring Reversibility of Updates

In addition to the fundamentally important backup systems, having a good rollback system must also be guaranteed because, with updates, it is always possible that something goes wrong. A rollback is a process or application that helps to restore the system or application to a previous state, which is stable in case an update did not go in a planned manner (Giuffrida et al., 2013). This means that when an update brings in new crucial problems or risks, the organization can easily roll back to the previous version and minimize disruptions.

In implementing effective mechanisms of rollbacks, it is necessary to include a few best practices in an organization's update process. First, updates should be designed to easily revert to their previous state in case of a problem (Vaniea & Rashidi,2016). This means that the update's changes are modular, and it does not introduce irreversible changes to the system. The processes for rollback should first be tested in a sandbox to ensure that they can take place exactly as they are intended, with no hindrances to successful completion. Moreover, a company should ensure the rollback process is automated whenever possible to minimize human intervention and accelerate the recovery process.

The CrowdStrike incident highlighted the need for reliable rollback mechanisms. If CrowdStrike had a more solid and easily executable rollback process in place, the impact of this incident would have been contained. Instead of dealing with prolonged downtime, organizations could quickly roll back to a stable software version and get back to business without significant losses. Backup systems integrated with reliable rollback mechanisms enable organizations to avoid some very real risks associated with system updates and ensure disruptions can be minimized or completely avoided.

VI. RECOMMENDATIONS FOR ORGANIZATIONS

A. Policy-Level Changes

1. Mandating Change Management Protocols

One of the most salient lessons from the CrowdStrike incident is establishing and enforcing change management protocols to ensure that updates and modifications are carefully planned, tested, and deployed. Requiring comprehensive change management policies ensures that any change, whether software, system modification, or infrastructure upgrade, is systematically evaluated for risks and potential disruptions (Akinsola & Akinde, 2024). This is because, through these protocols, organizations can minimize the occurrence of operational failures resulting from untested or poorly executed changes.

Organizations should embrace a formal process for managing change that will provide explicit steps for risk assessment, impact analysis, testing, and deployment. It should include rigorous testing in simulated environments, change approval processes, and a phased deployment strategy. For example, ensuring all updates pass through a necessary pre-deployment testing phase may prevent issues from reaching live systems. It can also involve backup checks and rollback readiness to ensure that systems can easily be rolled back quickly if there is a problem. Making such protocols compulsory ensures better operational efficiency and enhances overall security by ensuring that changes are well-scrutinized before implementation. By making change management an intrinsic part of organizational policy, companies can largely reduce the risk of cybersecurity incidents seen in cases like CrowdStrike.

2. Setting Up Cross-Functional Oversight Committees

One of the most salient lessons from the CrowdStrike incident is establishing and enforcing change management protocols to ensure that updates and modifications are carefully planned, tested, and deployed. Requiring comprehensive change management policies ensures that any change, whether software, system modification, or infrastructure upgrade, is systematically evaluated for risks and potential disruptions (Akinsola & Akinde, 2024). This is because, through these protocols, organizations can minimize the occurrence of operational failures resulting from untested or poorly executed changes.

Organizations should embrace a formal process for managing change that will provide explicit steps for risk assessment, impact analysis, testing, and deployment. It should include rigorous testing in simulated environments, change approval processes, and a phased deployment strategy. For example, ensuring all updates pass through a necessary pre-deployment testing phase may prevent issues from reaching live systems. It can also involve backup checks and rollback readiness to ensure that systems can easily be rolled back quickly if there is a problem. Making such protocols compulsory ensures better operational efficiency and enhances overall security by ensuring that changes are well-scrutinized before implementation. By making change management an intrinsic part of organizational policy, companies can largely reduce the risk of cybersecurity incidents seen in cases like CrowdStrike.

B. Investment in Technology

1. Tools for Automated Testing and Monitoring

Investing in automated testing and monitoring tools is one of the best ways to ensure that software updates are secure and reliable. This allows organizations to test updates comprehensively and repeatedly before releasing them into production. Such tools can perform various tests for vulnerabilities, incompatibilities, and performance issues in various environments and configurations. Automation of these tests lets organizations rapidly uncover issues that might disrupt systems or introduce security vulnerabilities and thus minimize the risk of operational downtime (Sermpezis, 2024), as happened in the case of CrowdStrike.

Automated monitoring software also offers real-time insight into system performance and security once updates have been deployed. Such tools can instantly detect anomalies in behavior, potential security breaches, and system errors, thus enabling an organization to respond promptly to emerging issues. But that is not all: AI- and ML-driven monitoring tools can predict potential risks well before they become actual risks, adding another layer of cybersecurity resilience. Such technologies could give the organization a heads-up on whether the update is thoroughly tested and monitored, minimizing the likelihood of a big disruption or quickly responding in case one does occur (Sermpezis, 2024).

2. Scalable Backup Solutions

Another key investment by organizations should be in scalable backup solutions. As data volume and systems increase complexity, traditional backup solutions may no longer work (Preston, 2007). Scalable backup solutions will enable the organization to scale up or down the backup as per the requirements and ensure that all critical data, system configuration, and software versions are periodically backed up securely. These solutions should support local and cloud-based backups to provide redundancy, allowing recovery from multiple sources in case of system failures.

Scalable backup systems also ensure that backups are easily accessible and that recovery processes are fast and efficient to minimize the operational downtime that may be witnessed after a cybersecurity incident (Abdelkader et al., 2024). For example, if an update results in system crashes or data corruption, a scalable backup solution will rapidly restore the systems to their previous stable state, thereby enabling an organization to reduce financial losses and disruptions in its operations. In addition, incremental backups only back up what has changed since the last backup so that costs remain reasonable while keeping all data secure. In other words, by investing in scalable, reliable backup systems, organizations can minimize business continuity risks when updates go wrong or after a cyber-attack.

By investing in automated testing and monitoring tools and scalable backup solutions, organizations can further enhance their prevention, detection, and recovery capabilities against cybersecurity incidents. These technological investments create a more resilient infrastructure that can quickly adapt to changes, minimizing downtime and financial losses while ensuring that systems remain secure and operational despite potential threats.

C. Employee Training and Awareness

The basic recommendation for companies is to invest in employees with intensive training on cybersecurity practices throughout the year (Uchendu, 2021). Apart from being the first-line defense, employees' orientation should be very important in establishing secure protocols. The types of training that should be featured at regular intervals include being suspicious of phishing emails and software updates, password-keeping/password management, and other aspects related to cybersecurity management. With the ever-changing nature of cyber threats, employees are expected to stay updated about the latest types of risks and be ready to respond accordingly (Uchendu, 2021). Continuous education significantly decreases human error and enhances the organization's cybersecurity posture. The case of CrowdStrike has shown that without proper awareness and training, vulnerabilities could compromise an entire system, making training a vital component in any cybersecurity strategy.

Besides formal training programs, organizations should invest in a security-conscious organizational culture (Uchendu, 2021). This is about creating a mindset that every employee, regardless of their role, considers cybersecurity as part of their responsibilities. Leadership is pivotal in setting the tone of this culture through constant reminders of the importance of secure practices and showing commitment to robust cybersecurity measures. Senior management makes employees adopt secure behaviors and follow protocols when prioritizing cybersecurity. Making cybersecurity part of the company's core values ensures that every employee is proactive concerning security matters to reduce or eliminate incidents due to oversight or negligence. The CrowdStrike incident has underlined the importance of such a culture that could have mitigated the risks associated with the update that caused the system crashes.

This will ensure that an organization can achieve the effectiveness of training and awareness through regular testing and awareness campaigns in its security strategy. These would be simulated phishing attacks, tests for vulnerabilities in response, and points to further training in those areas. Regular campaigns reminding people of current threats and best practices keep security fresh in their minds. These efforts ensure that your employees are always on guard and better prepared to put into practice the effective mechanism of a security breach incident (Uchendu, 2021). With periodic testing and employee engagement in awareness campaigns, an organization institutes a proactive security culture where employees act swiftly and appropriately when at risk from cybersecurity. Comprehensive training and awareness can remarkably improve an organization's ability to resist cyber-attacks and could have helped CrowdStrike avoid the rather costly incident.

VII. CONCLUSION

A. Restating the Importance of Operational Controls

Operational controls are one of the key factors to effective cybersecurity management (Abd & Zainol, 2021). In this regard, the incident related to CrowdStrike underlines the importance of organizations' ability to implement structured and rigorous operational procedures, including structured change management processes, testing, and rollback. Without controls, an organization exposes several critical risks: operational downtime, financial losses, and reputation loss. With cyber threats constantly evolving, a solid base of operational controls will ensure that companies can prevent, detect, and respond to incidents more effectively, thereby minimizing their impact and protecting their assets and data.

B. Summary of Key Insights From the CrowdStrike Case Study

The CrowdStrike case study provides key lessons on implementing comprehensive change management processes, pre-deployment testing, and reliable rollback mechanisms. It became clear how one tiny mistake in the deployment of an update can quickly snowball into a massive disruption, hitting millions of devices and numerous industries. The incident was further aggravated by a lack of thorough testing and effective rollback options, leading to prolonged and extensive downtime and operational setbacks. Understanding these failures helps organizations appreciate how rigorous procedures and preventive measures go a long way in averting similar system vulnerabilities.

C. Final Call to Action for Organizations to Enhance Cybersecurity Management Practices

With such excessive costs related to cybersecurity failures, organizations should enhance prioritizing cybersecurity management practices. This includes investments in strong change management frameworks, automating pre-deployment testing, and ensuring the systems have reliable backup and rollback mechanisms. This also includes continuous training and awareness to develop a security-conscious culture that will better equip employees to defend against active cyber threats. Through the proactive strengthening of cybersecurity infrastructures, organizations can reduce risks, ensure business continuity, and protect themselves from the financial and operational impacts that future incidents might cause. The time for action is now, and building a resilient cybersecurity framework has to be done quickly to deal with emerging challenges.

REFERENCES

Abdelkader, S., Amissah, J., Kinga, S., Mugerwa, G., Emmanuel, E., Mansour, D.-E. A., Bajaj, M., Blazek, V., & Prokop, L. (2024). Securing Modern Power Systems: Implementing Comprehensive Strategies to Enhance Resilience and Reliability Against Cyber-Attacks. *Results in Engineering, 23*, 102647–102647. DOI: 10.1016/j.rineng.2024.102647

Abd Majid, M., & Zainol Ariffin, K. A. (2021). Model for successful development and implementation of Cyber Security Operations Centre (SOC). *PLoS One, 16*(11), e0260157. DOI: 10.1371/journal.pone.0260157 PMID: 34797896

Alvarez Tech. (2024, August 14). *Crowdstrike Outage: What We Now Know – Alvarez Tech.* (2024, August 14). Alvarez Technology Group. https://www.alvareztg.com/crowdstrike-outage-what-we-now-know/

Fung, B. (2024, July 24). We finally know what caused the global tech outage - and how much it cost. CNN. https://edition.cnn.com/2024/07/24/tech/crowdstrike-outage-cost-cause/index.html

Ahlert, A. (2022). The Future of Vehicle Development Using Virtual Prototypes and an Interconnected Software Infrastructure. *Proceedings*, 229–243. DOI: 10.1007/978-3-658-37009-1_16

Ahmad, A., Maynard, S. B., Desouza, K. C., Kotsias, J., Whitty, M. T., & Baskerville, R. L. (2021). How can organizations develop situation awareness for incident response: A case study of management practice. *Computers & Security, 101*(1), 102122. DOI: 10.1016/j.cose.2020.102122

Ali, M., Khan, S. U., & Vasilakos, A. V. (2018). Security in cloud computing: Opportunities and challenges. *Information Sciences, 305*(1), 357–383. DOI: 10.1016/j.ins.2015.01.025

Akinsola, A., & Akinde, A. (2024). Enhancing Software Supply Chain Resilience: Strategy For Mitigating Software Supply Chain Security Risks And Ensuring Security Continuity In Development Lifecycle. *International Journal on Soft Computing, 15*(1/2), 01-18. DOI: 10.5121/ijsc.2024.15201

Burnstein, I. (2025). *Practical Software Testing*. Springer Professional Computing.

Johnson, R. (2024, August 9). *Lessons from Crowdstrike outage and incident response plan.* Cybersecurity and Cloud Services. Www.cai.iohttps://www.cai.io/resources/thought-leadership/cybersecurity-insights-and-prevention-strategies-from-the-crowdstrike-incident

Rittinghouse, J. W., & Hancock, W. M. (2025). *Cybersecurity Operations Handbook*. Elsevier Digital Press. Google Books. https://books.google.com/books?hl=en&lr=&id=BKYSfjEsi78C&oi=fnd&pg=PP1&dq=CISM

Jones, D. (2024, July 25). *CrowdStrike disruption direct losses to reach $5.4B for Fortune 500, study finds*. Cybersecurity Dive. https://www.cybersecuritydive.com/news/crowdstrike-cost-fortune-500-losses-cyber-insurance/722396/

DataCouch. (2024, September 3). *The Falcon's great Fall: The 2024 Update That Shook CrowdStrike's Legacy*. Medium; Medium. https://datacouch.medium.com/the-falcons-great-fall-the-2024-update-that-shook-crowdstrike-s-legacy-1d55c89e1ac1

De Zoysa. (2024, July 27). *Microsoft global outages caused by CrowdStrike software glitch*. https://www.researchgate.net/publication/382625564_Microsoft_global_outages_caused_by_CrowdStrike_software_glitch

Dissanayake, N., Zahedi, M., Jayatilaka, A., & Babar, M. A. (2022). Why, How and Where of Delays in Software Security Patch Management: An Empirical Investigation in the Healthcare Sector. *Proceedings of the ACM on Human-Computer Interaction, 6*(CSCW2), 1–29. DOI: 10.1145/3555087

Everett, G. D., & McLeod, R. (2025). *Software Testing*. John Wiley & Sons Inc. Google Books. https://books.google.com/books?hl=en&lr=&id=z8UdPmvkBHEC&oi=fnd&pg=PR7&dq=Everett

Fitzgerald, B., & Stol, K.-J. (2017). Continuous software engineering: A roadmap and agenda. *Journal of Systems and Software, 123*, 176–189. DOI: 10.1016/j.jss.2015.06.063

Giuffrida, C., Kuijsten, A., & Tanenbaum, A. S. (2013). Safe and automatic live update for operating systems. *SIGPLAN Notices, 48*(4), 279–292. DOI: 10.1145/2499368.2451147

Garousi, V., & Mäntylä, M. V. (2016). When and what to automate in software testing? A multi-vocal literature review. *Information and Software Technology, 76*, 92–117. DOI: 10.1016/j.infsof.2016.04.015

George, A. S. (2024). When Trust Fails: Examining Systemic Risk in the Digital Economy from the 2024 CrowdStrike Outage. *Partners Universal Multidisciplinary Research Journal, 1*(2), 134–152. DOI: 10.5281/zenodo.12828222

Hanmer, R. S. (2025). *Patterns for Fault Tolerant Software*. Wiley. Google Books. https://books.google.com/books?hl=en&lr=&id=jZgSAAAAQBAJ&oi=fnd&pg=PP12&dq=Hanmer

Highsmith, J. (2013). Adaptive Software Development: A Collaborative Approach to Managing Complex Systems. In *Google Books*. Addison-Wesley., https://books.google.com/books?hl=en&lr=&id=CVcUAAAAQBAJ&oi=fnd&pg=PR7&dq=Highsmith

Haapamäki, E., & Sihvonen, J. (2022). Cybersecurity in Accounting Research. *Routledge EBooks*, 182–214. DOI: 10.4324/9781003198123-10

Kopetz, H., & Steiner, W. (2022). *Real-Time Systems*. (2022). Real-time systems: design principles for distributed embedded applications. Springer Nature. https://tinyurl.com/2u62suk9

Lipner, S. (2018). The Trustworthy Computing Security Development Lifecycle. *20th Annual Computer Security Applications Conference*. DOI: 10.1109/CSAC.2004.41

Lindh, M., & Nolin, J. (2016). Information We Collect: Surveillance and Privacy in the Implementation of Google Apps for Education. *European Educational Research Journal, 15*(6), 644–663. DOI: 10.1177/1474904116654917

Ashare, M. (2024, July 25). *American Airlines credits IT teams with quick recovery from CrowdStrike disruption*. CIO Dive. https://www.ciodive.com/news/american-airlines-crowdstrike-outage-operatioins-recovery/722428/

Mircoserve. (2024, August 21). *CrowdStrike Incident: What Happened And What Did We Learn? | Microserve Canada*. Microserve Canada. https://www.microserve.ca/blog/crowdstrike-incident-summary-and-lessons/

Molyneaux, I. (2014). *The Art of Application Performance Testing*. O'Reilly. Google Books. https://books.google.com/books?hl=en&lr=&id=187UBQAAQBAJ&oi=fnd&pg=PR3&dq=Molyneaux

Munir, S., Kollnig, K., Shuba, A., & Shafiq, Z. (2024, April 4). *Google's Chrome Antitrust Paradox*. ArXiv.org. https://arxiv.org/abs/2406.11856

Neumann, P. G. (2000). Practical architectures for survivable systems and networks. Prepared by SRI International for the US Army Research Laboratory. https://shorturl.at/l6vOg

Stanford Law School. (2019). *TTLF Working Paper Series | Stanford Law School*. Stanford Law School. https://law.stanford.edu/transatlantic-technology-law-forum/ttlfs-working-paper-series/

Naseer, N. I. (2024). The crowdstrike incident: Analysis and unveiling the intricacies of modern cybersecurity breaches. *World Journal of Advanced Engineering Technology and Sciences, 13*(1), 728–733. DOI: 10.30574/wjaets.2024.13.1.0473

Nolan, L. (2024, July 29). *Consequences of Compliance: The CrowdStrike Outage of 19 July 2024*. USENIX. https://www.usenix.org/publications/loginonline/consequences-compliance-crowdstrike-outage-19-july-2024

Preston, W. C. (2007). Backup and Recovery: Inexpensive Backup Solutions for Open Systems. *Backup and Recovery*. (2025). O'Reilly. Google Books. https://books.google.com/books?hl=en&lr=&id=QgpIAgAAQBAJ&oi=fnd&pg=PR7&dq=Preston

Utting, M., & Legeard, B. (2010). Practical model-based testing: a tools approach. Elsevier. (2025). https://books.google.com/books?hl=en&lr=&id=8hAGtY4-oOoC&oi=fnd&pg=PP1&dq=Utting

Uchendu, B., Nurse, J. R. C., Bada, M., & Furnell, S. (2021). Developing a cyber security culture: Current practices and future needs. *Computers & Security*, *109*(1), 102387. DOI: 10.1016/j.cose.2021.102387

Kerner, S. M. (2024, October 29). *CrowdStrike outage explained: What caused it and what's next*. TechTarget. https://www.techtarget.com/whatis/feature/Explaining-the-largest-IT-outage-in-history-and-whats-next

Vaniea, K., & Rashidi, Y. (2016). Tales of Software Updates. *Proceedings of the 2016 CHI Conference on Human Factors in Computing Systems - CHI '16*, 3215–3226. DOI: 10.1145/2858036.2858303

KEY TERMS AND DEFINITIONS

Operational Controls: Safeguards or countermeasures that focus on the day-to-day security of systems and processes. These measures include procedures for monitoring, incident response, and ensuring that software or hardware changes do not compromise the overall security posture.

Change Management: A structured approach to planning, testing, and implementing system or software updates. It aims to minimize disruption by evaluating risks, communicating changes to stakeholders, and establishing clear protocols for deployment and rollback procedures.

Phased Rollouts: The practice of releasing updates or new features in incremental stages rather than all at once. This approach allows organizations to test for compatibility and stability on a smaller subset of systems before a full-scale deployment, reducing the risk of widespread disruption.

Rollback Plans: Predefined procedures to revert a system or application to its prior stable state if an update or change fails or causes significant issues. Rollback plans are a critical component of effective change management to quickly restore normal operations.

Endpoint Protection: A category of tools and strategies designed to secure end-user devices (e.g., desktops, laptops, mobile phones) against threats like malware, unauthorized access, and data breaches. Solutions typically include antivirus, intrusion detection, and continuous monitoring features.

Threat Intelligence: Information about current or emerging threats, malicious actors, vulnerabilities, and attack vectors. It helps organizations anticipate potential risks and tailor security controls to counter the most relevant dangers to their environment.

Compatibility Testing: The process of evaluating whether software, updates, or patches can operate seamlessly with existing systems, applications, or hardware. Proper compatibility testing helps prevent crashes, data corruption, or performance degradation after rollouts.

Misconfiguration: A vulnerability arising when system, network, or application settings are improperly implemented or left insecure by default. Misconfiguration can lead to unauthorized access, data leakage, or system failures.

Incident Response: The organized approach to detecting, managing, and recovering from security incidents. It typically includes processes for identifying a breach, limiting the damage, collecting evidence, and restoring normal operations while learning lessons to prevent recurrence.

Risk Management: The ongoing process of identifying, assessing, and mitigating risks that could adversely affect an organization's operations and objectives. In cybersecurity, risk management encompasses evaluating threats, establishing controls, and continuously monitoring for new or evolving vulnerabilities.

Chapter 2
Artificial Intelligence Strategies for Cleaner and Greener Manufacturing

Kathirvel Ayyaswamy
https://orcid.org/0000-0002-5347-9110
Department of Computer Science and Engineering, Saveetha Engineering College, Chennai, India

ABSTRACT

The journal aims to reduce energy usage that emits greenhouse gases by making products more productive and eco-friendlier. The writing deals with the issue of how the current trends in Industry 4.0 and AI systems can be used to protect the environment from the harms of pollution. It incorporates 1) conserving energy, implementing eco-friendlier workplaces, and reducing carbon footprints and 2) digital transformation with environmentally positive implications. Also, like in real manufacturing, it addresses the possibility of AI-driven manufacturing. It refers to Industry 5.0 as an evolutional road of communication and people and machines collaboration that transforms both society and individual; personalization as a result and higher productivity are just a few foundations to transform our perception of production and everyday life. Other Firstly, our guide will give some examples of preventive measures. This part stresses investing in R&D, collaborating, complying, and ensuring decision-making is informed by data running through the supply chain.

DOI: 10.4018/979-8-3373-2352-7.ch002

1. INTRODUCTION

This journal first questionnaire was eye-opening, because journal got information about AI techniques for clean and green production. Through this journal own personal research, it looked into the possible role between Artificial Intelligence and biodegradable packaging as a replacement to plastics. A practical option that has come to light is the utilization of starch amino as packing materials that offers a better option compared to traditional plastics.

AI has a number of applications that contribute to the optimum levels of biodegradable packaging materials usage as well. AI is capable of processing data related to the production, supply chain management logistics, and customer demand, which consequently, makes processes more streamlined and reduces the amount of waste. Such combinations of AI technologies can result in better utilization of available resources and can have a substantial impact in the reduction of harmful manufacturing practices.

Apart from this, measuring the success and effectivity of such measures also entails a period of monitoring and analysing results. Numbers like garbage recycling, carbon footprint reduction, and customer affinity to biodegradable packaging are useful indicators of how an artificial intelligence (AI)- based sustainability initiative is doing.

In the consideration of AI strategies as plausible sustainability improvements of biodegradable packaging, it should be stressed on by emphasizing the examples of successful implementation and best practices. Showcasing case studies that highlight the successful results of AI driven optimization solutions and the environmental benefits, is an effective way of making it clear for businesses.

In the end, AI strategies that target both the development of biodegradable packaging, economics and the possibility to scale up will get the first priority. Technology puts AI in manufacture with sustainability goals in mind, balancing out both sides thereby triggering positive environmental while at the same time meeting market demands.

2. PUBLIC SURVEY

The data of the AI application for cleaner and greener manufacturing was collected using a structured way in which different stakeholders representing varying perspectives and interests would be engaged. undefined

1. Survey Design: Overall, the first step was to build a detailed survey questionnaire that encompassed the main features of AI strategies, biodegradable packaging,

sustainable production, and opinions of the stakeholders regarding those themes. The survey instrument was carefully crafted in order to be understandable, precise and to the point as well as relevant so that the respondents will provide meaningful answers.

2. Target Audience: The choice of respondents comprised of people from both the public and private sectors who were involved in the manufacturing industry, including experts, researchers, academics, and policymakers. The mission was to collect a wide variety of views and authority related AI and Sustainability in manufacturing sector.
3. Distribution Channels: Numerous routes to market including the use of traditional and nontraditional media were employed to reach the audience effectively. These channels included digital platforms, industry meetings, professional groups, and direct applications to pertinent groups and agencies (Rithik et al, 2024). The research was presented in an email campaign, social media posts and joint collaborations with industry partners to increase the rate of visitor as much as possible (Kathirvel, A., and A. K. Naren, 2024e).
4. Data Collection: The online platforms were used in conducting a survey to make reaching and participation easier. Each participant has been provided with a link to the survey questionnaire and they are free to complete it on their own time. The questionnaire combined multiple choices, open-ended, and rating scales so as to collect data both objectively and subjectively.
5. Data Analysis: Which was the next step of processing the data from the responses in a systematic manner (Kathirvel A, and Maheswaran C P, 2023). I use qualitative data inclusive of demographic information and responses frequency to analyze the data using data statistical tools (Subramaniam et al, 2020). Advanced collection of the qualitative data collected through open-ended questions was analyzed thematically in order to reveal the recurring patterns, insights and themes expressed by the respondents.
6. Validation and Quality Assurance: In order to verify the accuracy and the reliability of the data, procedures such as data validation checks, anonymity assurances, and random sampling method was applied. As part of data quality checks, there were processes in place to ensure any mistakes or faults in the responses were identified and corrected.
7. Reporting: To conclude, this step was the publication of the results of the survey along with the insights gathered at the end as summary report. The report highlighted decisive points, forecasting's trends, guidelines for green AI manufacturing, and the importance of the upcoming research and practice.

The data collection procedures used in the survey was designed to ensure that the process was transparent and inclusive whilst creating a robust and factual construct which leveraged diverse viewpoints on AI strategies for more Cleaner and Greener Manufacturing.

3. THEORETICAL FRAMEWORK

Climate Change as a result of a transformation on the world environmental level has emerged as one of the most scale problems of advancement and economic development. Increasing of greenhouse gas levels with high intensity of the crude carbon dioxide (CO2) emissions is an appropriate nexus of the electricity production and consumption, which is slowly but surely represents great hindrances for the environment. (Climate Monitoring, 2020). International Zones established to fight the climate problems in some cases shifted the commercial activities related to these public good to other countries. (Aukker et al., 2013)

However, this has led to an insignificant transfer of emissions in preference to a proper reduction (Gobinath et al, 2024). This trouble worsens when manufacturing is relocated to countries that rely upon electricity sources with high carbon emissions or use technology that might be more power-efficient (Hamela and Dr.A.Kathirvel, 2019a).

In this case, developing international locations face an unequal proportion of obligation, contributing significantly to 63% of greenhouse gas emissions and enduring the bulk of the negative results of climate exchange. The economic impact of climate change is especially significant in these areas, currently standing at 78% and projected to rise to 87% by 2035. (Nordhaus, 2017). The susceptibility of those residing in tropical nations to natural calamities and their inferior living conditions exacerbate their difficulties. In poor countries, adopting traditional methods to reduce emissions, such as implementing pricing mechanisms or switching to cleaner energy sources, may need to be revised due to the impracticality of abandoning fossil fuels or pursuing nuclear energy in the short term. (Geissdoerfer, 2017)

Given these difficulties, the idea of a circular economy presents itself as a practical and viable alternative, at least in the foreseeable future (Hamela and Dr.A.Kathirvel,, 2019b).. The concepts of circular economy, which aim to decrease emissions without significantly modifying energy infrastructure, are perfectly compatible with intelligent technologies. As a fundamental component of the product supply system and a significant contributor to greenhouse gas emissions, manufacturing plays a crucial role in the fight against climate change. Incorporating intelligent technologies into manufacturing processes is essential for attaining a more environmentally friendly and efficient paradigm.

The transition from "Industry 4.0" to "Industry 5.0" indicates a strategic shift inside the industrial paradigm, highlighting the significance of planetary limitations and societal objectives in production and economic advancement. The notion of "Intelligence" has served as a forerunner to this shift, emphasizing the importance of capturing and monitoring manufacturing operations to guide them toward environmental sustainability (Sendler, 2017,44). Industry 5.0 presents a new method focusing on providing long-term service for ecological and societal advantages, such as prioritizing human needs, promoting sustainability, and enhancing resilience.

Given the circumstances, transforming innovative manufacturing systems into a more environmentally friendly model during the industry 5.0 era is reasonable and crucial. Implementing intelligent technologies, known as "Intelligent manufacturing (GIM)," is a new and integrated manufacturing approach that facilitates the achievement of green objectives. (Deif, 2011). This research suggests that intelligent technologies can achieve different green and sustainable goals. It emphasizes the importance of continuously evaluating and improving the sustainability of these systems using green metrics. In the face of climate change, combining innovative technologies and eco-friendly production offers a hopeful path toward sustainable and ecologically aware industrial progress. (Atlas & Florida, 1998)

Currently, the emphasis on safeguarding the environment has grown increasingly vital. As societies globally acknowledge the pressing necessity to tackle environmental concerns, the notion of Green Smart Manufacturing (GSM) has evolved as a crucial contributor to this international endeavour. (Heller & Shukla, 2003) Since the industrial sector plays a significant role in economic advancement and energy usage, incorporating artificial intelligence (AI) into Green Manufacturing projects has become crucial to promoting sustainability. (Breque, 2021)

Governments actively promote the transition to Green Smart production because they recognize the importance of environmentally conscious production. (Zhou et al., 2019). The German Industry 4.0, Remaking America, and Made in China 2025 initiatives demonstrate a shared dedication to promoting sustainability in industrial methods. The recent (Kathirvel et al, 2024 a & b) upsurge in government backing has significantly increased industry and research on green manufacturing. (Duan et al., 2024)

Integrating artificial intelligence into Green Manufacturing processes, namely through the deployment of conversational and expressive robots, has significant promise. AI enhances industrial performance and aligns with the Sustainable Development Goals (SDGs), facilitating sustainable growth. By utilizing AI technologies, industries may make significant and purposeful contributions to the global environmental agenda.

Incorporating Artificial Intelligence into Green Manufacturing is crucial in today's rapid technical progress and environmental consciousness. In the 21st century, combining technology and environmental preservation is essential for creating a sustainable and resilient future.

The Development and Evolution of Greentelligent Engineering: Paving the Way for The Green Revolution in AI Strategies for Cleaner and Greener Manufacturing

The paper discusses the evolution and framework of Greentelligent Manufacturing, which aims to promote cleaner and greener manufacturing practices. It highlights the role of artificial intelligence strategies in driving the green revolution in manufacturing. (Sundar and Kathirvel, 2019).

Figure 1. Evolution of AI strategies

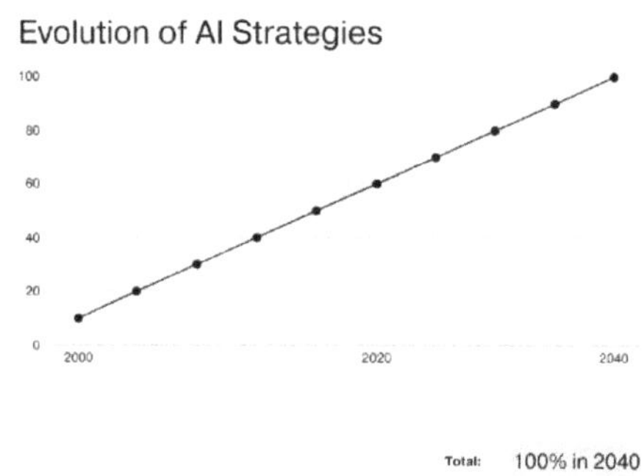

Three degrees may be distinguished inside the evolution of intelligent manufacturing (GIM): emergent, transitional, and synergetic (Figure 1). The authentic desires of Intelligent Manufacturing (IM) and Green Manufacturing (GM) were sustainability and the exceptional use of available resources. GM and IM collaborated and pooled their talents to accomplish their objectives throughout the transitional segment. When GM and IM reached the synergetic degree, they laboured properly collectively, coordinating their goals and utilizing devices designed with each paradigm in thought. The evolution led to the development of intelligent manufacturing (GIM) as an intellectual manufacturing paradigm based upon humans and environmentally benign.

Figure 2. Framework of artificial intelligent strategies for cleaner and greener manufacturing

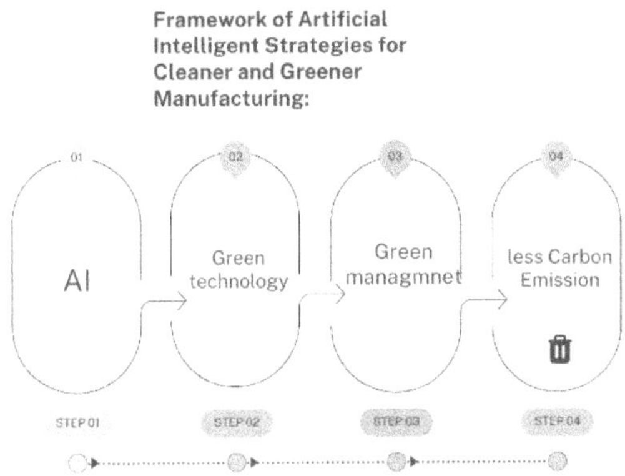

"Greentelligent Manufacturing" aims to maximize efficiency, sustainability, and control in manufacturing processes by fusing green practices with intelligent technologies. The Greentelligent Manufacturing framework has been meticulously designed to encompass an extensive array of novel processes and materials, such as clean energy generation methods and the creation of eco-friendly products 'Intelligent' refers to incorporating contemporary sensor technologies, automation, and process optimization within the manufacturing environment, encompassing intelligent infrastructure, programs, and networked solutions (Kathirvel et al, 2020). In addition, it includes specialized "Information and Communication Technologies-ICT" that enable the real-time tracking of Waste, consumption, and greenhouse gas (GHG) emissions. It also facilitates the real-time control of energy, productivity, and costs across many sites. (Nimbalkar, 2017)

Integrating sensible technology into Green intelligent manufacturing is vital for achieving sustainable desires, staying aggressive, and enhancing the fee of advanced production industries. The framework ensures that business operations are green and environmentally responsible by integrating clever infrastructure and actual-time tracking.

Its objective is to achieve a more environmentally friendly approach by modifying industrial processes and reimagining product designs. Additionally, it prioritizes using ecologically friendly practices in manufacturing, such as decreasing emissions, optimizing resource utilization, and improving energy efficiency. Finally, it evaluates the environmental sustainability of the intelligent methods used in the production system. (Kumar & Rao, 2018)

In the following sections, we will examine Greentelligent Manufacturing more extensively, investigating the mechanisms that enable it and the tools and processes that support it. As we progress through this transformation, incorporating advanced technologies and environmentally friendly approaches becomes crucial for cleaner, more sustainable manufacturing practices. It is a significant milestone in the pursuit of the green revolution.

4. MATERIAL AND METHODS

This journal had the pleasure to do public questionnaire to help me understand AI strategies oriented towards cleaner and greener manufacturing. The reactions revealed an array of opinions and ideas that not only brought into focus the possible role of AI in manufacturing sustainability but also its major game changer character in this regard.

A highly ranked finding from the study was the role of AI in managing predictive maintenance. Participants agreed that AI-based predictive analytics is of great importance in preventing the emergence of defects in operation beforehand. With early detection of such problems, manufacturers can prevent machine downtimes and minimize material wastage with the potential to gain better operating efficiency in line with the environmentally friendly manufacturing approach.

Not only did the survey provided the optimism but it also showed how AI could double up in promoting the circular economy in the manufacturing sector. AI applications in supply chain management related to the product lifecycle emerged as highly sought after, particularly design optimization, reduction in overproduction using predictive demand forecast and planning, and intelligent routing (Kathirvel, 2024e). These tactics, in their view, should play a big role in making environmental footprint of the industrial operations less bulky.

It is interesting that some of the respondents remarked of the ethical implications of the introduction of AI in manufacturing. They then raised issues about data privacy, algorithmic biases and the need for transparency ownership in AI driven decision making processes. They argued that addressing these specific concerns would pave way for trust in artificial intelligence technologies and proper use of them in powering sustainability goals (Jolin et al, 2025).

The research also found that AI adoption is facing some challenges in the manufacturing sector. Low understanding of AI capabilities, high initial costs of implementation, and skills required for this field are among problems mentioned by topics experts (Kathirvel, 2024f0. Meanwhile, a number of the participants expressed their confidence in the possibility of an alliance between the players of industry, academy, and governmental institutions whose aims include overcoming the barriers and stimulating the adopttion of AI which is aimed at green and clean manufacturing processes.

Lastly, the public survey on AI strategies for manufacturing that can be both cleaner and greener showed that the residents of the community hold a wide array of opinions and viewpoints. AI goes a long way in boosting resourcing efficiency to predictive maintenance and circular economy frameworks and, therefore, presents tremendous potential in leading the way for manufacturing sustainability.

Solving ethical issues as well as removal of barriers will be an important factor in using the AI to drive and achieve better environmental sustainability with industries.

5. EMERGING STUDIES THAT SUPPORT THE AI STRATEGIES IN GREEN MANUFACTURING: MANUFACTURING: A JOURNEY TOWARDS GREENER INNOVATION

Chen, Jiang, Yang, and Gao (2023) reported that the Global Cleaner manufacturing Conference (GCPC) 2023 showcased notable progress in cleaner manufacturing methodologies. Within the field of Greentelligent Manufacturing, Life Cycle Assessment (LCA) plays a crucial role as a standardized method for assessing environmental implications. Automation and artificial intelligence improve the efficiency of LCA by streamlining cost evaluations and connecting them to specific production processes for future projections. Advanced Information and Communication Technologies (ICTs) and the Internet of Things (IoT) allow for the continuous monitoring of CO2 emissions, which supports implementing a pricing model that considers the environmental impact. Furthermore, carbon taxes and Emissions Trading Systems (ETS) incentivize environmentally friendly behaviours, influencing producers and consumers worldwide. (Wara, 2007)

"Carbon Capture and Storage (CCS)" is a promising solution for achieving carbon neutrality but has obstacles. Norway is at the forefront of implementing "Carbon Capture and Storage (CCS)", viewing it as a significant endeavour comparable to a "Moon mission" in reducing carbon emissions, according to the authors Pérez-Fortes et al. in 2014. Intelligent technologies offer answers, which include virtual twins that verify strength usage and IoT tracking for optimizing plant operations. As we move towards sustainable production, these tools are essential for optimizing processes, minimizing emissions, and promoting a more environmentally friendly future.

Reconfigurable Manufacturing: Adapting for Tomorrow

Reconfigurable manufacturing (RM) demonstrates its ability to adapt and effectively handle wastewater and emissions by employing systematic reconfiguration. Integrating IoT technologies and AI in RM systems improves their capabilities by enabling early detection of machine faults, minimizing defects, and promoting efficient and sustainable manufacturing processes.

6. SIGNIFICANCE OF IMPLEMENTATION OF THE AI GREEN REVOLUTION

In today's increasing globalization and industrialization age, ensuring sustainability has become a top priority for enterprises. The expanded consciousness regarding environmental, social, and economic difficulties requires the implementation of ethical and sustainable business practices throughout supply chains. Sustainability, as defined by the World Commission on Environment and Development, refers to a type of development that meets the current generation's requirements while also considering the ability of future generations to fulfil their own needs. This definition recognizes the constraints imposed by limited natural resources (WCED, n.d).

To successfully navigate the intricate terrain of sustainability, it is necessary to tackle the social, economic, and environmental aspects, each of which has its own set of obstacles and changing importance as time progresses (Andrews, 2015). Attaining the entire sustainability of an employer poses a challenging task, requiring a complete approach that encompasses remodelling the commercial enterprise. This reorganization prioritizes the incorporation of Industry 4.0 (IDY four.0) technologies, "sustainable cleaner production", and "circular financial system-CE" practices.

Industry four.0 technology, which encompasses artificial intelligence techniques for more excellent environmentally friendly manufacturing, is becoming a critical element in this change. Artificial intelligence (AI), capable of making choices primarily based on data and automated approaches, offers organizations an effective device to improve their sustainability projects (Kathirvel et al, 2025). AI-enabled cleaner manufacturing techniques can reduce environmental effects and resource use. The round financial system, facilitated by utilizing superior technologies, promotes the most significant usage of resources through recycling and remanufacturing processes.

Figure 3. Waste management cycle

AI techniques are becoming increasingly crucial for cleaner and greener production because they contain the answers to sustainability challenges in the best form. Incorporating Industry 4.0 technology is an excellent approach to increasing operational efficiency, reducing environmental impact, and promoting a circular economy. Users experience a complex picture of reality, and it is no longer only technological development but also an imperative strategic necessity as it is aligned with environmental sustainability and social welfare. AI programs are a tipping point for corporations, be it as gift essentials or as a way of ensuring that the future generation can do as well and not be left out of the equation. (Call for Papers - Journal of Cleaner Production I ScienceDirect.com by Elsevier, n.d.)

7. ADOPTION OF AI AND ITS IMPACT ON SUSTAINABLE PRODUCTION

Adopting AI innovations is a revolutionary force that propels manufacturers into an era of greater competitiveness, resilience, and environmental responsibility in pursuing sustainable manufacturing. AI strategies are characterized by the adoption of modular, automated processes that are guided by data. It allows for specific management of supply networks and fabric flows. The numerous benefits include more suitable competition, improved overall performance, and greater profitability. This wave of innovation may want to disrupt the production panorama by transforming production and transport techniques. It can also create a CO2 gasoline-free atmosphere and sell environmentally friendly production techniques.

Smart Factory technology, a defining characteristic of AI strategies, carries robotics, machine-to-system communication, and immediate decision-making into manufacturing operations. The final result is a more advantageous manufacturing cycle, ending in a faster product era, even optimizing capital expenditures. Incorporating synthetic intelligence (AI) techniques in Industry 4.0 enhances those benefits, facilitating the transition towards more environmentally friendly production methods. Data democratization and insight's introduction are prioritized to allow a seamless link past the flower production limits. It guarantees that sustainability concerns are incorporated into each part of the production environment. (Müller et al., 2018)

AI strategies necessitate a transformational industrial policy to create a sustainable environment. This approach should incorporate ongoing retraining and upgrading, spotting the dynamic nature of generation and automation. Establishing comprehensive commercial coverage for AI strategies is crucial to bringing together digital breakthroughs in different markets and areas. This policy alternate requires people to increase new capabilities that prioritize flexibility, the capacity to apply actual-time facts efficiently, and the potential to evolve line setups to fulfil daily requirements and adjustments. The emergence of Industry four.0 represents a vast transformation, necessitating a reevaluation of traditional factors of industries, consisting of production traces and supply chains, driven through novel technical possibilities and facts assets. (Habib & Chimsom, 2019)

The "Internet of Things-IoT" is critical in driving "Industry 4.0" with AI strategies projects by facilitating gathering statistics from numerous gadgets and sensors. Using AI and systems to gain knowledge of gear with records evaluation bureaucracy inspires sustainable manufacturing. The concept of Industry 4.0 facilitates integrating machines and programs into gadgets, resulting in an unbroken cycle of operation and machine-gaining knowledge. Organizations adopting Industry four.0 technology, including the "Internet of Things-IoT", synthetic intelligence (AI), and system getting to know, have experienced accelerated profitability and advanced performance in their operations. (Ammar et al., 2021) "Industry 4.0" is applied to the manufacturing sector to promote sustainable practices.

AI strategies effortlessly integrate with the current focus on sustainable manufacturing, facilitating the incorporation of sustainable development principles into the industrial sector. This integration leads to increased environmental, social, and economic efficiency. Industry 4.0 is a concept that encompasses the integration of digitalization technologies, big data, Cyber-Physical Structures, virtual reality, and cloud computing. Industry 4.0 has significant promise in sustainable manufacturing to increase productivity, streamline processes, and improve overall corporate efficiency. Nevertheless, the production sector has challenges and risks requiring sustainable methods. (Piccarozzi et al., 2018)

Big data, analytics, and deep learning are becoming critical factors in sustainable manufacturing, providing enhanced communication and efficiency in daily operations. In the energy industry, a significant change is happening, with digital electronic devices replacing paper. This transition is leading to new methods of functioning, communicating, and working with clients. (Chong et al., 2018)

AI strategies go beyond automation and include implementing sustainable practices in intelligent production. This evolution impacts smart grids, green energy management, and distributed output, contributing to a comprehensive approach to sustainability. As hardware vendors and software development businesses collaborate to construct and integrate corporate applications, the emphasis turns to ensuring internal reliability and adopting environmentally sustainable methods. The process of digitization, driven by AI strategies, not only provides new and creative ways of doing business but also accelerates the generation of renewable energy and the implementation of environmentally friendly energy supply strategies.

8. ANALYTICAL APPROACH

Integrating the principles pursuing sustainable development goals:

The idea of "Pollution Prevention Pays" (PPP) combined with "Life Cycle Thinking" (LCT) to contribute to poverty reduction, climate change and social inequality can be realized by adopting a holistic environmental approach. The pollutant prevention program (PPP) adopts the strategy of catching and removing pollution right at the starting phase when it is still easy to deal with. It highlights that if pollution can be avoided, it will benefit the environment and the economy. By applying pollution control measures, organizations can decrease the amount of trash created, minimize the environmental impact, and cut down on waste disposal and treatment expenses. The order in which the mentioned factors have been placed is in line with SDG 12 (Responsible et al.), as it provides the necessary impetus for resource efficiency, waste reduction and sustainable practices.

LCT, or Life Cycle Thinking, is not limited to just one portion of the product or process. It is a broader view of the life cycle of a product or process, which incorporates the extraction of raw materials, the production process, and the final disposal. It aims to understand the surroundings and make products more effective from the design phase.

The results provided by the authors Chen, Jiang, Yang, & Gao, 2023). at the Global Cleaner Production Conference (GCPC) in September 2023 underline the relevance of sustainable production techniques. The cooperation framework of the PPPs and LCTs with sustainable development demanded a holistic strategic plan, which covered coordination between sectors, governments, and NGOs as the first step. Such culture must be acknowledged and perpetuated while allocating financial resources for technology and method development to prevent pollution. It could be that undertaking detailed environmental assessments, using sustainable production methods and cleaning up using the ecosystem principles are some ways of mitigating environmental impact. Furthermore, companies may apply the tools for lifecycle assessment and sustainability certificates to determine and spread information about the environmental impact of their products or services.

Governments have a crucial role in stabilizing and controlling sustainable practices by laying down the necessary policy and regulatory frameworks. Governments can establish pollution control regulations, provide financial incentives for environmentally friendly investments and help businesses adopt these methods through green procurement policies. Furthermore, governments should promote knowledge exchange and capacity-building programs as part of the strategy to transfer knowledge and skills that will help introduce PPP and LCT concepts to more sectors.

Civil society establishments, which include non-governmental businesses (NGOs), academics, and community groups, are critical in raising awareness, advocating for, and concerning stakeholders in sustainable improvement. Civil society may create top trade and ensure duty for environmental consequences by promoting pollutant avoidance and life cycle thinking, lobbying for legislative changes, and actively interacting with companies and legislators.

Ultimately, including pollution prevention and existence cycle wondering in pursuing sustainable development goals affords a radical approach to tackling environmental issues and promoting economic growth and social development. Businesses also lessen their environmental impact, improve aid performance, and help sustainable development objectives by enforcing proactive pollutant manipulation measures and thinking about the whole life cycle of their services or products. Practical cooperation among enterprises, governments, and civil society is crucial in promoting sustainable practices and advancing the shift towards a more sustainable and resilient future.

9. RESULTS

Incorporating Artificial Intelligence (AI) has become a powerful catalyst in driving sustainable and eco-friendly production. Although AI holds the potential to transform processes, minimize inefficiencies, and address the issue of greenhouse gas emissions, its deployment is full of risks and problems. Mastering those vital elements is essential for the effective use of AI in achieving waste-unfastened and greenhouse gasoline-unfastened manufacturing. (Bag, 2022).

Given the heavy reliance of AI systems on records, ensuring the privacy and safety of touchy information is an extensive problem. Highbrow property theft is drastically risky in economic enterprises, where special techniques and designs are giant. AI systems will rely on vast datasets for learning, and if data is peculiarly used or tampered with, it could have dangerous implications. To minimize those security issues, adequate cybersecurity measures must be implemented and comply with statistical security laws.

Figuring out the ethical form of using AI for industrial purposes is becoming more demanding daily. We can increase social, economic, and environmental inequalities with biases in AI algorithms. It occurs through the evolution of the gaps. For example, greener production might resort to an algorithm that is skewed techniques or components, subsequently hindering the original aim of sustainability. Ethical and fair processes must be considered when using artificial intelligence to avoid negative consequences. (Garetti, M, 2012).

Many manufacturing facilities use old structures that want to be mainly built to support superior technology consisting of synthetic intelligence (AI). Incorporating AI into the present-day infrastructure provides a significant obstacle. Manufacturers may be discouraged from adopting AI for environmentally friendly operations due to compatibility issues, retrofitting costs, and manufacturing interruptions during the changeover.

Deploying AI technology necessitates a considerable initial expenditure on hardware, software programs, and training. Manufacturers may be hesitant because of the ambiguity surrounding the return on investment (ROI) and the length required to attain demonstrable blessings. The capability for economic losses and the requirement for a long-term long-term outlook is probably intimidating. Effective dissemination of capacity lengthy-term benefits and conducive economic climate cultivation is essential for selling the significant adoption of AI within the production sector.

Introducing new technology, especially in industries with established techniques, now and again requires assistance with alternate resistance. Obtaining the help of stakeholders, control, and employees for AI's advantages in promoting environmentally pleasant production can be met with doubt and hesitance. Implementing change management processes, engaging in effective verbal exchanges, and highlighting early achievements

It is crucial to overcome resistance and inspire a way of life that is open to innovation.

Although implementing AI in manufacturing aims to minimize the environmental footprint, it is essential to behave through environmental impact checks (EIA). It is crucial to guarantee that AI operations no longer lead to pollutants or beneficial resource depletion. In addition, manufacturers should not forget the proper disposal of AI-related technology when giving up its existence cycle and mitigating any capacity environmental effects.

Manufacturing organizations must be subject to strict ecological regulations, and AI solutions do not simplify things. Verifying the AI methods in line with the established environmental requirements and gaining regulatory approvals may be complex and time-consuming. AI-enabled models present specific compliance challenges to manufacturers that need to direct assets and legal expertise to examine these complexities thoroughly but still need to match adherence to rules and operations requirements.

AI intelligence can immensely assist in enhancing supply chain transparency and traceability, the demolition of which is of much concern as far as sustainability is concerned.Also, as environmental authorities consider implementing devices in a challenging global supply chain, they encounter several issues. The implementation strategy for the sustainability of the production process must include the routine check-up of all materials and elements to meet the required criteria. This is why the collaboration with providers and blockchain technology we can do to traceability is at its best.

For AI systems to bring about lower manufacturing tactics and operating costs, manufacturing AI hardware often results in ecological expenditures. Challenges arise from the mining and processing uncommon elements for the AI era, electricity-intensive manufacturing tactics, and digital waste control. Achieving a harmonious equilibrium between the blessings of synthetic intelligence and the ecological effect of its hardware necessitates a complete and all-encompassing strategy in the direction of sustainability.

Integrating AI in business industries gives capacity advantages and problems as the purpose is to reap waste-free and greenhouse gas-loose operations. Thorough deliberation is required because of the hazards related to statistics privacy, moral concerns, the integration of outdated structures, and the environmental consequences of the manufacturing AI era. To surmount those problems, a collective endeavour must encompass prominent figures in the region, policymakers, and the labour pressure. By adopting a scientific and accountable method, synthetic intelligence (AI) can function as an influential associate in accomplishing environmentally friendly and green manufacturing methods, thereby facilitating the improvement of a sustainable business future.

10. STRATEGICAL RECOMMENDATION FROM RESULTS

Above are the challenges which can be associated with the following recommendations: By using artificial intelligence (AI) to achieve environmentally friendly and pollution-free manufacturing processes, it is possible to develop several strategic suggestions to tackle these crucial issues (Jovane et al.,2008)

Dedicate resources to R&D endeavours to create AI technologies customized for sustainable manufacturing. It includes financial programs promoting advancements in renewable energy, waste minimization, and carbon capture technology. Bhamra (2016)

Promote cooperation among industry players, government agencies, academic institutions, and technology suppliers to expedite the implementation of AI-powered solutions. Collaborative endeavours may facilitate the exchange of optimal methods, combine resources, and stimulate joint efforts to achieve sustainability objectives.

Keep updated with changing rules and standards for environmental protection and emissions reduction. Efficiently incorporate these criteria into industrial processes and allocate resources to technology that guarantees adherence to present and future laws.

Adopt a method of making decisions based on data using AI analytics to maximize the use of resources, reduce waste, and find ways to increase efficiency. Develop and deploy reliable data gathering and analysis systems to monitor environmental performance parameters and facilitate ongoing improvement efforts.

Allocate resources towards implementing training initiatives that enhance the skills and capabilities of workers, enabling them to run AI-enabled industrial systems proficiently. Establish and foster an organization's sustainability and environmental stewardship culture to align with its strategic goals.

Broaden the use of AI beyond internal industrial operations to include the entire supply chain. Engage with suppliers and logistics partners to deploy artificial intelligence-based solutions to manage inventories, optimize transportation, and implement sustainable sourcing practices.

Establish mechanisms for ongoing monitoring and assessment of environmental performance measures to measure progress towards sustainability objectives— Utilise real-time data analytics to pinpoint areas of improvement and adapt strategy appropriately.

Investigate potential investments in renewable energy sources, such as solar, wind, and hydroelectric power, to decrease dependence on fossil fuels and carbon emissions linked to industrial processes. (Arnold, Kiel, and Voigt 2016)

Manufacturers may become leaders in sustainable industrial practices by prioritizing these strategic guidelines, which will help them overcome the hurdles of applying AI for greener and cleaner production.

11. APPLICATIONS: FOR AI STRATEGIES FOR ACHIEVING CLEANER AND GREENER MANUFACTURING

AI techniques significantly improve within the commercial zone, wherein physical sports and virtual generation are integrated, resulting in a transformative impact. AI techniques usher in a new generation of optimal performance, approaches, and development in production through mixing devices, gaining knowledge of and real-time facts processing. This advancement also contributes to a cleaner and more environmentally friendly production technique. This paradigm shift enhances productiveness, efficiency, and flexibility and promotes sustainability, leading to extended profitability and toughness for companies. (Sarmiento et al., 2020)

Factories Which are Sustainable and Clever

One of the number-one ways to introduce Intry 4.0 is to convert production facilities into environmentally pleasant and intelligent factories. Companies are reorganizing their production procedures to beautify their environmental friendliness and sustainability. It includes integrating interconnected production gadgets, energy structures empowered with synthetic intelligence, and gadgets for the industrial Internet of Things. Implementing AI technologies helps with accountable intake and improvement by effectively dealing with natural resources through circular financial system concepts and weather cognizance.

Minimized Carbon Emissions and Pollution Management

AI techniques are essential in mitigating carbon emissions and managing pollutants in many industries. These sustainability dreams are achieved with robotics, renewable energy, statistics collection, IoT, and digitalization. Industry 4.0 complements development in fields that include solar power consumption, energy safety, and lightweight materials by reducing the reliance on conventional fossil fuels and optimizing aid usage. (Dincer and Acar, 2015)

Eco-Friendly Structures

Industry 4.0 has many applications in creating sustainable buildings, from architecture to continuing management. Architects utilize Building Information Modeling (BIM) software to enhance the sustainability of buildings. Digital technologies facilitate the use of eco-friendly bacteria that possess the inherent ability to repair structures, thereby demonstrating the potential of sustainable design and architecture. Intelligent systems actively control heating and cooling to optimize energy usage in real time, improving overall environmental effectiveness.

Utilizing Digital Information for Beneficial Environmental Influence

Industry 4.0 incorporates digital information and communication technology to address and reduce the favourable environmental effects caused by different businesses. Analyzing manufacturing processes and quantifying the positive consequences of intelligent manufacturing are achieved through digital technologies. It entails a thorough digital transformation endeavour to improve operational efficiency, workplace health and safety, and collaboration with product design departments.

Increased Sustainable Advantages

AI strategies and technologies provide a comprehensive solution for dealing with the intricacies of technology, manufacturing, and sustainability. The advantages of sustainability are improved by assessing and grouping production procedures according to enabling technologies such as 5G cellular wireless connectivity, IoT, machine learning, and augmented reality. Practical applications arise, enhancing operational procedures, environmental friendliness, and collaboration between manufacturers, suppliers, and customers.

Service Management

AI strategies achieve efficient service management by connecting measurement devices with manufacturing businesses' comprehensive information and automation infrastructure in energy and services management. It entails gathering, transmitting, and retaining immense energy supply utilization, generation, and shift data. The widespread availability of data and improved accessibility to computing resources (Kathirvel et al, 2024c) enable the utilization of advanced artificial intelligence methods for identifying variables and analyzing patterns. (Waibel et al., 2017)

Enhancement of Productivity

One of the main objectives of Industry 4.0 is to enhance operations' efficiency, competitiveness, and overall financial commitment. Industry 4.0 enhances proactive resource use in enterprises by prioritizing energy management. Different power generation sources must be integrated into a market that is both increasingly demanding and spread out to maximize energy efficiency (Kathirvel, 2024d).

Improving Environmental Innovation

Industry 4.0 encompasses environmental advancements through optimizing automated manufacturing processes, leading to improved efficiency and less waste generation. The Internet of Things (IoT) is a network that links machines, sensors, actuators, and computers together to gather and exchange information. Digital twins are virtual representations of natural properties and systems that offer valuable insights for future planning, data collection, and device surveillance. Cyber-physical systems combine computational, network, physical processes, and environmental advancements within the system (Chin et al.,2019)

Enhancing Production Efficiency

Cloud computing networks work together to supply data to optimize production, predict process failures, and reduce downtime. Interoperability facilitates the effective exchange of knowledge among various entities such as units, sensors, actuators, devices, robots, and human beings. Big data and analytics pertain to the extensive and ever-changing datasets obtained from diverse sources of machine learning technology. Industry 4.0 is a field that focuses on developing strategies, ideas, and solutions to optimize safety and production in industries. It, in particular, emphasizes the use of prevention techniques. (Nahavandi,2019)

Enhance Proficiency and Adaptability in Automation

Training and practice structures are essential in equipping people with the competencies to thrive in developing Industry 4.0 professions. The past few centuries' commercial enterprise and industrial sector advancements encompass various technological components associated with Industry 4.0. Robots are essential for implementing bendy automation and offer numerous benefits, such as extra excellent manipulation, a more secure printing environment, reduced bottlenecks, improved performance, and enhanced worker pride. Robotic integration can improve environmentally sustainable strategies

Eco-Friendly

Elevated degrees of automation enhance manufacturing and worker protection. Heavy machinery may additionally be managed using far-flung control and haptic remarks technology over 5G networks.

Tackling Climate Change

AI strategies offer practical techniques and instruments to tackle climate change and other sustainability goals, leading to favourable industry outcomes. Partnerships among technological pioneers, scientists, private enterprises, and non-profit entities play a crucial role in the swift progress of the worldwide economy. The advent of digital technology brings forth novel consumer prospects and transforms business practices, thereby impacting the long-term sustainability of economies. This technology can significantly influence the protection, inclusivity, affordability, and long-term growth of all those involved.

Manage Entire Industrial Operations

Industries that aim to automate their industrial operations recognize the importance of access to current and relevant data. Connecting to cloud storage may ensure all pertinent data is accessible anytime and anywhere. Industry 4.0 technology, such as cameras and sensors, offer supplementary data to assist engineers in achieving jobs with more efficiency. Integrating nanotechnology with 3D printing enhances production by increasing flexibility and improving energy efficiency.

Reduce Waste

The automotive sector wholeheartedly adopts lean methods, prioritizing eliminating waste in all manufacturing parts. Adopting lean thinking allows manufacturers to reduce resource consumption, including packaging, raw materials, and energy. The response to climate change presents an opportunity to increase revenue, expand industries, and cultivate a sustainable image. Implementing intelligent manufacturing techniques can effectively reduce waste and minimize the emission of greenhouse gases while enhancing production processes.

12. IMPLEMENTING INNOVATIVE SUPPLY CHAIN MANAGEMENT PRACTICES TO ACHIEVE SUSTAINABILITY GOALS IN THE ERA OF CARBON TRADING

In the midst of the developing worry for natural maintainability and the pressing need to lessen fossil fuel byproducts, production network the executives (SCM) systems have acquired huge significance in achieving manageability targets, particularly in carbon exchanging. In the midst of the gigantic extension of the worldwide economy, fossil fuel byproducts have turned into a significant block to accomplishing economical turn of events. Producing firms, which assume a critical part in fossil fuel byproducts, face developing requests to carry out low-carbon rehearses all through their stockpile chains. Moreover, there is a developing accentuation on carrying out reusing and remanufacturing answers for items that have arrived at the finish of their life cycle. It is finished to help the shift towards a round economy, which plans to expand asset utilization and save energy.

To address these difficulties, creative supply chain management strategies must be used to promote carbon reduction and improve sustainability outcomes. Carbon trading systems, which facilitate the exchange of carbon credits between businesses, have become prominent as efficient instruments for controlling carbon emissions from industrial facilities. Governments are also regulating by creating regulation laws on carbon emissions monitoring to make carbon trading an integral part of worldwide initiatives on climate change management. So this is why a good supply chain management (SCM) strategy application should be aimed at the period of carbon trading in order to accomplish sustainability objectives and considerably reduce carbon emissions.

This special issue wants to have a research section that includes all studies that are innovatively focused on designing supply chain management systemic methods that can meet the carbon trading era requirements. The discussions and encouragements provided in this study will develop exploitable concepts and techniques that facilitate trading costs and, thus, the sustainability achieved by concentrating on transformative advances in SCM.

Introducing emissions of carbon issues into the supply chain management process is a significant feature signifying what the focus is on. Conventionally, cost and productivity have led enterprises to develop supply chain strategies. However, organizations that trade carbon must deal with both sides of the coin and focus on making their procedures environmentally friendly and with fewer carbon emissions. Through the promulgation of carbon emissions data into a decision support system, businesses can now develop advanced supply chain management methods and make science-based choices. The former makes reusing and recycling the primary components, increasing the product lifecycle and reducing the environmental load.

Furthermore, ensuring that the materials are purchased sustainably is essential for promoting carbon offset within the supply chains. Organizations may greatly reduce emissions by obtaining them independently or through suppliers with the least carbon consequence. The latest SCM (Supply chain management) is technology-driven and employs data analytics that utilizes information on suppliers' eco-friendliness to find issues that need cooperation and enhancements. By forming long-term alliances with suppliers who constantly push for environmental sustainability, the concept of the supply value chain can be boosted, encouraging greener production chains and global carbon footprint reduction.

We also focus on applying eco-friendly logistical and transport management systems. As transportation, to a considerable extent, enables CO2 emissions within the logistics chain, completing its processes efficiently that considers the environmental impact is the key to minimizing the negative effects. The eco-friendly SCM approach focuses on improving carrier routes, adopting high-tech vehicle types, and promoting other ways of transportation, such as rail and marine transport. Besides that, shifting to electric vehicles and using alternative renewable energies for logistics activities result in significant carbon target achievement.

13. FUTURE SCOPE

Within the manufacturing industry, the future is poised to provide several prospects and breakthroughs due to the incorporation of AI techniques to achieve cleaner and more environmentally friendly production. A vital development place is the ongoing improvement and broadening of Industry 4.0 technology. With the growing recognition of this technology, we may assume a shift in production techniques towards improved sustainability and environmental friendliness.

Industry 4.0 has established the basis for greater sensible and practical manufacturing by incorporating automation, records analytics, and device getting-to-know.

The destiny improvement toward Industry 5.0, defined by progressed cooperation and communique among humans and machines, has exceptional capacity. This trade will adjust the interplay between human beings and machines, creating a more collaborative and flexible manufacturing environment.

In addition, the capacity for simulated intelligence in assembling goes past the capacity's substantial space and comprises of the whole organization of suppliers and business frameworks (Sundar and Kathirvel, 2020a). Through digitization and availability, makers can improve asset use effectiveness, decline waste, and diminishing nursery fuel outflows over the creation cycle. Taking on this far-reaching way to deal with manageability is fundamental for handling critical natural issues and accomplishing carbon impartiality goals.

Furthermore, incorporating AI-powered technology will empower manufacturers to get the right of entry to higher productivity, efficiency, and creativity stages. AI technologies can beautify competitiveness and pressure corporate growth by enabling predictive renovation, satisfactory control, custom-designed product creation, and actual-time decision-making (Sundar and Kathirvel, 2020b).

AI is fast becoming a reality so that producers can take over the current bottlenecks, and the future provides a playground for digital manufacturers. Incorporating AI technology to improve the manufacturing techniques of the business realm can be instrumental in creating a more sustainable and responsible business zone that will ultimately help the betterment of the forthcoming generations.

14. CONCLUSION

Journals survey on the employment of AI tools for Cleaner and Green Manufacturing has yielded useful information and views on the role AI can play in the process of providing sustainability inside manufacturing. Journal have utilized a quantitative method of gathering data through a structured survey methodology which has helped us understand the stakeholder perspectives, trends and opportunities in this area.

The level of attention and understanding on the part of industry players on the applications of AI in driving cleaner and greener manufacturing activities is high with the business sector. The feedback given encouraged awareness in the growing concern of the negative role traditional manufacturing processes play and the need for sustainable solutions.

The survey portrayed AI as a powerful tool for the optimization of resource utilization, predictive maintenance, and supply chain management as the leading themes. Citizen comments focused on the ability of AI to be used in algorithms to make data analyses for real-time changes, less waste utilization, and improved production efficiency, which contribute to greener manufacturing.

While on one hand AI-oriented sustainability approaches hold a promise, they have their dark side being the high cost, skills necessary to use them and ethical issues among which. Nevertheless, it was stated that the joint initiatives involving industry partners, research institutions and governance were catalysts for overcoming these obstacles and to moving towards greener production processes.

A hypothesis can be developed from the survey results, which then would recommend some strategies to optimize AI systems in Cleaner and Greener Manufacturing. These are consisting of nurturing cross-sector partnerships, facilitating talent for AI, regulating frameworks that trigger responsible practice, and constantly using AI for progress and innovation.

As a whole, the survey illustrates the capabilities of AI as a powerful tool that enables a positive environmental output in the manufacturing industry. Bridging AI-driven strategies, using ecofriendly materials such as biodegradable packaging, and addressing the challenges through taking measures collectively, the manufacturers can build the foundation that the future will rely on to have its sustainability goal accomplished.

Nevertheless, regardless of those boundaries, the advantages of integrating AI into business operations outweigh the potential drawbacks. Multiple case studies and research effects have proven that AI-driven solutions notably beautify operational efficiency, product first-rate, and environmental sustainability. By using artificial intelligence (AI) to improve industrial procedures, companies may also enhance their competitive gain even by actively participating in international initiatives to deal with weather change and conserve herbal assets.

Nevertheless, the robust incorporation of AI into manufacturing requires collaborative endeavors from stakeholders in each public and business domain name. Governments need to offer beneficial guidelines and incentives to promote AI generation. Simultaneously, industry leaders should allocate resources closer to instructing and growing their personnel to facilitate an unbroken transition to AI-pushed commercial processes.

REFERENCES

Ammar, M., Haleem, A., Javaid, M., Walia, R., & Bahl, S. (2021). Improving material quality management and manufacturing organization systems through Industry 4.0 technologies. *Materials Today: Proceedings*, *45*, 5089–5096. DOI: 10.1016/j.matpr.2021.01.585

Andrews, D. (2015). The circular economy, design thinking, and education for sustainability. *Local Economy*, *30*(3), 305–315. DOI: 10.1177/0269094215578226

Arnold, C., Kiel, D., & Voigt, K.-I. (2016). How the Industrial Internet of Things changes business models in different manufacturing industries. *International Journal of Innovation Management*, *20*(8), 1640015. DOI: 10.1142/S1363919616400156

Atlas, M., & Florida, R. (1998). Green manufacturing. In Handbook of Technology Management, 1385–1393.

Aukker, T., De Koning, A., & Wood, R., (2013). EXIOPOL–development and illustrative analyses of a detailed global MR EE SUT/IOT. *Economic Systems Research*, *25*(1), 50–70. DOI: 10.1080/09535314.2012.761952

Ayyaswamy, K. (2024e). Enhancing Digital Technology Planning, Leadership, and Management to Transform Education. In Bhatia, M., & Mushtaq, M. T. (Eds.), *Navigating Innovative Technologies and Intelligent Systems in Modern Education* (pp. 1–9). IGI Global., DOI: 10.4018/979-8-3693-5370-7.ch001

Bag, S., & Pretorius, J. H. C. (2022). Relationships between industry 4.0, sustainable manufacturing and circular economy: Proposal of a research framework. *The International Journal of Organizational Analysis*, *30*(4), 864–898. DOI: 10.1108/IJOA-04-2020-2120

Behrendt, A., Odenwälder, P., Müller, N., & Schmitz, C. (n.d.). Industry 4.0 Demystified—Lean's Next Level. McKinsey, McKinsey Co. Retrieved January 9, 2020, from https://www.mckinsey.com/business-functions/operations/our-insights/industry-4-0-demystified-leans-next-level

Bhamra, T. (2016). *Design for Sustainability*. Informa UK Limited. DOI: 10.4324/9781315576664

Braccini, A. M., & Margherita, E. G. (2018). Exploring Organizational Sustainability of Industry 4.0 under the Triple Bottom Line: The Case of a Manufacturing Company. *Sustainability (Basel)*, *11*(1), 36. DOI: 10.3390/su11010036

Breque, M., De Nul, L., & Petridis, A. (2021). *Industry 5.0: Towards a sustainable, human-centric, and resilient European industry*. European Commission, Directorate-General for Research and Innovation.

Call for papers - Journal of Cleaner Production | ScienceDirect.com by Elsevier. (n.d.). https://www.sciencedirect.com/journal/journal-of-cleaner-production/about/call-for-papers#supply-chain-management-innovation-practices-for-sustainability-achievement-under-carbon-trading-era

Campbell, T., Williams, C., & Ivanova, O., (2011). *Could 3D printing change the world? Technologies, Potential, and Implications of Additive Manufacturing*. Atlantic Council.

Chen, B., Jiang, X., Yang, X., & Gao, X. (Eds.). (2023). Global Cleaner Production Conference (GCPC) 2023. Journal of Cleaner Production https://www.sciencedirect.com/journal/journal-of-cleaner-production/special-issues

Chin, T., Li, G., Jiao, H., Addo, F., & Jawahar, I. (2019). Career sustainability during manufacturing innovation. *Career Development International*, *24*(6), 509–528. DOI: 10.1108/CDI-02-2019-0034

Chong, S., Pan, G. T., Chin, J., Show, P. L., Yang, T. C. K., & Huang, C. M. (2018). Integration of 3D printing and Industry 4.0 into engineering teaching. *Sustainability (Basel)*, *10*(11), 3960. DOI: 10.3390/su10113960

ClimateWatch. (2020). Historical GHG Emissions. Retrieved June 24, 2021, from https://www.climatewatchdata.org/ghg-emissions?end_year=2018&start_year=1990

Deif, A. M. (2011). A system model for green manufacturing. *Journal of Cleaner Production*, *19*(14), 1553–1559. DOI: 10.1016/j.jclepro.2011.05.022

Dincer, I., & Acar, C. (2015). A review on clean energy solutions for better sustainability. *International Journal of Energy Research*, *39*(5), 585–606. DOI: 10.1002/er.3329

Duan, W., Khurshid, A., Khan, K., & Călin, A. C. (2024). Transforming industry: Investigating 4.0 technologies for sustainable product evolution in China through a novel fuzzy three-way decision-making process. *Technological Forecasting and Social Change*, *200*, 123125. DOI: 10.1016/j.techfore.2023.123125

Elliott, R. N. (2016). Energy efficiency and industry: The national trend. Washington DC: American Council for an Energy-Efficient Economy. Retrieved from http://aceee.org/blog/2015/12/energy-efficiency-and-industry

Epureanu, B. I., Li, X., Nassehi, A., & Koren, Y. (2020). Self-repair of intelligent manufacturing systems by deep reinforcement learning. *CIRP Annals, 69*(1), 421–424. DOI: 10.1016/j.cirp.2020.04.008

Garetti, M., & Taisch, M. (2011). Sustainable manufacturing: Trends and research challenges. *Production Planning and Control, 23*(2-3), 83–104. DOI: 10.1080/09537287.2011.591619

Garetti, M., & Taisch, M. (2012). Sustainable manufacturing: Trends and research challenges. *Production Planning and Control, 23*(2-3), 83–104. DOI: 10.1080/09537287.2011.591619

Geissdoerfer, M., Savaget, P., Bocken, N. M., & Hultink, E. J. (2017). The Circular Economy–A New Sustainability Paradigm? *Journal of Cleaner Production, 143*, 757–768. DOI: 10.1016/j.jclepro.2016.12.048

Gobinath, V. M., Kathirvel, A., Rajesh Kanna, S. K., & Annamalai, K. (2024). "Chapter 5: Smart Technology in Management Industries: A Useful Perspective", Artificial Intelligence Applied to Industry 4.0, Wiley Publiser, USA, 1st Edition, July 2024, pp.93-106, DOI: 10.1002/9781394216147.ch5

Habib, M. K., & Chimsom, C. (2019). Industry 4.0: Sustainability and design principles. In 2019 20th International Conference on Research and Education in Mechatronics (REM) (pp. 1–8). IEEE.

Kanagasundaram, H. and Kathirvel, A. (2019), EIMO-ESOLSR: energy efficient and security-based model for OLSR routing protocol in mobile ad-hoc network. IET Communications, 13: 553-559. https://doi.org/10.1049/iet-com.2018.5564DOI: 10.1049/iet-com.2018.5564

Kanagasundaram, H. and Kathirvel, A. (2019b), Multi Objective ALO based Energy Efficient and Secure routing OLSR Protocol in MANET", International Journal of Intelligent Engineering and Systems, Vol. 12, No. 1, pp. 74-83, 2019. Publisher: Intelligent Network and Systems Society, ISSN 2185310X, DOI: DOI: 10.1049/iet-com.2018.5564

Heller, T. C., & Shukla, P. R. (2003). Development and climate: Engaging developing countries. In Beyond Kyoto: Advancing the international effort against climate change, 111-140.

Jabbour, A., Jabbour, C.J.C., Foropon, C., & Filho, MG (2018). When titans meet—Can Industry 4.0 revolutionize the environmentally sustainable manufacturing wave? The role of critical success factors. Technol. Soc. Chang., pp. 132, 18–25.

Jovane, F., Yoshikawa, H., Alting, L., Boër, C., Westkamper, E., Williams, D., Tseng, M., Seliger, G., & Paci, A. (2008). The incoming global technological and industrial revolution towards competitive, sustainable manufacturing. *CIRP Annals, 57*(2), 641–659. DOI: 10.1016/j.cirp.2008.09.010

Jolin, J. S., Theophilus, A., and Kathirvel, A. (2025). Two factor mutual authentication with fingerprint and MAC Address Validation, International Journal of Communication Networks and Information Security, Vol. 16, No. 6, 2024, pp. 56 – 68. Publisher:Institute of Information Technology, Kohat University of Science and Technology, ISSN:2076-0930 E-ISSN:2073-607X, DoI:DOI: 10.5815/ijcnis.2024.06.05

Junior, J. A. G., Busso, C. M., Gobbo, S. C. O., & Carreão, H. (2018). Making the links between environmental protection, process safety, and Industry 4.0. *Process Safety and Environmental Protection, 117*, 372–382. DOI: 10.1016/j.psep.2018.05.017

Kathirvel, A. (2024d). Applications of Serverless Computing: Systematic Overview. In Aluvalu, R., & Maheswari, U. (Eds.), *Serverless Computing Concepts, Technology and Architecture* (Vol. 221-233). IGI Global., DOI: 10.4018/979-8-3693-1682-5.ch014

Kathirvel, A. (2024f). Innovation and Industry Application: IoT-Based Robotics Frontier of Automation in Industry Application. In Satishkumar, D., & Sivaraja, M. (Eds.), *Internet of Things and AI for Natural Disaster Management and Prediction* (pp. 83–105). IGI Global., DOI: 10.4018/979-8-3693-4284-8.ch004

Kathirvel, A., Gobinath, V. M., & Annamalai, K. (2024c), "Chapter 1: A Review on Additive Manufacturing in Industrial Environment", Advances in Pre- and Post-Additive Manufacturing Processes, Taylor & Francis Publiser, CRC Press, London, 1st Edition, May 2024, pp. 1-17. DOI: 10.1002/9781394216147.ch5

Kathirvel, A., Gobinath, V. M., Naren, A. K., & Maheswaran, C. P. (2025). AI-based automated disease detection based on symptoms healthcare for pets and birds. In *AI and the Revival of Big Data* (pp. 311–345). IGI Global., DOI: 10.4018/979-8-3693-8472-5.ch014

Kathirvel, A., & Maheswaran, C. P. (2023), "Chapter 8: Enhanced AI-Based Intrusion Detection and Response System for WSN", Artificial Intelligence for Intrusion Detection Systems, CRC Publiser/Chapman and Hall, New York, 1st Edition. DOI: 10.1201/9781003346340-8

Kathirvel, A., & Naren, A. K. (2024e). Diabetes and Pre-Diabetes Prediction by AI Using Tuned XGB Classifier. In Khang, A. (Ed.), *Medical Robotics and AI-Assisted Diagnostics for a High-Tech Healthcare Industry* (pp. 52–64). IGI Global., DOI: 10.4018/979-8-3693-2105-8.ch004

Kathirvel, A., Naren, A. K., & Santhoshi, B. (2024b). Business Intelligent and Blockchain in Entrepreneurship. In *Entrepreneurship Innovation and Education for Performance Improvement*. IGI Global., DOI: 10.4018/979-8-3693-7903-5.ch015

Kathirvel, A., Naren, A. K., & Subramanian, C. (2024a). Intelligent Serverless Computing Technology and Recent Trends: A Review. In *Driving Transformative Technology Trends with Cloud Computing*. IGI Global., DOI: 10.4018/979-8-3693-2869-9.ch002

Kathirvel, A., Subramaniam, M., Navaneethan, S., & Sabarinath, C. (2021), "Improved IDR Response System for Sensor Network", Journal of Web Engineering, Vol. 20 1, 53–88, DOI: 10.13052/jwe1540-9589.2013

Kerr, W., & Ryan, C. (2001). Eco-efficiency gains from remanufacturing: A case study of photocopier remanufacturing at Fuji Xerox Australia. *Journal of Cleaner Production*, *9*(1), 75–81. DOI: 10.1016/S0959-6526(00)00032-9

Khezri, A., Benderbal, H. H., & Benyoucef, L. (2019). A sustainable reconfigurable manufacturing system design focusing on environmentally hazardous wastes, in 2019 24th IEEE International Conference on Emerging Technologies and Factory Automation (ETFA), September, 317–324.

Kumar, R., & Rao, P. (2018). Green manufacturing technology - solution for environmental impact and waste. *Sustainable Development*, *4*(12), 532–535.

Leong, W. D., Lam, H. L., Ng, W. P. Q., Lim, C. H., Tan, C. P., & Ponnambalam, S. G. (2019). Lean and green manufacturing—A review of its applications and impacts. *Process Integration and Optimization for Sustainability*, *3*(1), 5–23. DOI: 10.1007/s41660-019-00082-x

Li, B. H., Zhang, L., & Wang, S. L., (2010). Cloud manufacturing: A new service-oriented networked manufacturing model. *Jisuanji Jicheng Zhizao Xitong*, *16*(1), 1–7.

Li, X., Bayrak, A. E., Epureanu, B. I., & Koren, Y. (2018). Real-time teaming of multiple reconfigurable manufacturing systems. *CIRP Annals*, *67*(1), 437–440. DOI: 10.1016/j.cirp.2018.04.051

Li, X., Li, N., Kolmanovsky, I., & Epureanu, B. I. (2021). Stochastic model predictive control for remanufacturing system management. *Journal of Manufacturing Systems*, *59*, 355–366. DOI: 10.1016/j.jmsy.2021.02.002

Müller, J. M., Kiel, D., & Voigt, K. I. (2018). What drives the implementation of Industry 4.0? The role of opportunities and challenges in the context of sustainability. *Sustainability (Basel), 10*(1), 247. DOI: 10.3390/su10010247

Nahavandi, S. (2019). Industry 5.0—A Human-Centric Solution. *Sustainability (Basel), 11*(16), 4371. DOI: 10.3390/su11164371

Naren, A. K., Kathirvel, A., & Santhoshi, B. (2024). Chapter 5: Critical Approaches to Data Engineering Systems Innovation and Industry Application Using IoT. In Critical Approaches to Data Engineering Systems and Analysis, Hershey, PA: IGI Global, 2024.DoI: DOI: 10.4018/979-8-3693-2260-4.ch005

Nimbalkar, S., Guo, W., & Petri, C., (2017). *Innovative manufacturing technologies and data analytics for improving energy efficiency in industrial energy systems*. Oak Ridge National Laboratory.

Nordhaus, W. (2017). Integrated assessment models of climate change. NBER Reporter, pp. 16, 16–20.

Pérez-Fortes, M., Moya, J. A., Vatopoulos, K., & Tzimas, E. (2014). CO2 capture and utilization in cement and iron and steel industries. *Energy Procedia, 63*, 6534–6543. DOI: 10.1016/j.egypro.2014.11.689

Piccarozzi, M., Aquilani, B., & Gatti, C. (2018). Industry 4.0 in management studies: A systematic literature review. *Sustainability (Basel), 10*(10), 3821. DOI: 10.3390/su10103821

Plex Systems Inc. (n.d.). Plex manufacturing cloud. Retrieved from https://www.plex.com/

Rithik, G., Kathirvel, A., & Naren, A. K. (2024). The IoT of Robotics: The Frontier of Automation. In *Artificial Intelligence-Enabled Digital Twin for Smart Manufacturing, Wiley Publiser- Scrivener Publishing LLC, Online*. Print., DOI: 10.1002/9781394303601.ch13

Salam, A. (2020). *Internet of Things in sustainable energy systems. In the Internet of Things for Sustainable Community Development*. Springer.

Sarmiento, J. R. R., Monroy, J., Moreno, F.-A., Galindo, C., Bonelo, J.-M., & González-Jiménez, J. (2020). *A predictive model for maintaining industrial machinery in the context of Sendler, U. (2017). The Internet Internets: IThingsie 4.0 unleashed*. Springer.

Subramaniam, M., Kathirvel, A., Sabitha, E., & Anwar Basha, H. (2021). "Modified Firefly Algorithm and Fuzzy C-Mean Clustering Based Semantic Information Retrieval", Journal of Web Engineering, Vol. 20 1, 33–52. DOI: 10.13052/jwe1540-9589.2012

Sundar, R. and Kathirvel, A. (2020a), "Aggressively delivered mechanism over variable length density using a simulated annealing algorithm in mobile ad hoc network", Transactions on Emerging Telecommunications Technologies, pp. 1 – 13. Wiley-Blackwell. DOI: 10.1002/ett.3863

Sundar, R. and Kathirvel, A. (2020b), "Enhanced Cluster Based Stable Path for Load Balancing and Reducing Overhead using Artificial Bee Colony in Manets", International Journal of Vehicle Information and Communication Systems, Vol.5, No.1, pp. 41 -54. Inderscience Publishers Ltd. John Wiley & Sons Ltd. DOI: 10.1002/ett.3863

Waibel, M., Steenkamp, L., Moloko, N., & Oosthuizen, G. (2017). Investigating the Effects of Smart Production Systems on Sustainability Elements. *Procedia Manufacturing*, *8*, 731–737. DOI: 10.1016/j.promfg.2017.02.094

Wang, S., Wan, J., Li, D., & Zhang, C. (2016). Implementing Smart Factory of Industrie 4.0: An Outlook. Int. J. Distrib. Sens. Netw., p. 12, 3159805–3159810.

Wara, M. (2007). Is the global carbon market working? *Nature*, *445*(7128), 595–596. DOI: 10.1038/445595a PMID: 17287794

WCED. (n,d). Our common future. Retrieved from https://sustainabledevelopment .un.org/content/documents/5987our-common-future.pdf

Wismann, S. T., Engbæk, J. S., Vendelbo, S. B., Bendixen, F. B., Eriksen, W. L., Aasberg-Petersen, K., Frandsen, C., Chorkendorff, I., & Mortensen, P. M. (2019). Electrified methane reforming: A compact approach to greener industrial hydrogen production. *Science*, *364*(6442), 756–759. DOI: 10.1126/science.aaw8775 PMID: 31123131

Yang, J., Ye, Y., Li, X., Lü, X., & Chen, R. (2018). Flexible, conductive, and highly pressure-sensitive graphene-polyimide foam for pressure sensor application. *Composites Science and Technology*, *164*, 187–194. DOI: 10.1016/j.compscitech.2018.05.044

Zhang, X., Ao, X., Cai, W., et al. (2019). A sustainability evaluation method integrating the energy, economy, and environment in remanufacturing systems. Journal of Cleaner Production, p. 239, 118100.

Zhou, J., Zhou, Y., Wang, B., & Zang, J. (2019). Human–cyber–physical systems (HCPSs) in the context of new-generation intelligent manufacturing. *Engineering (Beijing)*, *5*(4), 624–636. DOI: 10.1016/j.eng.2019.07.015

Chapter 3
IT Service Information Security Management

Binastya Anggara Sekti
https://orcid.org/0000-0001-5489-4888
Universitas Esa Unggul, Indonesia

ABSTRACT

Information security has become a cornerstone of modern IT service management, driven by the increasing reliance on digital infrastructure and the ever-evolving landscape of cyber threats. IT security is essential to protect sensitive data, ensure operational continuity, and build trust among stakeholders. As organizations adopt complex IT environments, the need for a systematic approach to managing information security within IT services has never been greater. IT Service Information Security Management outlines strategies for safeguarding the confidentiality, integrity, and availability of IT services while aligning with organizational goals and compliance requirements. Key topics include implementing proactive security measures, conducting risk assessments, managing vulnerabilities, and orchestrating incident response processes. Many case studies and examples are included to provide practical insights into overcoming challenges and adopting best practices in IT service information security management.

1. INTRODUCTION

1.1 Information Technology Services Management

Information Technology (IT) services are a series of activities, solutions, or products provided by IT service providers to support the needs of businesses and end-users. These services enable a business organization to effectively manage,

DOI: 10.4018/979-8-3373-2352-7.ch003

store, access, and process information, and support day-to-day operations, decision-making, and the achievement of strategic objectives. IT services are needed by companies because every company needs to manage complex business processes, namely analysis, acceleration, and process optimization (Serhiienko, Mashchenko, Samorodov, Babichev, & Klimenko, 2024).

IT services basically function to align information technology with business needs, i.e. ensure that infrastructure, applications, and information systems can be used optimally to support productivity, innovation, and efficiency. IT services are typically designed on service-oriented principles, where the main focus is on the value provided to the customer or user, not just on the technology itself. Customer demand for quick solutions often means ignoring risk management (Engemann & Miller, 2024).

IT Infrastructure Management is the management of hardware, software, network, and data. The development of information systems has become increasingly complex and poses various problems that must be solved. The addition or change of new technologies, products, and application models makes the management of the information system that runs more difficult to maintain (Varga, Barreto, & Battaglin, 2020).

Cloud computing is a new type of service that changes IT governance, where Cloud services focus more on remote IT infrastructure management. Cloud computing is a computing paradigm that allows remote access over the Internet without the need to directly install information technology resources such as servers, platforms, and software (Park, Kim, Yun, & Yeom, 2020). Examples of cloud-based service provision such as SaaS (Software as a Service), PaaS (Platform as a Service), and IaaS (Infrastructure as a Service) (Nordli, Haugeland, Nguyen, Song, & Chauvel, 2023).

Support for end-users is one of the important domains of IT management. This support includes technical assistance in the form of helpdesk, remote support, or onsite support. In cloud computing, which is currently the fastest growing domain in modern business, there has also been an increase in demand access to data resources. However, at the same time, there are many concerns about the security of such solutions. Often the information that users decide to store online is sensitive. In a sense, there are some risks involved when using cloud computing because the beneficiaries must trust and rely on the service provider. On the other hand, the increasing number of users taking advantage of cloud solutions is forcing cloud providers to ensure the appropriate level of security. So, more and more organizations are deciding to move their data to the cloud (Poniszewska-Maranda, Matusiak, Kryvinska, & Yasar, 2020).

The characteristics of Information Technology Services reflect the basic principles that ensure the services are effective and relevant to users. First, IT services must be customer-oriented, meaning that the main focus is on meeting the needs and expectations of users, both in terms of functionality and user experience. These services must also be measurable, where service performance is evaluated through clear parameters such as Service Level Agreement (SLA), so that organizations can ensure service levels are in accordance with agreed standards. In addition, IT services are dynamic, able to adapt to changing business needs, technological developments, and changing market conditions. Finally, these services must be value-based, which provide real benefits to businesses such as increasing operational efficiency, reducing costs, speeding up processes, and strengthening information security. These four characteristics are an important foundation in the management of quality and sustainable IT services.

The importance of Information Technology Services in the era of digital transformation cannot be ignored, because this service is a vital component in supporting business sustainability and growth. One of its main roles is to improve operational efficiency through business process automation and more optimal resource management, so that organizations can work faster and cost-effectively. In addition, IT services also support business innovation by providing a technology platform that enables the development of new products and services to meet the changing needs of the market. Security is also a crucial aspect, where IT services play an important role in improving the protection of data and systems from increasingly complex cyber threats. In terms of customer relationships, IT services contribute to improving the customer experience through the provision of fast, secure, and reliable services. Last but not least, IT services help organizations ensure compliance with applicable industry regulations and laws, which are an absolute requirement for doing business in various sectors. Thus, the role of IT services is fundamental in building an adaptive, innovative, and highly competitive organization in the midst of dynamic technological changes.

In the increasingly advanced digital era, information technology (IT) services not only serve as operational support for the organization, but also as a strategic foundation in business value creation. With the high reliance on IT services, there is a critical need to ensure that the information managed through those services remains safe, secure, and available. Therefore, information security management in IT services (IT Service Information Security Management) is the main pillar in maintaining reliability, confidentiality, integrity, and availability of data. The agile implementation of IT Service management with an effective risk management approach can be done with an agile framework (Engemann & Miller, 2024).

IT Service Information Security Management integrates information security principles into the IT service lifecycle, from planning, provisioning, to service maintenance. This practice focuses on the development of security policies, the implementation of technical and administrative controls, and the monitoring of risks related to IT services. International standards such as ISO/IEC 27001 and frameworks such as ITIL (Information Technology Infrastructure Library) provide guidance in establishing a systematic approach to service security management (Mishra, Alzoubi, Gill, & Anwar, 2022).

In this context, organizations are faced with increasingly complex challenges, such as increasing cyber threats, strict regulations regarding data protection, and the need to maintain customer trust. Through effective IT service information security management, organizations can minimize the risk of security incidents, meet compliance requirements, and maintain operational continuity.

In today's digital era, all organizations are increasingly relying on information technology (IT) services to drive their business operations in improving customer satisfaction and creating a competitive advantage. This dependence, however, makes them vulnerable to various cyber-threats, i.e. data breaches and sophisticated ransomware attacks. Therefore, integrating strong information security management within IT service frameworks has become essential to protect sensitive information, ensure service continuity, and maintain stakeholder trust. Standards like ISO/IEC 27002, CIS®, COBIT®, ISA/IEC 62443, and NIST Special Publication 800-53 can be used to achieve robust information security (Kaur, Gabrijelčič, & Klobučar, 2023; Malatji, Marnewick, & Von Solms, 2022). Among these, ISO/IEC 27001 is the most widely recognized standard for information security and ranks as the third most prevalent ISO certification (Culot, Nassimbeni, Podrecca, & Sartor, 2021).

1.2 Information Security Management

Information Security Management (ISM) in IT services aims to protect data confidentiality, data integrity, and of course the availability of information. Confidentiality ensures sensitive information can only be accessed by those authorized; integrity to keep data accurate and reliable; and data availability ensures information and services are available when needed. To be able to achieve this goal requires a holistic understanding that includes technical matters, policies from the organization, and consideration of human factors. A large amount of data activity can increase the possible risks, for example, data leaks, unauthorized access, leaks of sensitive information, and leaks of privacy matters (Singh, Sanwar Hosen, & Yoon, 2021; Yang, Xiong, & Ren, 2020).

Due to the increasing complexity of cyber threats, various frameworks and standards have been developed to help organizations implement effective information security management (ISM) practices. For example, the ISO/IEC 27001 standard provides a structured approach to managing sensitive company information by establishing an information security management system (ISMS). ISO/IEC 27001 standard focuses on risk management and continuous improvement, enabling organizations to identify potential vulnerabilities and apply appropriate controls (Kaur et al., 2023; Singh et al., 2021).

In recent years, the presence of big data technology has significantly improved information security management capabilities. By leveraging big data analytics technology, organizations can continuously monitor and assess large amounts of data to identify system anomalies and various potential security threats in real-time. This proactive strategy not only helps reduce risks to information systems and ensure compliance with regulatory standards, but also allows companies to build a competitive advantage (Misra et al., 2022; Singh et al., 2021).

Additionally, embracing a comprehensive framework that addresses operational, technical, human, and physical security aspects is recommended to address the intricacies of contemporary cybersecurity threats. This all-encompassing strategy ensures that every aspect of information security is considered, fostering a culture of awareness of security and strength within the organization. In other words, as organizations continue to address the complexities of the digital world, integrating robust information security management within an IT service framework has become a necessity rather than just a best practice. By adopting a standard framework, leveraging the latest technology, and promoting a culture of security awareness, organizations can successfully manage risk and ensure the robustness of their IT services.

2. ROLE OF INFORMATION SECURITY IN IT SERVICE MANAGEMENT

Information security within ITSM is designed to ensure the protection of data and IT services from unauthorized access, disruption, and damage. Key elements include:

2.1 Confidentiality

Confidentiality ensures that sensitive information is accessible only to authorized individuals. This is achieved through mechanisms such as encryption, role-based access controls (RBAC), and secure authentication protocols. Protecting confidentiality prevents unauthorized disclosure of critical business and customer data, reducing the risks of identity theft and corporate espionage (Bhatt et al., 2021; Bu & Cho, 2020).

2.2 Integrity

Integrity refers to maintaining the accuracy, consistency, and trustworthiness of data throughout its lifecycle. This involves implementing hash functions, digital signatures, and secure database management practices. Ensuring data integrity prevents unauthorized alterations, accidental modifications, and malicious tampering, thereby enhancing the reliability of IT services.

2.3 Availability

Availability ensures that IT services and data are accessible whenever needed by authorized users. High availability is achieved through redundancy, disaster recovery plans, and real-time monitoring tools. Downtime caused by cyberattacks, natural disasters, or system failures can disrupt business operations, making availability management a critical component of IT service security.

2.4 Authentication

An authentication mechanism validates the identity of a service user attempting to access a system or IT service. Techniques such as multi-factor authentication (MFA) can perform biometric verification, and digital certificates strengthen authentication, reducing the likelihood of unauthorized access (Amft et al., 2023; Ogbanufe & Baham, 2023; Vasudev, Harini, & Neethu, 2023).

2.5 Authorization

Authorization controls define the level of access granted to authenticated users. This ensures that individuals can only perform operations within their designated permissions, minimizing the risk of privilege escalation attacks and insider threats.

2.6 Non-Repudiation

Non-repudiation provides proof of the origin and integrity of data transactions, preventing entities from denying their actions. This is commonly achieved through cryptographic signatures, audit logs, and forensic analysis, ensuring accountability in IT service management.

2.7 Accountability

Accountability ensures that all security-related actions and changes within an IT service environment can be traced to specific individuals or systems. Log management, access tracking, and security information and event management (SIEM) solutions help enforce accountability, aiding in compliance audits and forensic investigations (González-Granadillo, González-Zarzosa, & Diaz, 2021; Radoglou-Grammatikis et al., 2021).

By incorporating these key elements into IT service management, organizations can build a robust security framework that protects critical assets while aligning with the organization's business and regulatory goals.

3. IMPLEMENTING THE PROACTIVE SECURITY MEASURE

A proactive approach to IT service security can include several things:

3.1 Security Policies and Governance

Implementing well-defined security policies that adhere to industry standards such as ISO 27001, NIST, and GDPR ensures consistent and enforceable security measures across the organization. These policies should outline data protection practices, acceptable use guidelines, and security responsibilities at all organizational levels (Culot et al., 2021; Kaur et al., 2023).

3.2 Risk Assessments

Performing the regular risk assessments to help identify vulnerabilities, threats, and potential impacts on IT services. Organizations should use structured methodologies such as the NIST Risk Management Framework (RMF) and ISO 27005 Risk Assessment Methodology to systematically assess and mitigate security risks. Figure 1 represents the Risk Management Framework (RMF).

Figure 1. Risk Management Framework (RMF)

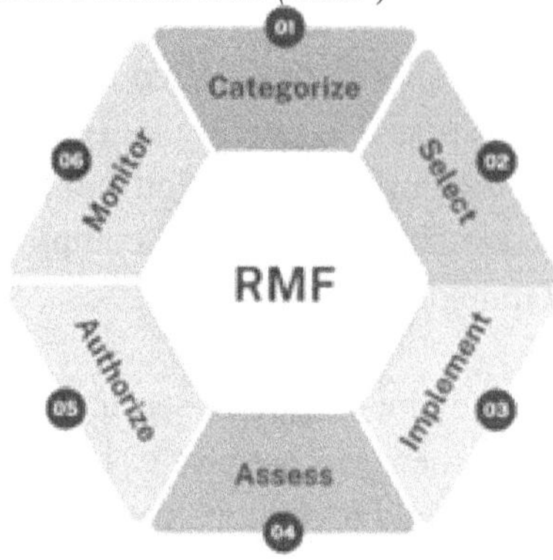

3.3 Control Against Access

Implement robust access controls, such as role-based access control (RBAC), multi-factor authentication (MFA), and the principle of least privilege, to ensure that only certain authorized personnel can log into critical IT services and data. These measures help prevent unauthorized access and insider threats.

3.4 Security Awareness Training

Training employees to recognize and respond to various security threats such as phishing attacks, social engineering, and malware is essential to reduce human-related security risks. Organizations need to hold security training programs regularly and conduct simulations from the results of the training.

3.5 Threat Intelligence and Monitoring

Using real-time threat intelligence platforms and Security Information and Event Management (SIEM) tools allows organizations to detect and respond to security threats proactively. AI-driven threat detection solutions can identify anomalies and mitigate cyber threats before they cause damage (González-Granadillo et al., 2021; Radoglou-Grammatikis et al., 2021).

3.6 Patch and Vulnerability Management

Regularly updating software, operating systems, and applications with security patches helps eliminate known vulnerabilities. Organizations need to implement an automated patch management system so that updates are always happening and the risk of exploitation can be avoided.

3.7 Incident Response Planning

Developing and testing an incident response plan (IRP) ensures that organizations can respond effectively to security incidents. This includes defining roles and responsibilities, establishing communication protocols, and conducting incident response drills to ensure preparedness for cyberattacks.

3.8 Security Audits and Compliance Checks

Conducting periodic security audits and compliance checks ensures adherence to industry regulations and best practices. Third-party security audits and penetration testing help identify security gaps and improve the overall IT service security posture. Implementing these measures will boost IT security, reduce risks, and improve resilience against cyber threats.

4. RISK ASSESSMENT AND VULNERABILITY MANAGEMENT

Risk assessment and vulnerability management are important aspects of IT service security management. These processes assist organizations in identifying, evaluating, and mitigating security risks and vulnerabilities within their IT environment.

4.1 Risk Assessment Frameworks

Organizations should use structured methodologies to evaluate risks and decide on mitigation strategies. Important risk assessment frameworks are presented in Table 1 below.

Table 1. Risk assessment frameworks

Framework	Description
NIST Risk Management Framework (RMF)	Provides a structured process for managing cybersecurity risk, including security categorization, control selection, implementation, and monitoring (NIST, 2023).
ISO 27005 Risk Assessment Methodology	Aligns with the ISO 27001 standard, offering a comprehensive approach to risk management by identifying threats, vulnerabilities, and mitigation strategies (ISO/IEC 27005, 2022).
OCTAVE (Operationally Critical Threat, Asset, and Vulnerability Evaluation)	A self-directed, flexible approach for evaluating security risks based on operational needs and business goals (Caralli et al., 2022).

4.2 Vulnerability Management

Vulnerability management involves identifying, assessing, prioritizing, and mitigating security vulnerabilities to reduce risk. Key steps in this process include:

4.2.1 Asset Identification

Asset Identification is a very important first step in information security management, where organizations must identify and catalog all Information Technology (IT) assets it has. These assets include various components such as hardware, software, networking, databases, and cloud services. By having a complete and accurate list of assets, organizations can better understand the level of risk exposure that each asset has, so that it can prioritize protection based on the value and criticality of those assets to business operations. This identification process is also the basis for the development of security strategies, compliance audits, and emergency response planning, so that organizations can be more proactive in dealing with potential threats that develop.

4.2.2 Vulnerability Scanning

Vulnerability Scanning is an important process in maintaining the security of information systems, where organizations routinely conduct scans of their IT assets to detect potential security gaps and weaknesses that can be exploited by irresponsible parties. This activity is generally carried out using automated tools such as Nessus, Qualys, or OpenVAS, which are able to identify various vulnerabilities ranging from misconfigurations, software that is not updated, to weaknesses in network communication protocols. By conducting regular scans, organizations can get a more accurate picture of the security condition of their assets and can take remedial actions before these vulnerabilities are exploited by attackers. In addition, vulnerability scanning also plays an important role in meeting compliance requirements with industry standards such as ISO 27001 or PCI DSS, as well as strengthening the overall security posture of an organization amid the ever-changing threat landscape.

4.2.3 Risk-Based Prioritization

Risk-Based Prioritization is a strategic approach in vulnerability management, where organizations not only identify existing weaknesses, but also evaluate and prioritize their handling based on the level of risk posed. This evaluation considers several important factors such as the severity of the vulnerability, the likelihood of the vulnerability being exploited, and the potential impact on business operations if the vulnerability is attacked. To support this, many organizations use the Common Vulnerability Scoring System (CVSS), an internationally standardized scoring method that provides quantitative scores of vulnerabilities based on technical factors and the business environment. By leveraging CVSS, organizations can determine which vulnerabilities should be addressed immediately and which can be prioritized later, so that security resources can be effectively allocated to mitigate the most critical risks to business continuity and integrity.

4.2.4 Patch and Remediation Management

Patch and Remediation Management is a structured process that aims to ensure that security patches are applied in a timely manner to all of your organization's IT assets to close previously identified vulnerabilities. By implementing a systematic process, organizations can narrow the risk window between vulnerability discovery and remedial implementation. The use of automation solutions, such as patch management tools, is highly recommended because it can increase efficiency, speed up the distribution of patches to various systems, and minimize human error that often occurs in manual processes. In addition, an effective patching program should include a risk evaluation process prior to patch implementation, staging environments, and patch status reporting to monitor compliance with security policies. Good patch management not only reduces the risk of vulnerabilities-based cyberattacks, but also helps organizations maintain operational stability and meet various industry compliance standards.

4.2.5 Penetration Testing

Conducting periodic penetration tests helps validate the effectiveness of vulnerability remediation efforts and identify security gaps that may not be detected through automated scans.

Penetration testing is an important step in a cybersecurity strategy, where testing is conducted periodically to assess the effectiveness of vulnerability remediation efforts and identify additional security gaps that may not be detected by automated scanning. In this process, ethical hackers simulate real-world attacks on organizations' systems, applications, and networks with the goal of exploiting existing vulnerabilities before malicious parties do. Penetration testing not only verifies that patches and security controls have been implemented correctly, but also provides insight into the combination of vulnerabilities that can be exploited together to gain wider access to the system. In addition, penetration test results help organizations fix structural weaknesses, optimize security policies, and increase risk awareness among management and users. It can be said that penetration testing is an integral part of building a more resilient and proactive security posture against evolving cyber threats.

4.2.6 Monitoring and Continuous Improvement

Monitoring and Continuous Improvement is a critical component of the vulnerability management lifecycle, where security personnel must actively monitor the ever-changing cyber threat landscape and dynamically adjust vulnerability management practices. Monitoring is carried out not only on internal systems to detect anomalies or potential intrusions, but also on external trends, such as new exploits, newly discovered vulnerabilities, and the latest attack techniques reported through various threat intelligence sources. By integrating this information into security strategies, organizations can build more proactive defenses, accelerate responses to threats, and identify areas that require continuous improvement. Continuous improvement also includes regular evaluations of existing security policies, procedures, and technologies, as well as the implementation of changes based on learnings from previous incidents or the results of periodic security tests. With this approach, organizations not only maintain resilience to today's attacks, but also strengthen their ability to address future cybersecurity challenges. Figure 2 illustrates the Vulnerability Management Lifecycle.

Figure 2. Vulnerability management lifecycle

Organizations can significantly avoid various cyber threats and improve the resilience of IT services by adopting thorough risk assessments and vulnerability management practices. Effective IT Service Information Security Management can protect IT services from multitude of cyber threats. Organizations need to take a risk-based, proactive approach, use advanced security technologies, and promote a security-focused culture. Integrating security into an ITSM framework improves service reliability, regulatory compliance, and stakeholder trust.

5. INCIDENT RESPONSE AND RECOVERY

Incident response and recovery are essential to protecting an organization from the adverse effects of cybersecurity incidents. These processes ensure that when an attack or breach occurs, the organization can effectively handle, mitigate, and recover from it.

5.1 Framework of Incident Response

Effective incident response activities require a structured framework for handling security incidents in a coordinated manner. Table 2 presents the framework, outlining the description of several critical phases.

Table 2. Incident response framework

Phase	Description
Preparation Threats	The first step is preparing for potential incidents by developing an Incident Response Plan (IRP), defining roles and responsibilities, and ensuring all team members are trained. Communication protocols should also be established, and stakeholders (internal and external) need to be informed.
Identification of Incidents	This phase focuses on monitoring systems and networks to identify potential incidents. Tools like SIEM (Security Information and Event Management) and IDS (Intrusion Detection Systems) are crucial for real-time detection. Once an incident is detected, it's analyzed to understand its scope, impact, and origin.
Containment of Threats	Containment involves isolating affected systems to prevent further damage. The containment strategy could involve shutting down systems, restricting access, or disconnecting compromised networks. The goal is to reduce the incident's reach and impact.
Recovery & Restoration	After containment, the next step is eliminating the threat. This includes removing malicious code, closing vulnerabilities, and ensuring no further compromise remains. Recovery involves restoring systems to normal operational levels while ensuring all security measures are intact.
Feedback and Refinement	After recovering from the incident, an in-depth analysis is conducted to understand what went wrong, identify weaknesses in processes or systems, and improve future response strategies. Continuous improvement is the key to a successful security program.

Figure 3. Incident response lifecycle

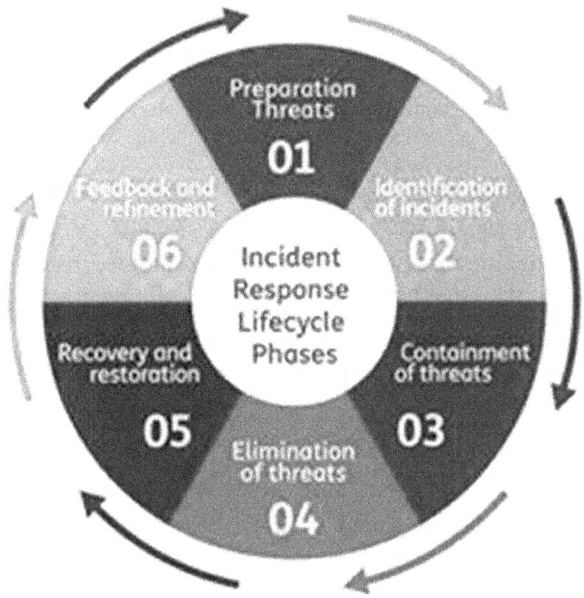

This image represents the structured cycle of incident response, which can be used to guide decision-making and resource allocation during each phase of an incident.

5.2 Key Components of Recovery

The initial response to an incident is vital, but recovery is essential for resuming normal operations quickly. Key components of recovery include:

5.2.1 Business Continuity Planning

Business Continuity Planning (BCP) is an important strategy for organizations, which is to ensure that organizations can maintain essential operations during and after an incident. By having an effective BCP, organizations are able to minimize the impact of disruptions on services, maintain customer trust, and speed up the recovery process. This planning begins by identifying the critical functions, i.e. the most important business operations that must remain running in an emergency situation. Once these functions are defined, organizations need to define Recovery Time Objectives (RTOs), which are the maximum acceptable time limits for disruption to each critical function before it has a significant impact on the business. In addition, redundancy planning is a key aspect of BCP, by implementing backup systems such as alternative data centers or cloud-based services that can take over operations if the main system fails. Through this approach, organizations can build strong resilience to a wide range of operational risks.

5.2.2 Data Backup and Restoration

Data Backup and Restoration is a crucial element in an information security strategy, as data loss is one of the most severe consequences of a security incident. For this reason, organizations must have a comprehensive and structured data backup and recovery strategy. The first step is to perform regular backups, ensuring that all important data is copied regularly to offsite locations or cloud-based storage, with encryption protections to keep the data private. In addition to backing up, organizations also need to conduct periodic data restore tests to ensure that the backed up data can be restored smoothly and without errors when needed. Next, organizations must establish the right backup frequency, which is determining how often data should be backed up based on the level of data criticality and business needs, while considering the available storage capacity. By applying this approach consistently, organizations can minimize the risk of data loss, accelerate the operational recovery process, and increase resilience to various forms of disruption.

5.2.3 Post-Incident Reporting

Post-Incident Reporting is an important process in incident management that aims to document in detail all aspects related to the incident, from the chronology to the lessons learned. This report should include an incident timeline, which is a detailed chronology of the event, from the moment of detection to recovery, as well as all actions taken throughout the process. In addition, the report must contain an impact assessment, which is a clear assessment of the impact of the incident on the business and operations of the organization. The next step is to conduct a root cause analysis, with the aim of identifying the main cause of the incident, whether it is system vulnerability, human negligence, or other contributing factors. Based on this analysis, the report must contain recommendations for improvement, namely suggestions to improve policies, procedures, or technical protections so that similar incidents can be prevented in the future. By consistently implementing post-incident reporting practices, organizations can strengthen their security posture, improve response to incidents, and build better resilience to evolving threats.

The Incident Recovery Process is the various stages of the recovery process, emphasizing the main actions that must be taken after detention and before resuming normal operating conditions. An effective incident response and recovery strategy is essential to minimize the damage caused by security incidents, ensure business continuity with minimal disruption, and improve the overall security posture of the organization. Adequate preparation, prompt detection, rapid containment, and comprehensive recovery are essential to significantly reduce the impact of cybersecurity threats.

6. SECURITY COMPLIANCE AND REGULATORY CONSIDERATIONS

Organizations must comply with security frameworks and regulations to protect sensitive data and IT services. Security compliance includes meeting legal obligations, maintaining efficiency, and preserving stakeholder trust. This section will discuss key compliance needs, regulation impacts, and how security frameworks aid in compliance.

6.1 Key Regulatory Requirements

Various global and regional regulations mandate how organizations must safeguard sensitive information and ensure data security. Listed below are some of the most significant regulations affecting security compliance. The General Data Protection Regulation (GDPR) and Health Insurance Portability and Accountability Act (HIPAA) aim to protect health data as a special category of personal data, highlighting the importance of obtaining explicit consent or authorization from the data owner before processing or disclosing information (Jurczuk & Suprynowicz, 2024). Table 3 presents key regulatory requirements.

Table 3. Key regulatory requirements

Regulation	Description
General Data Protection Regulation (GDPR)	The General Data Protection Regulation (GDPR) is a European Union regulation that establishes strict guidelines for how businesses handle and protect personal data. It mandates requirements such as ensuring data subject rights (e.g., access, rectification, and erasure), obtaining explicit consent for data processing, and conducting Data Protection Impact Assessments (DPIAs) to identify and mitigate privacy risks.
Health Insurance Portability and Accountability Act (HIPAA)	HIPAA establishes regulations in the U.S. for safeguarding sensitive patient health information. It requires the implementation of specific measures for data encryption, privacy protection, and the secure transmission of medical records.
Payment Card Industry Data Security Standard (PCI DSS)	PCI DSS is a collection of security guidelines aimed at safeguarding cardholder data during payment transactions. It outlines best practices for securely managing credit card information and mandates regular vulnerability assessments and risk evaluations
Sarbanes-Oxley Act (SOX)	SOX mandates that publicly traded companies in the U.S. establish internal controls and cybersecurity protocols to ensure the accuracy of financial reporting and maintain data integrity
Federal Information Security Management Act (FISMA)	FISMA mandates that U.S. federal agencies and their contractors protect information systems and adopt comprehensive risk management strategies.

6.2 Impact of Regulations on IT Security Practices

Adhering to security compliance requirements impacts IT service management in the following ways:

6.2.1 Data Protection

Regulations like GDPR and HIPAA require organizations to safeguard personal and confidential data. Data protection is data encryption, access control, and conducting regular security audits.

6.2.2 Risk Management

Regulations such as SOX and FISMA mandate that organizations carry out regular risk assessments, implement security controls, and manage vulnerabilities. These measures help organizations in detecting, preventing, and responding to potential risks.

6.2.3 Documentation and Reporting

Regulatory compliance necessitates that organizations maintain comprehensive records of their security protocols, incident reports, and compliance undertakings. These records are essential for audits and for showcasing conformity with regulatory mandates.

6.2.4 Penalties and Fines

Failure to comply with regulations can lead to financial penalties, legal consequences, and potential damage to reputation. For instance, GDPR violations may result in fines of up to 4% of annual global revenue or €20 million, whichever is greater.

6.3 Security Frameworks for Compliance

To fulfill regulatory requirements, organizations may implement various security frameworks and standards. These frameworks offer systematic methodologies for managing security and ensuring compliance. Among the most widely recognized frameworks are those presented in Table 4 below.

Table 4. Security frameworks for compliance

Framework	Purpose	Compliance Link
ISO/IEC 27001	A widely recognized standard for establishing an Information Security Management System (ISMS), aiding organizations in fulfilling data protection and risk management obligations.	GDPR, PCI DSS, FISMA
NIST Cybersecurity Framework (CSF)	A versatile framework created by NIST to assist organizations in enhancing their cybersecurity resilience, structured around five key functions: Identify, Protect, Detect, Respond, and Recover	HIPAA, SOX
COBIT	A governance and management framework for enterprise IT that aligns IT goals with business objectives, ensuring regulatory compliance and effective IT oversight	SOX, FISMA
SOC 2	A framework specifically for service organizations to ensure they manage data securely and comply with privacy regulations.	GDPR, PCI DSS

6.4 The Role of Audits in Compliance

Security audits need to be conducted regularly to ensure compliance with the organization's regulations. These audits are for independent evaluation of measures and ensure the security of the organization, helping to uncover vulnerabilities and highlight areas that need improvement. Common types of audits include:

- Internal Audits: Conducted by internal teams to assess adherence to security policies and regulatory requirements. Internal audits help ensure ongoing compliance and operational efficiency.
- External Audits: Conducted by an independent third-party auditor to assess the organization's compliance with existing industry standards and regulatory requirements. These audits are especially critical for obtaining certifications such as SOC 2 or PCI DSS.
- Compliance Audits: Designed to verify adherence to existing organization regulations, such as HIPAA, GDPR, or SOX. These audits typically include comprehensive evaluations of documentation, security measures, and operational practices.

Security compliance is crucial for IT service management, ensuring legal and regulatory adherence while protecting data. By adopting frameworks, conducting audits, and staying updated with regulations, organizations can mitigate non-compliance risks and strengthen security. Effective programs prevent fines and build trust with customers, partners, and stakeholders.

7. EMERGING TRENDS AND FUTURE DIRECTIONS

As cyber threats evolve, organizations must adapt to new technologies, methods, and security strategies. The following trends highlight emerging directions in IT service information security, helping organizations enhance defenses and stay compliant with regulations.

7.1. The Machine Learning and Artificial Intelligence in Cybersecurity

AI and ML are influencing cybersecurity by offering tools for threat detection, analysis, and response. These technologies allow systems to process large amounts of data and identify patterns, improving the detection of anomalies and enabling real-time responses to new threats. Table 5 presents Machine Learning and Artificial Intelligence in Cybersecurity.

Table 5. Machine learning and artificial intelligence in cybersecurity

Technology	Impact on Cybersecurity
AI for Detection of Threat	AI-based systems can quickly analyze vast data sets to identify threats more efficiently than traditional approaches. They can recognize behavioral patterns and detect anomalies, including zero-day attacks.
ML for Predictive of Security	Machine learning models predict potential security events by analyzing historical data, improving proactive defense measures. The system is constantly evolving to adapt to emerging threats.

7.2. Zero Trust Security Model

The Zero Trust security model follows the principle of "never trust, always verify." It assumes no user, device, or application is trusted by default, whether inside or outside the network. Access is only granted after strict identity verification to mitigate risks from internal threats and unauthorized access. Table 6 presents the Zero Trust Security Model.

Table 6. Zero trust security model

Aspect	Zero Trust Features
Identity & Access Management (IAM)	Zero Trust relies on robust Identity and Access Management (IAM) frameworks, incorporating multi-factor authentication (MFA), role-based access control (RBAC), and identity federation to ensure that only authorized users can gain access.
Network Segmentation	By segmenting networks and applications, Zero Trust limits lateral movement and reduces the overall attack surface.

7.3. Cloud Security and Hybrid Environments

As organizations increasingly migrate to the cloud, ensuring the security of hybrid cloud environments is becoming more critical. Cloud security involves securing applications, data, and systems hosted in public or private clouds. The rise of hybrid cloud models, which integrate on-premises infrastructure with cloud services, creates challenges for maintaining consistent security policies across environments. Table 7 presents Cloud Security and Hybrid Environments.

Table 7. Cloud security and hybrid environments

Trend	Description
Securing Hybrid Cloud	The need to secure hybrid cloud environments has led to the development of integrated security solutions that provide consistent protection across both cloud and on-premises systems.
Cloud-Native Security	Cloud-native security solutions, like cloud workload protection platforms (CWPP), are increasingly being adopted to secure workloads running in cloud environments.

7.4. Security Orchestration, Automation, and Response (SOAR)

SOAR technologies are gaining traction as they enable security teams to automate repetitive tasks, streamline incident response workflows, and improve decision-making. SOAR tools integrate with other security technologies, such as SIEM, to orchestrate responses to security events based on predefined rules. Table 8 presents Security Orchestration, Automation, and Response.

Table 8. Security orchestration, automation, and response

Feature	SOAR Benefits
Automated Response	SOAR systems can automatically respond to certain types of security incidents, such as isolating compromised systems or blocking malicious IP addresses.
Incident Management	SOAR enables security teams to collaborate and manage incidents more efficiently by centralizing incident details and automating tasks.

7.5. 5G and IoT Security

The expansion of 5G networks and the growing number of IoT devices pose significant challenges for information security. 5G promises faster speeds and more connected devices, but also increases the potential attack surface, especially in industrial IoT systems and critical infrastructure. Table 9 presents 5G and IoT Security,

Table 9. 5G and IoT security

Technology	Security Challenges
5G Networks	5G technology introduces new security challenges, including increased device connectivity and the need for end-to-end encryption across the network (.
IoT Devices	The vast number of IoT devices, many of which have limited security capabilities, makes it difficult to manage vulnerabilities and prevent unauthorized access.

7.6. Privacy-Enhancing Technologies (PETs)

With the increasing amount of personal data being processed, privacy-enhancing technologies (PETs) are essential in ensuring that data privacy regulations, such as GDPR, are upheld. PETs help organizations safeguard individuals' privacy while still allowing for data analysis and processing. Table 10 presents Privacy-Enhancing Technologies.

Table 10. Privacy-Enhancing technologies

Technology	PET Applications
Homomorphic Encryption	Allows data to be processed while it is still encrypted, ensuring privacy even during analysis.
Differential Privacy	Involves adding noise to datasets to protect individual privacy while still gaining valuable insights.

Emerging trends in cybersecurity, such as AI-driven threat detection, Zero Trust models, cloud security, SOAR solutions, and the security challenges of 5G and IoT, are reshaping the way organizations approach information security. As cyber threats become more and more widespread, organizations must be quick to adapt by integrating new technologies and adopting a proactive and holistic approach to security. By staying ahead of these trends, organizations can mitigate risks, enhance security practices, and ensure the protection of sensitive data and critical systems.

8. CASE STUDIES AND REAL-WORLD APPLICATIONS

Examining how information security practices are implemented in real-world situations can offer every organization a good insight into improving their own information security. We will review several case studies that illustrate the implementation of security frameworks, risk management, and incident response, along with lessons derived from these experiences.

8.1. Case Study: Implementing a Zero Trust Security Model at a Financial Institution

A major financial institution transitioned to a Zero Trust Security Model to address growing concerns about insider threats and data breaches. The Zero Trust framework was adopted after the institution faced several internal security challenges, including unauthorized access to sensitive financial data by employees with elevated privileges (Azad, Abdullah, Arshad, Lallie, & Ahmed, 2024; Daah, Qureshi, Awan, & Konur, 2024; Daah et al., 2024; Hale, van Bossuyt, Papakonstantinou, & O'Halloran, 2021).

Key Actions Taken:

- Identity and Access Management (IAM): The institution integrated multi-factor authentication (MFA) and single sign-on (SSO) solutions to strengthen user authentication, ensuring that all users were verified before gaining access to sensitive systems.
- Micro-Segmentation: The network was divided into smaller, isolated segments, with stringent access controls enforced between them to limit lateral movement.
- Continuous Monitoring: Real-time security monitoring was implemented using Security Information and Event Management (SIEM) tools to detect and respond to any suspicious activity.

Outcome:

By adopting the Zero Trust model, the financial institution was able to reduce unauthorized access incidents significantly. The framework also allowed for better visibility and control over user activities, thereby mitigating insider threats and improving overall security posture.

Lessons Learned:

- Continuous Verification: The institution learned that ensuring continuous verification of users and devices is key to minimizing risk.
- User Education: Provide employees with awareness and knowledge of the importance of security policies and the importance of Zero Trust principles in ensuring compliance and minimizing human error.

8.2. Case Study: Ransomware Attack Response at a Healthcare Provider

A healthcare provider experienced a devastating ransomware attack, which encrypted critical patient data and brought down many of the institution's IT systems. The attack was attributed to a phishing email that led to the installation of ransomware on a user's computer (Ghayoomi, Laskey, Miller-Hooks, Hooks, & Tariverdi, 2021; Tully, Selzer, Phillips, O'Connor, & Dameff, 2020; Wilner, Luce, Ouellet, Williams, & Costa, 2021).

Key Actions Taken:

- Incident Response Plan (IRP): Healthcare providers activate incident response plans (IRPs), in isolating systems against the spread of malware.
- Data Backups: The organization immediately restored data from offline backups, ensuring that critical patient records could be recovered without paying the ransom.
- Communication and Transparency: The healthcare provider communicated openly with patients, employees, and regulatory bodies about the breach, maintaining transparency about the impact and recovery efforts.

Outcome:

The healthcare provider was able to recover from the attack in a relatively short time frame due to the availability of secure backups. No ransom was paid, and the attack highlighted the importance of robust incident response plans and data backup procedures.

Lessons Learned:

- Importance of Regular Backups: The case demonstrated how essential it is to maintain secure and regular backups to quickly recover from ransomware attacks.
- Employee Training: It is urgent to train employees to recognize the dangers of phishing emails, which are attacks on lay users.

8.3. Case Study: Cloud Security Implementation at a Retail Business

A retail business implemented a cloud security strategy to secure its customer data stored in cloud environments. The move to the cloud was driven by the need for greater scalability and flexibility in managing large volumes of customer data, especially during peak shopping seasons (Ge, 2025; Padmaja & Seshadri, 2021).

Key Actions Taken:

- Cloud Access Security Broker (CASB): The organization deployed a CASB solution to monitor and enforce security policies across multiple cloud platforms, ensuring data security, compliance, and visibility.
- Data Encryption: All customer data, whether at rest or on the go, is encrypted using the best encryption algorithms to prevent unauthorized activity.
- Vendor Risk Management: The organization conducted thorough risk assessments of its cloud service providers, ensuring that they met required security standards (e.g., ISO 27001, SOC 2).

Outcome:

Cloud security implementations improve the ability of companies to scale and maintain a high level of security. Retailers can always improve compliance with data security protection regulations and ensure customer information is stored and accessed securely.

Lessons Learned:

- Vendor Due Diligence: It's important to evaluate the security features of a cloud vendor before making a choice to ensure that they align with your organization's security regulations and standards.
- Ongoing Monitoring: Continuous monitoring of cloud services was necessary to detection some unauthorized access attempts or vulnerabilities.

8.4. Case Study: SOC 2 Compliance at a SaaS Company

A Software-as-a-Service (SaaS) company aimed to achieve SOC 2 compliance to build trust with potential customers and demonstrate that it handled sensitive data securely. Achieving SOC 2 compliance was particularly important for the company as it sought to expand its customer base and work with enterprise clients (Chang et al., 2022; Pallavi & Jayarekha, 2022).

Key Actions Taken:

- Security Controls: The company implemented strict security controls, including role-based access control (RBAC) for employee access to sensitive data, and regular penetration testing to identify vulnerabilities.
- Monitoring and Log: The company set up continuous monitoring and notes of user activity to detection and respond to incidents of IT security promptly.
- Third-Party Audits: External auditors performed a comprehensive assessment of the company's security practices, ensuring that they met SOC 2's trust service criteria (security, availability, processing integrity, confidentiality, and privacy).

Outcome:

The SaaS company successfully achieved SOC 2 compliance, which enhanced its credibility and attracted enterprise clients. The compliance process also led to improved internal security practices, better incident response capabilities, and increased transparency.

Lessons Learned:

- Documentation and Reporting: Thorough documentation of security processes and incident logs was essential for meeting SOC 2 compliance requirements.
- Continuous Improvement: Achieving SOC 2 compliance wasn't a one-time event but an ongoing process that required continual monitoring, updates, and improvements.

These case demonstrate how organizations in various industries are implementing comprehensive security frameworks to mitigate risks, enhance resilience, and maintain compliance with industry regulations. By applying the lessons learned from these real-world applications, businesses can better prepare for and respond to cyber threats, while continuously improving their security practices.

9. CONCLUSION

In the digital landscape, IT service security is vital for business continuity, data protection, and stakeholder trust. This chapter covers Information Security in IT Service Management (ITSM), detailing strategies and best practices to protect IT infrastructure and services. It emphasizes integrating security into ITSM frameworks, highlighting proactive measures, risk management, compliance, and response strategies to ensure resilient IT services.

9.1 Key Benefits of the Chapter

9.1.1 Holistic Understanding of IT Security

Holistic Understanding of IT Security: This chapter provides a well-rounded understanding of how information security integrates into IT service management, touching on everything from data confidentiality and integrity to availability and incident response. By emphasizing the need for a comprehensive security approach, organizations can appreciate the interconnectedness of various IT service components and the pivotal role security plays in their overall success.

9.1.2 Proactive Security Strategies

Proactive Security Strategies: This chapter covers proactive measures like risk assessments, vulnerability management, and frameworks such as Zero Trust and

SOAR. These strategies help organizations anticipate and mitigate threats early, reducing downtime and damage.

9.1.3 Compliance with Regulatory Requirements

Compliance with Regulatory Requirements: This chapter discusses the importance of security compliance in IT service management. It covers various regulatory requirements (e.g., GDPR, HIPAA, PCI DSS) and security frameworks (e.g., ISO/IEC 27001, SOC 2).

9.1.4 Improved Incident Response and Recovery

Improved Incident Response and Recovery: This chapter outlines how important it is to have a well-structured incident response plan, which covers all stages from detection and analysis to containment and recovery. Through the use of real-world case studies and best practices, it demonstrates how organizations can efficiently recover from cyber threats, thereby minimizing downtime and ensuring business continuity. The focus on lessons learned following incidents encourages organizations to continuously enhance their security posture based on previous experiences.

9.1.5 Emerging Trends and Future Directions

Emerging Trends and Future Directions: The chapter discusses upcoming trends in the cybersecurity field, such as the use of AI and ML in threat detection, the Zero Trust security model, and the increasing importance of cloud security and IoT security concerns. These trends indicate changes in cyber threats and suggest that organizations need to adopt new technologies and strategies to address these developments.

9.1.6 Case Studies and Real-World Applications

The chapter showcases how different industries use information security practices to tackle challenges. By examining these case studies, readers gain practical insights into implementing security measures and their benefits, encouraging tailored security frameworks for specific needs.

9.1.7 Actionable Insights for Organizations

The insights in this chapter—like robust security policies and continuous monitoring—guide organizations to improve security. Integrating these practices into ITSM can enhance both security and operational efficiency.

In summary, this chapter highlights the essential need for incorporating security measures within IT service management to counter the growing complexity of cyber threats. The advantages of adopting a proactive, organized, and regulatory-compliant security approach are evident: minimized risk, improved operational resilience, better adherence to regulations, and increased stakeholder confidence. By implementing the strategies and lessons presented in this chapter, organizations can establish a strong security framework that ensures business continuity, encourages innovation, and meets the evolving demands of the digital landscape.

REFERENCES

Amft, S., Höltervennhoff, S., Huaman, N., Krause, A., Simko, L., Acar, Y., & Fahl, S. (2023). "We've Disabled MFA for You": An Evaluation of the Security and Usability of Multi-Factor Authentication Recovery Deployments. In *CCS 2023 - Proceedings of the 2023 ACM SIGSAC Conference on Computer and Communications Security* (pp. 3138–3152). DOI: 10.1145/3576915.3623180

Azad, M. A., Abdullah, S., Arshad, J., Lallie, H., & Ahmed, Y. H. (2024). Verify and trust: A multidimensional survey of zero-trust security in the age of IoT. *Internet of Things: Engineering Cyber Physical Human Systems*, *27*, 101227. DOI: 10.1016/j.iot.2024.101227

Bhatt, S., Pham, T. K., Gupta, M., Benson, J., Park, J., & Sandhu, R. (2021). Attribute-Based Access Control for AWS Internet of Things and Secure Industries of the Future. *IEEE Access : Practical Innovations, Open Solutions*, *9*, 107200–107223. DOI: 10.1109/ACCESS.2021.3101218

Bu, S.-J., & Cho, S.-B. (2020). A convolutional neural-based learning classifier system for detecting database intrusion via insider attack. *Information Sciences*, *512*, 123–136. DOI: 10.1016/j.ins.2019.09.055

Chang, V., Golightly, L., Modesti, P., Xu, Q. A., Doan, L. M. T., Hall, K., Boddu, S., & Kobusińska, A. (2022). A Survey on Intrusion Detection Systems for Fog and Cloud Computing. *Future Internet*, *14*(3), 89. DOI: 10.3390/fi14030089

Culot, G., Nassimbeni, G., Podrecca, M., & Sartor, M. (2021). The ISO/IEC 27001 information security management standard: Literature review and theory-based research agenda. *The TQM Journal*, *33*(7), 76–105. DOI: 10.1108/TQM-09-2020-0202

Daah, C., Qureshi, A., Awan, I., & Konur, S. (2024). Enhancing Zero Trust Models in the Financial Industry through Blockchain Integration: A Proposed Framework. *Electronics (Basel)*, *13*(5), 865. DOI: 10.3390/electronics13050865

Engemann, K. J., & Miller, H. E. (2024). Toward revealing concealed risks for agile IT service management practices. *Information Systems and e-Business Management*. DOI: 10.1007/s10257-023-00666-8

Ge, X. (2025). Analysis of legal framework solutions to protect retail consumers. *International Journal of Retail & Distribution Management*, *53*(2), 1–16. DOI: 10.1108/IJRDM-02-2023-0055

Ghayoomi, H., Laskey, K., Miller-Hooks, E., Hooks, C., & Tariverdi, M. (2021). Assessing resilience of hospitals to cyberattack. *Digital Health*, *7*, 20552076211059366. DOI: 10.1177/20552076211059366 PMID: 34868621

González-Granadillo, G., González-Zarzosa, S., & Diaz, R. (2021). Security information and event management (SIEM): Analysis, trends, and usage in critical infrastructures. *Sensors (Basel)*, *21*(14), 4759. DOI: 10.3390/s21144759 PMID: 34300500

Hale, B., van Bossuyt, D. L., Papakonstantinou, N., & O'Halloran, B. (2021). A zero-trust methodology for security of complex systems with machine learning components. In *Proceedings of the ASME Design Engineering Technical Conference* (Vol. 2). DOI: 10.1115/DETC2021-70442

Jurczuk, M., & Suprynowicz, M. (2024). Consent in Data Privacy: A General Comparison of GDPR and HIPAA. *Adam Mickiewicz University Law Review*, *16*, 173–194. DOI: 10.14746/ppuam.2024.16.07

Kaur, R., Gabrijelčič, D., & Klobučar, T. (2023). Artificial intelligence for cybersecurity: Literature review and future research directions. *Information Fusion*, *97*, 101804. DOI: 10.1016/j.inffus.2023.101804

Malatji, M., Marnewick, A. L., & Von Solms, S. (2022). Cybersecurity capabilities for critical infrastructure resilience. *Information and Computer Security*, *30*(2), 255–279. DOI: 10.1108/ICS-06-2021-0091

Mishra, A., Alzoubi, Y. I., Gill, A. Q., & Anwar, M. J. (2022). Cybersecurity Enterprises Policies: A Comparative Study. *Sensors (Basel)*, *22*(2), 1–35. DOI: 10.3390/s22020538 PMID: 35062504

Misra, N. N., Dixit, Y., Al-Mallahi, A., Bhullar, M. S., Upadhyay, R., & Martynenko, A. (2022). IoT, Big Data, and Artificial Intelligence in Agriculture and Food Industry. *IEEE Internet of Things Journal*, *9*(9), 6305–6324. DOI: 10.1109/JIOT.2020.2998584

Nordli, E. T., Haugeland, S. G., Nguyen, P. H., Song, H., & Chauvel, F. (2023). Migrating monoliths to cloud-native microservices for customizable SaaS. *Information and Software Technology*, *160*, 107230. https://doi.org/https://doi.org/10.1016/j.infsof.2023.107230. DOI: 10.1016/j.infsof.2023.107230

Ogbanufe, O. M., & Baham, C. (2023). Using Multi-Factor Authentication for Online Account Security: Examining the Influence of Anticipated Regret. *Information Systems Frontiers*, *25*(2), 897–916. DOI: 10.1007/s10796-022-10278-1

Padmaja, K., & Seshadri, R. (2021). Analytics on real time security attacks in healthcare, retail and banking applications in the cloud. *Evolutionary Intelligence, 14*(2), 595–605. DOI: 10.1007/s12065-019-00337-z

Pallavi, G. B., & Jayarekha, P. (2022). Secure and efficient multi-tenant database management system for cloud computing environment. *International Journal of Information Technology : an Official Journal of Bharati Vidyapeeth's Institute of Computer Applications and Management, 14*(2), 703–711. DOI: 10.1007/s41870-019-00416-5

Park, J., Kim, U., Yun, D., & Yeom, K. (2020). Approach for Selecting and Integrating Cloud Services to Construct Hybrid Cloud. *Journal of Grid Computing, 18*(3), 441–469. DOI: 10.1007/s10723-020-09519-x

Poniszewska-Maranda, A., Matusiak, R., Kryvinska, N., & Yasar, A. U. H. (2020). A real-time service system in the cloud. *Journal of Ambient Intelligence and Humanized Computing, 11*(3), 961–977. DOI: 10.1007/s12652-019-01203-7

Radoglou-Grammatikis, P., Sarigiannidis, P., Iturbe, E., Rios, E., Martinez, S., Sarigiannidis, A., Eftathopoulos, G., Spyridis, Y., Sesis, A., Vakakis, N., Tzovaras, D., Kafetzakis, E., Giannoulakis, I., Tzifas, M., Giannakoulias, A., Angelopoulos, M., & Ramos, F. (2021). SPEAR SIEM: A Security Information and Event Management system for the Smart Grid. *Computer Networks, 193*, 108008. DOI: 10.1016/j.comnet.2021.108008

Serhiienko, O., Mashchenko, M., Samorodov, B., Babichev, A., & Klimenko, O. (2024). Simulation and Optimisation of Business Process Management: Case Study of IT Company. *Business Systems Research, 15*(1), 67–90. DOI: 10.2478/bsrj-2024-0004

Singh, S., Sanwar Hosen, A. S. M., & Yoon, B. (2021). Blockchain Security Attacks, Challenges, and Solutions for the Future Distributed IoT Network. *IEEE Access : Practical Innovations, Open Solutions, 9*, 13938–13959. DOI: 10.1109/ACCESS.2021.3051602

Tully, J., Selzer, J., Phillips, J. P., O'Connor, P., & Dameff, C. (2020). Healthcare Challenges in the Era of Cybersecurity. *Health Security, 18*(3), 228–231. DOI: 10.1089/hs.2019.0123 PMID: 32559153

Varga, S., Barreto, G., & Battaglin, P. D. (2020). A holistic IT infrastructure management framework. *International Journal on Computer Science and Engineering, 21*(1), 1–9. DOI: 10.1504/IJCSE.2020.105222

Vasudev, R., Harini, N., & Neethu, M. R. (2023). Multi-Factor Authentication System With ID Card Credentials For Secure Transactions. In *2023 14th International Conference on Computing Communication and Networking Technologies, ICCCNT 2023*. DOI: 10.1109/ICCCNT56998.2023.10308252

Wilner, A. S., Luce, H., Ouellet, E., Williams, O., & Costa, N. (2021). From public health to cyber hygiene: Cybersecurity and Canada's healthcare sector. *International Journal (Toronto, Ont.)*, *76*(4), 522–543. DOI: 10.1177/00207020211067946

Yang, P., Xiong, N., & Ren, J. (2020). Data Security and Privacy Protection for Cloud Storage: A Survey. *IEEE Access : Practical Innovations, Open Solutions*, *8*, 131723–131740. DOI: 10.1109/ACCESS.2020.3009876

Chapter 4
Risk Management and Cost Calculation in Software Projects

Sezi Güngörmüş
https://orcid.org/0009-0000-4709-556X
Dumlupinar University, Faculty of Engineering, Department of Software Engineering, Turkey

Ömer Batıner Türkbay
https://orcid.org/0009-0006-7381-1914
Dumlupinar University, Faculty of Engineering, Department of Software Engineering, Turkey

Çiğdem Bakır
https://orcid.org/0000-0001-8482-2412
Dumlupinar University, Faculty of Engineering, Department of Software Engineering, Turkey

ABSTRACT

Software projects are one of the most critical elements that determine the success of businesses in today's technological world. However, the management of these projects is quite complex and includes many uncertainties. Along with uncertainties and complexities, effective management of risks and accurate cost estimation are necessary for the successful completion of projects. Therefore, risk management and cost calculation are among the basic elements of strategic decision-making processes in software projects. In this study, the types of risks encountered in software projects, risk management strategies and cost calculation methods are discussed. In this study, considering all these situations, the relationship between risk management and cost calculation processes is examined and various suggestions are presented

DOI: 10.4018/979-8-3373-2352-7.ch004

for the effective implementation of these processes. The purpose of this study is to emphasize the importance of risk and cost management processes in software projects and to reveal the role of these processes in increasing the success rate of projects.

INTRODUCTION

Today, the complexity and uncertainty of software projects make risk management and cost calculations mandatory in these projects. Risks in software projects can arise from various sources such as technical errors, organizational problems and external factors. Correct identification and management of these risks ensures that projects are completed on time, within budget and with the desired quality. On the other hand, cost calculation is a critical process for budget planning of projects and preventing possible budget overruns. This study examines the importance of risk management and cost calculations in software projects and examines the methods and strategies to improve these processes.

Risk and cost analysis in software projects should not be limited to the discipline of software engineering, but should also be linked to other areas such as project management, finance, psychology, and organizational behavior. For example, project management principles provide a critical framework for identifying and managing risks at an early stage, while financial analysis techniques provide basic tools for accurate cost calculations and budget estimates. Similarly, psychology and organizational behavior can help understand team communication and team dynamics, which contributes to preventing communication problems frequently encountered in software projects. This interdisciplinary approach allows for the assessment of risks encountered in software projects from a broader perspective and the development of more effective solutions.

In addition, in order to successfully implement risk and cost analysis in software projects, it is also important to integrate with areas such as systems engineering and data analytics. Systems engineering can help identify and manage risks correctly by correctly analyzing the general building blocks and components of software projects. Data analytics can be used to make cost and risk estimates more accurate based on existing data in projects. This interdisciplinary collaboration allows software projects to be planned and managed more effectively, thus increasing the chances of success.

Risk management and cost calculation processes in software projects are subjects that are widely discussed in the academic literature and many studies have been conducted on. The findings in this literature focus on the various difficulties encountered in the software development process, risks and the effectiveness of cost calculation methods. Some important findings of academic studies on risk management and cost calculations in software projects are summarized below.

Many academic studies emphasize the role of risk management in the success of software projects. Identifying and managing risks in advance increases the completion rates of projects on time and within budget. In particular, researchers such as Boehm (1989) and Sommerville (2011) have indicated the importance of identifying risks in the early stages of projects. According to these studies, starting the risk management process early allows project managers to manage resources and schedules more efficiently. In addition, identifying risks helps in predicting the costs of the project (Boehm, 1989) and (Sommerville, 2011).

In the academic literature, many different methods are suggested for cost calculation in software projects. Boehm's COCOMO (Constructive Cost Model) model is one of the most widely used methods for estimating software development costs. It has been found that COCOMO makes cost estimates depending on the project size and complexity and helps in determining how risks in projects will affect the cost. Although various studies indicate that the accuracy of COCOMO may vary depending on the project type and scale, this model is generally an effective estimation tool. In addition, concepts such as Parkinson's Law have an important place in the literature on how the correct management of time and resources in software development processes affects costs. Parkinson's Law argues that work should be managed correctly with existing resources and that excess resources will increase costs. This finding emphasizes the importance of cost calculation methods that prevent unnecessary resource use in software projects. The literature also draws attention to the importance of the integration of risk management and cost calculations. This integration allows software projects to be planned and executed more healthily. Kendall and Kendall (2009) stated that the proper management of risks has a direct impact on the cost control of the project (Kendall and Kendall, 2009). Similarly, Kloppenborg and Anantatmula (2013) emphasize that integrating risks into cost calculations in software projects is a critical factor in increasing the success rate of the project (Kloppenborg and Anantatmula, 2013).

The literature also reveals that project size and complexity have a significant impact on software costs. Jones (2007) stated that cost estimates for large and complex projects are generally more difficult and that such projects generally carry more risks. In complex projects, each new function and feature added leads to increased risks and thus increased costs. This finding shows that cost calculations should be adapted according to the project size and complexity (Jones, 2007).

Mohapatra and Mishra have done significant work on providing information, engaging in conversations, assisting with tasks, and providing creative suggestions using deep learning techniques on various web texts (Mohapatra and Mishra, 2024). AI Tool is a powerful large language model (LLM) designed to produce human-like responses in providing information, engaging with conversations, assisting with tasks, and generating creative insights by being trained on web data. At the core of AI Tool is a transformative neural network that can successfully capture long-range dependencies in text. With 175 billion parameters, this model is one of the most comprehensive LLMs developed to date. This research aims to examine the impact and overall performance of the responses generated by AI Tool across various industrial sectors, in line with the principles of data analytics (Mohapatra and Mishra, 2024).

Time management plays an important role in cost calculation processes. Hoch and others have shown that proper time management in software projects can directly affect costs and that the extension of the project delivery period can increase costs (Hoch, et.al, 2000). Therefore, the combined application of time management and risk management strategies in software projects provides a great advantage in estimating and controlling costs. Studies in the academic literature show how risk management and cost calculation are intertwined in software projects and how these processes affect each other. An effective risk management strategy is an important tool in estimating and controlling project costs. Similarly, proper cost calculation methods make it possible to take the necessary precautions to minimize the effects of risks. Findings in the literature reveal the importance of addressing risk and cost management in an integrated manner in order to increase the success rates in software projects.

Our study addresses the importance of risk management and cost calculation in software projects and needs some improvements to create a deeper impact. First, the addition of real-world case studies that will show how theoretical concepts are applied in practice will help readers adapt to the subject more easily. In addition, incorporating recent developments in the field, especially technologies such as artificial intelligence and machine learning, into the theoretical framework will increase the timeliness of the study. Finally, comparing the proposed solutions with existing methods will highlight the value of the study by revealing their advantages and areas for improvement more clearly. These improvements will expand the scope of the study and provide a deeper understanding of the subject.

Since risk management and cost calculation in software projects are frequently encountered problems, there are many studies on these topics in the existing literature. However, the aim of this study is to clearly present the best practices and strategies in these areas and to create a solid foundation that can guide professionals and project managers. Correct management of risks and costs is of critical importance not only theoretically but also in practice, and therefore, repetition of known methods contributes to the development of the field.

However, considering the suggested criticism, we also accept that future studies should focus on new perspectives in order to provide more innovative solutions. For example, integrating modern technologies such as artificial intelligence and machine learning into risk management and cost calculation can allow for more dynamic and accurate analyses in this area. In addition, addressing risk and cost analyses in software projects with a more data-driven approach can make project management more effective. Such innovative approaches will allow future research to provide more original and forward-looking contributions.

OVERVIEW OF RISK MANAGEMENT IN SOFTWARE PROJECTS

Risk is a concept that, in general, combines the probability of an event or situation occurring with the consequences of this event. In software projects, risk is defined as uncertainties and potential problems that may prevent the project from achieving its goals or make the process of achieving these goals difficult. These goals may include elements such as on-time delivery, staying within budget, and meeting desired quality standards. Risk can have both positive and negative consequences by its nature.

Software projects face various types of risks, such as technical, organizational, and external risks (Figure 1). Technical risks are errors or deficiencies that occur during software development; organizational risks can result from lack of communication and cooperation within the team, while external risks arise from external factors such as market conditions or legal regulations. These types of risks can negatively affect the completion of projects on time and within budget, so it is vital to develop an effective risk management strategy.

Figure 1. Software risk management paradigm

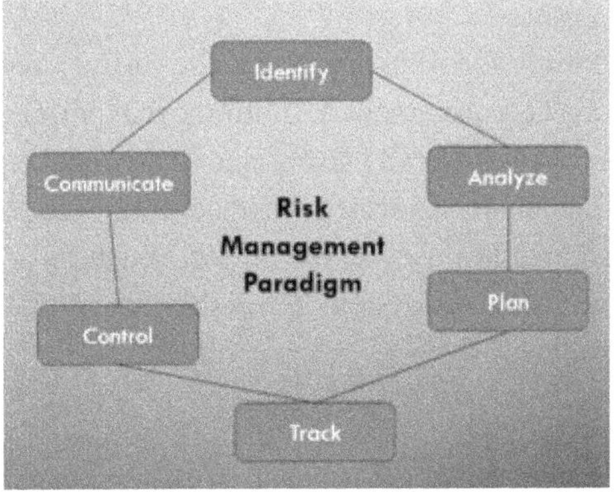

Table 1. Risks in software projects

Risks
Staff shortages
Unrealistic timelines and budgets
Developing the wrong functionality and features
Designing the wrong user interface
Unnecessary overdevelopment ("Gold-plating")
Constantly changing requirements
Shortages of outsourced components
Shortages of outsourced tasks
Real-time performance issues
Strengthening computer science capabilities

Although risk in software projects is often associated with negative impacts, there are also opportunity risks that bring positive results. For example, the use of a new technology may initially create uncertainty, but if successfully implemented, it can give the project a competitive advantage. Therefore, risk management should focus not only on reducing negative impacts, but also on evaluating potential opportunities.

The importance of risk management in software projects is evident in its effects on the completion of projects on time and within budget. Effective risk management ensures that projects are completed within the planned time and cost, while also improving quality. Timely detection and management of risks reduces the failure rate of projects and allows for more efficient use of resources; therefore, risk management in software projects is not only a necessity, but also a critical element for the sustainability of projects.

The sources of risks in a software project can be various. Factors such as technical complexities, incorrect requirement definitions, inexperience of team members, inadequate budget or scheduling can cause risks to arise during the project.

Technical Risks: Technical risks arise from uncertainties related to the technology, tools, and technical approaches used in the project. Such risks usually occur when technical decisions are made incorrectly during the project or unexpected technical problems occur. Examples:

- Difficulties encountered in using a new programming language or framework.
- Failure of the system to meet scalability or security requirements.
- Inadequate documentation of the technology involved.

Operational Risks: Operational risks arise from problems encountered in the daily operations of the project. Such risks may arise from the performance of individual team members or from the processes used during project execution. Examples:

- Inadequate or unrealistic preparation of project plans.
- Problems with time management.
- Lack of critical resources (people or equipment).

Organizational Risks: Organizational risks arise from factors related to the structure, project management processes, or human resources within the company. Management deficiencies, lack of clear definition of tasks, or communication problems between team members are examples of such risks. Examples:

- Inadequate leadership or project manager experience.
- Lack of clear goals and processes.
- The team does not have sufficient technical knowledge or experience.

External Risks: External risks arise from uncontrollable factors that occur outside the project. These risks are usually affected by economic, political, environmental, or legal changes. Examples:

- Changes in legal regulations.
- Natural disasters or epidemics affecting the project.
- Failure of suppliers or failure to provide resources on time.

Risk Process in Software Projects

Effective risk management is necessary to ensure success in projects. Correctly identifying and categorizing risks is an important step in ensuring successful completion of projects. In the literature, risks encountered in software projects are divided into various categories. In the study conducted by Murthi (2002), the risk categories specified are as follows (Murthi, 2002):

1) Requirements: Unclear or constantly changing requirements are one of the most common risks that can cause projects to fail.
2) Technology: Failure of the technologies used to meet expectations poses a significant risk in the development process.
3) Business: Business-related decisions and partnerships can cause projects to be delayed or stopped.
4) Political: Power struggles in large organizations can lead to project obstruction.
5) Resources: Insufficient resources can negatively affect the project schedule and team morale.
6) Skills: Lack of knowledge and skills of team members can make it difficult for the project to progress.

7) Deployment and Support: Lack of required infrastructure or support staff can prevent the project from being completed on time.
8) Integration: Incompatible applications can threaten the integrity of the system.
9) Schedule: Timing issues can make deliveries and project progress difficult.
10) Maintenance and Development: Inadequate documentation and training can make it difficult to maintain the software.
11) Design: Poor design decisions can negatively impact the software's performance and user experience.
12) Miscellaneous: Unforeseen events, such as natural disasters or failures, can disrupt the project.

Identifying and Reducing Risks

In software projects, correctly identifying and managing risks is critical to the success of the projects. However, risk management can become more complex in projects with geographical and socio-cultural differences. Various risks can be encountered in these projects, ranging from communication deficiencies to coordination difficulties and control problems. In the study conducted by Nurdiani et al. (2011), risks in software projects were examined comprehensively and detailed under the headings of communication, coordination and control (Nurdiani, 2011).

1) Communication: Lack of synchronized communication, delayed feedback and communication difficulties due to geographical distance can negatively affect the efficiency of projects.
2) Coordination: Determining an appropriate software development process, incompatibility of tools in different locations and unclear distribution of tasks are among the risks that make project management difficult.
3) Control: Aligning the goals of the stakeholders, making project progress and status visible, and managing security vulnerabilities are critical for the successful management of projects.

Table 2. Risk identification: Communication

COMMUNICATION	
Risk Category	**Reasons and Difficulties**
Lack of synchronized communication	Limited instant communication opportunities among team members.
Feedback delays	It leads to loss of time in decision-making and problem-solving processes.
Lack of team cohesion	The decrease in the sense of teamwork weakens cooperation.
Data loss	Errors or losses experienced during information transfer.
Cultural diversity	Communication and cooperation problems arising from different cultures.

Table 3. Risk identification: Coordination

Coordination	
Risk Category	**Reasons and Difficulties**
Inconsistency of working hours	Team members work in different time zones, making simultaneous collaboration difficult.
Lack of transparency in roles and responsibilities	Project scope and task distribution are unclear.
Proper software development process definition	Lack of clarity in processes makes workflow difficult.
Limited experience as a team	A team that has never worked together before has difficulty adapting.
Clear definition of project scope	The project's goals and boundaries are unclear.

Table 4. Risk identification: Control

Control	
Risk Category	**Reasons and Difficulties**
Feedback delays	Loss of time in project monitoring and control processes.
Accurate effort estimation	Incorrect workload estimates create problems in resource management.
Managing team dependencies	Lack of coordination between team members or subgroups.
Managing cost growth	Unplanned expenses and budget overruns.
Managing staff turnover	Loss of information due to team member departure or replacement.

After identifying the risks, strategies to reduce these risks are also discussed under the same headings and are indicated in tables. The identified risks and the precautions that can be taken against these risks are presented below, respectively.

Table 5. Risk reduction: Communication

Communication	
Strategy	**Explanation**
Shifting working hours	Increase communication time by aligning working hours.
Reducing communication hierarchy	Reduce communication hierarchy to encourage direct communication.
Using groupware tools	Use technological tools to support team collaboration.
Encouraging frequent communication	Daha fazla bilgi paylaşımı ve iş birliği için sık iletişimi teşvik etme.
Assigning a contact person	Appointing a representative to facilitate communication between teams.
Developing a specialized terminology glossary	Creating a glossary to use within the team to ensure common understanding.

Table 6. Risk reduction: Coordination

Coordination	
Strategy	**Explanation**
Allocate tasks in line with software architecture	Properly distributing tasks to independent parts of the software
Encourage frequent deliverables	Scheduling frequent deliveries to keep work moving.
Create a team member guide	Creating a guide that includes team members' areas of expertise and responsibilities.
Hold a face-to-face kickoff meeting	Arranging a face-to-face meeting at the beginning of the project to ensure alignment.
Ensure that tools are compatible and consistent	Checking the compatibility of tools used by different teams.
Evaluate team members assigned to the project	Evaluating employees' suitability for the project and their performance.

Table 7. Risk reduction: Control

Control	
Strategy	**Explanation**
Provide regular real-time communication	Organizing regular and synchronous meetings among team members.
Agree on cost and effort estimates	Agreeing on estimates as a team at the beginning of the project.
Consider inflation rates in different countries	Taking economic differences into account when doing cost planning.
Share expectations and guidelines early	Explaining the project requirements and rules with team members early.
Update project status regularly	Provide frequent status updates to monitor project progress.
Ensure senior management support	Making progress with the support of managers throughout the project.
Provide training	Arranging necessary training to improve the skills of team members.

Cost Calculation in Software Projects

Cost is the monetary value of the total resources spent for the production, development or delivery of a product or service, and includes elements such as labor, equipment, software licenses, infrastructure, training and outsourcing in software projects. Correct cost calculation is critical to the sustainability and success of the project. Cost plays an important role in planning and budgeting projects; accurate estimates ensure that the project is completed on time and with the specified resources. In addition, monitoring costs throughout the project helps to use resources more efficiently and prevents unnecessary expenses. Cost is an important element in calculating the return on investment of a software project; incorrect estimates may lead to failure to achieve the expected profit or benefit from the project. In addition, cost estimates are also important in terms of determining and preventing risks that may be encountered during the project in advance. Transparent and accurate cost management creates trust in the sponsors and stakeholders of the project and contributes to the approval of the project. In short, cost is not only a financial data, but also a strategic element that affects the overall success of the project.

Cost Calculation Methods

Cost calculation in software projects is a critical process for determining the project scope, allocating resources, and creating the budget. Cost calculation can be performed with different methods and is usually applied with an approach selected according to the size, complexity, and goals of the project.

Expert Opinion Based Method: Cost estimation is made based on the opinions of experienced team members or industry experts. Although this method is fast and practical, it requires careful evaluation because it is subjective.
Analog Method: Estimation is made by referencing the cost information of previously completed similar projects. This method makes it easier to benefit from historical data, but differences between projects should be taken into account.
Parametric Method: Cost is calculated using certain parameters and criteria for project components. For example, standard unit prices such as cost per line of code can be used in the software development process.
Bottom-Up Estimation Method: The costs of all tasks within the scope of the project are estimated separately, and these costs are brought together to calculate the total project cost. This method provides more detailed and precise results, but it is time-consuming.
Estimation Based on Agile Methods: In Agile projects, cost calculations are usually done over short cycles (sprints). The total cost is calculated by estimating the resources and effort required for each sprint.

Software Cost Estimation Models

Accurate cost estimation in software projects is a fundamental element for successful project management. In the literature, different estimation tools have been developed and their scope and areas of use have been discussed. In this section, the general features of these tools and their effects on software projects are discussed. Cost estimation in software projects is a critical step for determining the budget and managing project resources correctly. These estimates are usually made based on historical data, standard methods and mathematical models. Software cost estimation models provide more accurate calculations of costs by taking into account the size, scope and complexity of the projects.

COCOMO (COnstructive COst MODel) Model: COCOMO is a mathematical model widely used to estimate the costs of software projects. It is applied at three different levels according to the project type:

- Basic COCOMO: The size of the project is evaluated according to the number of lines of code. It is suitable for simple and medium-level projects.
- Intermediate COCOMO: In addition to the size of the project, factors such as project management, team experience and complexity are also evaluated.
- Detailed COCOMO: More detailed analyses are performed for each stage in the software development process. Suitable for complex projects.

Function Point Analysis (FPA): This model estimates the cost by measuring the functionality of the software. Functions are determined based on user requirements and each function is scored according to its complexity. FPA focuses on the services the software offers to the user rather than the number of lines of code and is therefore preferred especially in business-oriented projects.

PUTNAM Model: The PUTNAM model is another mathematical model used to optimize resource use in software projects. It estimates costs by taking into account variables such as project duration, number of employees and labor efficiency. It is usually used in large-scale software projects.

Delphi Method: The Delphi method involves experts coming together to make independent estimates and then consolidating these estimates. Since it is an iterative process, it makes estimates more precise and reliable.

Artificial Intelligence-Based Models: In recent years, machine learning and artificial intelligence techniques have been used for cost estimation in software projects. These models analyze past project data to provide cost estimates for future projects. They are very effective when the amount of data is large.

Agile Estimation Models: In agile software development methods, cost estimation is done over sprints and iterations. The total cost is calculated by estimating the resources and effort required for each iteration. This model is frequently preferred in agile projects due to its flexible structure.

Table 8. Estimation tools

Vehicle Name	Scope and Use
COCOMO II	Very comprehensive, can be used for different software projects.
CoStar	Advanced estimating model, especially suitable for large projects.
CostModeler	Provides advanced cost estimating for in-house software projects.
SEER	A comprehensive estimating tool, compatible for various types of software.
SoftCost	Suitable for small and medium-sized projects.

In the study conducted by Jones (2005), the role of cost estimation tools in managing uncertainties in software projects and in the effective use of resources was emphasized (Jones, 2005). In addition, typical activity rates performed in different software projects were examined in Table 9. For example, the fact that coding activities take place in 30% of Web-based projects, 20% in MIS projects and 23% in commercial software projects shows that each project has different priorities and this diversity should be taken into account in cost estimation and resource planning.

Table 9. Typical activity ratios

Activity	Web Based Applications	Management Information Systems	Commercial Software
Determining Requirements	5.00%	7.50%	4.00%
Prototyping	10.00%	2.00%	1.00%
Initial Design	8.00%	7.00%	7.00%
Detailed Design	7.00%	8.00%	6.00%
Coding	30.00%	20.00%	23.00%
Preparing User Documentation	10.00%	7.00%	12.00%
Performing Unit Tests	30.00%	4.00%	2.50%
Functional Tests	6.00%	5.00%	5.00%
Performing System Tests	7.00%	5.00%	5.00%
Project Management	10.00%	12.00%	11.00%

The Relationship Between Risk Management and Cost Estimation

The relationship between risk management and cost estimation in software projects is a critical element for successful project management. Both processes complement each other so that projects can be completed on time and within budget. Proper risk management allows for more accurate cost estimates, and conversely, accurate cost calculations make it easier to better understand project risks and take precautions against them. Risk management and cost estimation are two important processes that are interconnected and support each other for the successful completion of a software project. Proper identification and management of risks make cost calculations more accurate and effective. Similarly, accurate cost calculations make it easier to recognize risks in advance and take necessary precautions. Achieving this balance contributes to the successful completion of software projects with the targeted budget, time and quality.

REAL WORLD EXAMPLES

Let's take an example of an e-commerce website development project. In such projects, risks usually focus on areas such as user experience (UX), system security, payment integrations, and scalability. In such a project, the following risks and cost management strategies can be considered:

- Risks:

Timeout Risk: Project delivery time estimates often include not fully understanding user demands and security requirements of web applications. This can lead to timeout.

Technical Risks: The integration of complex payment systems and security protocols can lead to technical errors and compromise of the system.

User Experience (UX) Risk: Users not being able to use the application as expected or design errors can lead to user dissatisfaction and low sales.

- Cost Management Strategies: A realistic time frame and resource allocation should be made for the project, and additional costs should be taken into account for risks. Additional costs that will be created by technical debt and security vulnerabilities should be anticipated, and a budget should be allocated especially for security audits and system tests. By investing in user testing and prototype design at early stages, additional costs resulting from UX errors can be prevented. Risk and cost management in software projects are indispensable elements of project management. The risks encountered in different software projects and the cost management strategies applied against these risks are shaped according to the characteristics and requirements of each project. Identifying risks at early stages and implementing appropriate cost strategies contribute greatly to the successful completion of projects.

Risk management and cost calculation processes in software projects are widely discussed and many studies have been conducted in the academic literature. The findings in this literature focus on the various difficulties encountered in the software development process, risks, and the effectiveness of cost calculation methods. Some important findings of academic studies on risk management and cost calculation in software projects are summarized below.

Relationship between Risk Management and Success: Many academic studies emphasize the role of risk management in the success of software projects. Identifying and managing risks in advance increases the completion rates of projects on time and within budget. In particular, researchers such as Boehm (1989) and Sommerville (2011) have emphasized the importance of identifying risks in the early stages of projects. According to these studies, starting the risk management process early allows project managers to manage resources and timelines more efficiently. In addition, identifying risks helps in predicting project costs.

Effectiveness of Cost Calculation Methods: In the academic literature, many different methods are suggested for cost calculation in software projects. Boehm's COCOMO (Constructive Cost Model) model is one of the most widely used methods for estimating software development costs. It has been found that COCOMO makes cost estimates depending on project size and complexity and helps in determining how risks in projects will affect costs. Although various studies indicate that the accuracy of COCOMO may vary depending on the type and scale of the project, this model is generally an effective estimation tool. In addition, concepts such as Parkinson's Law have an important place in the literature on how the correct management of time and resources in software development processes affects costs. Parkinson's Law argues that work should be managed correctly with existing resources and that excess resources will increase costs. This finding emphasizes the importance of cost calculation methods that prevent unnecessary resource use in software projects.

A. The Virtual Case File (VCF) Project

The Virtual Case File (VCF) Project was initiated by the FBI in 2000 and was a project aimed at modernizing the digital file management system (Cook, 2000). The project was developed so that the FBI could manage its criminal files more securely, quickly and systematically. However, the project was canceled due to the lack of clear requirements, frequently changing project goals and technological inadequacies. VCF was associated with both financial losses and the disruptions experienced by the FBI in its technological transformation processes.

1) Requirements: The requirements of the VCF project were not clear, realistic or constant throughout the project process, and the project experienced confusion due to frequently changing and unclear requirements. For example, the lack of a well-defined enterprise architecture led to inconsistencies between the project goals and the delivered outputs (Cook, 2000).
2) Technology: The technologies selected for the VCF project did not meet expectations and created significant development challenges. The project relied on outdated technologies and was not integrated properly, which prevented it from adapting to modern IT environments (Cook, 2000).
3) Business: Decisions, partnerships, and contracting arrangements related to business processes caused delays and inefficiencies. The FBI's reliance on a single contractor (Science Applications International Corp) for the VCF development process created competitive pressures and reduced accountability, which led to cost increases and missed deadlines (Cook, 2000).
4) Political: Internal conflicts and external political factors significantly hampered the VCF project. The project came under scrutiny from Congress and the National Research Council, which increased pressure and stalled progress (Cook, 2000).
5) Resources: Resource allocation, especially in terms of budget and personnel, was inadequate. The project was held back by budget cuts and a lack of qualified personnel.

6) Skills: The project team's areas of expertise, especially in IT management and software development, were inadequate. This lack of talent led to poor project execution and oversight.
7) Deployment and Support: The infrastructure and support provided for the VCF project were inadequate. There were significant problems with the deployment of software updates and support for users, which led to low morale among the project team.
8) Integration: Integration problems were common, especially with existing FBI systems. Compatibility issues arose due to the use of different technologies, which complicated the development process and delayed the project.
9) Timeline: The project's timeline was unrealistic and the delivery date was not met. The initial schedule did not take into account the difficulties of developing a comprehensive IT system.
10) Maintenance and Development: Documentation and training for the VCF project were inadequate, which had a negative impact on long-term maintenance and development. The lack of clear documentation made it difficult for new team members to understand the system.
11) Design: Design decisions made for the VCF project negatively impacted performance and usability. The system's architecture did not adequately meet user needs, leading to inefficiencies and user dissatisfaction.
12) Other Factors: Unforeseen events, such as leadership changes and shifts in organizational priorities, disrupted the VCF project. These events often led to reassessments of project goals and scope.

The key risks identified in the FBI's Virtual Case File project were unclear requirements, inadequate technology and resources, lack of skills, and poor integration and support processes. This highlights the importance of clear communication, solid planning, and stakeholder engagement throughout the project lifecycle. By addressing these factors, future projects can avoid similar mistakes.

B. Denver International Airport (DIA) Baggage Handling System Project

The Denver International Airport (DIA) Baggage Handling System Project was initiated in 1995 by the Denver International Airport administration to automate baggage handling processes. The aim of the project was to provide fast and error-free baggage handling using innovative technologies. However, the project failed due to the complexity of the system, technological problems and insufficient resources. Due to high cost overruns and technical problems, a manual handling system had to be returned.

1) Requirements: The Denver International Airport baggage handling system project experienced significant problems due to the requirements not being clear and fixed. The uncertainty and frequent changes in the requirements caused confusion and rework among the project team, which negatively affected the project's timeline and budget. In particular, the complexity of the system and the constantly changing needs of the airport led to frequent revisions of the requirements (Finkelstein, 1993).
2) Technology: The technology used within the scope of the project was one of the most innovative and complex systems of the period. However, the reliability of this technology is low and its integration is quite difficult. This situation caused serious difficulties and delays in the project development process (Fountain, 2025).
3) Resources: The project experienced difficulties due to insufficient resources such as budget and competent personnel. In particular, the initially estimated budget was insufficient and this led to cost overruns (Cundiff, et.al, 2018).
4) Skills: The project team's lack of expertise in managing such a complex and innovative system was effective in the failure. In particular, their lack of knowledge in the areas of software development, integration and project management negatively affected the project (Cundiff, et.al, 2018).
5) Integration: The integration of different systems and components posed a major challenge for the project. Compatibility issues and lack of coordination between systems caused delays and system failures (Fountain, 2025).
6) Timeline: The project's timeline was unrealistic and was exceeded many times. Complexity and frequent changes in requirements made the feasibility of the schedule even more difficult (Cundiff, et.al, 2018).
7) Maintenance and Development: Inadequate documentation and training negatively affected long-term maintenance and development efforts (Fountain, 2025).
8) Design: Flaws in the design of the system negatively affected performance, usability, and scalability (Cundiff, et.al, 2018).

The failure of the Denver International Airport baggage handling system project was due to a number of factors, including unclear and unstable requirements, complex and unreliable technology, inadequate resources, skill gaps, poor integration, unrealistic timelines, and inadequate maintenance and development planning. This project demonstrates the importance of comprehensive planning, realistic expectations, a strong risk management approach, and effective communication and collaboration. Learning from such mistakes can help future projects avoid similar pitfalls and achieve successful results.

C. London Ambulance Service Computer Aided Direction System (LASCAD) Project

London Ambulance Service Computer Aided Direction System (LASCAD) was initiated by London Ambulance Service in 1992 to speed up emergency interventions. This project was designed to track the location of ambulances in real time and direct the most appropriate unit to the scene. However, the project failed due to software errors in the system, inadequate testing processes and infrastructure deficiencies. This failure caused serious operational problems throughout London.

1) Requirements: Research indicates that the requirements of the LASCAD project were not clear and stable. The requirements were both vague and constantly changing throughout the project development life cycle. This vagueness and variability caused confusion and misunderstandings between developers and users. The failure to fully test the system and the failure to test the hardware under full load were the main reasons for the project failure (Hougham, 1996).
2) Technology: Although the technology used in LASCAD was advanced for its time, significant difficulties were encountered. The complexity of the system and the lack of sufficient technical research and development were the reasons for the failure. The integration of the various components, especially Automatic Vehicle Location (AVL) and mobile data terminals, created problems (Hougham, 1996).
3) Business: Business decisions in the LASCAD project were problematic. The pressure to develop a successful and rapid application resulted in hasty decisions and inadequate planning. The lack of adequate risk assessment and emergency planning further exacerbated the situation (Leveson and Turner, 1993).
4) Political: Internal conflicts and power struggles within the London Ambulance Service contributed to the failure of the project. Lack of consensus and inadequate cooperation among stakeholders hindered effective decision-making and problem-solving processes (McGrath, 2024).
5) Resources: The resources of the LASCAD project, including budget, personnel and infrastructure, were inadequate. In addition, the lack of adequate training of staff further exacerbated this problem (Hougham, 1996).
6) Skills: Lack of skills in the project team is also a significant factor affecting LASCAD failure. Inadequate knowledge in areas such as software development, system integration, and project management hindered project progress (Landry, 1996).
7) Deployment and Support: The infrastructure and support provided to the LASCAD system was inadequate. The lack of a backup system and inadequate user support led to the failure of the system (Hougham, 1996).

8) Integration: Integration of the different components of the LASCAD system was difficult. Compatibility problems and data inconsistencies further increased these problems (Hougham, 1996).
9) Timeline: The project timeline was unrealistic and could not be adhered to. Unrealistic dates, hasty decisions, and inadequate testing processes resulted (Hougham, 1996).
10) Maintenance and Development: Inadequate documentation and training hindered long-term maintenance and development. This made it difficult to solve problems and make necessary improvements (Hougham, 1996).
11) Design: Design flaws in the LASCAD system significantly affected the performance, usability, and scalability of the system. The complexity and user-friendliness of the system led to errors and a great deal of frustration for users (Montealegre and Keil, 2000).

The failure of the LASCAD project was the result of a number of factors, including unclear requirements, inadequate technology assessment, poor business decisions, internal conflicts, inadequate resources, skill deficiencies, poor infrastructure, integration problems, unrealistic timelines, poor documentation, design flaws, and the accumulation of these factors. These factors should be taken into account in future projects to prevent similar failures.

D. Healthcare.gov Project

The Healthcare.gov Project was developed by the US government in 2013 as part of the Affordable Care Act. This platform aimed to enable citizens to easily select and purchase health insurance plans. However, problems in the design and integration of the system resulted in major technical setbacks during the project launch. Undelivered features and performance issues cost the US government both financially and reputationally.

1) Requirements: The requirements of the Healthcare.gov project faced significant problems. Although the project had a seemingly simple task, the requirements were not clearly defined, leading to a problematic project with late deliveries and multiple contractors. Unclear specifications and last-minute changes to key features further complicated the development (Olszewski and Wingreen, 2011).
2) Work: The involvement of many contractors with different levels of experience and expertise led to inefficiencies and conflicts of interest. An expedited timeline and high-pressure environment negatively impacted quality and detailed planning (Olszewski and Wingreen, 2011).

3) Politics: The highly politicized nature of the Affordable Care Act greatly impacted the Healthcare.gov project. Intense criticism of the project from both supporters and opponents, combined with the 2013 government shutdown, made the development and deployment process challenging. External political pressures influenced decision-making and resource allocation, which undermined the project's success (Shah, 2015).
4) Skills: The complexity of the project required high skill levels, but research has indicated potential skill gaps. The involvement of multiple contractors led to inconsistencies in quality and performance (Olszewski and Wingreen, 2011).
5) Deployment and Support: The initial deployment of Healthcare.gov presented significant deployment and support issues. The website experienced accessibility and functionality issues due to long waiting times, server errors, and other technical issues (Shah, 2015).
6) Integration: Integration of different systems and components posed a significant challenge. The integration of numerous software components from contractors led to incompatibility and bug issues (Olszewski and Wingreen, 2011).
7) Timeline: The project's timeline was unrealistic and targeted dates were not met. Missed deliveries and rushed development led to numerous bugs and glitches on the website.
8) Maintenance and Development: There was a lack of adequate documentation and training to support long-term maintenance and development. This deficiency made it difficult to resolve issues experienced after the initial deployment of the website.
9) Design: The design of Healthcare.gov had a negative impact on performance, usability, and scalability. The complexity of the website and poor user interface led to user confusion and frustration (Silvis-Cividjian, 2024). The failure of the Healthcare.gov project was due to a combination of risk factors such as unclear requirements, inadequate resource allocation, insufficient skills, integration issues, unrealistic timelines, and a highly political environment. Future projects can mitigate these risks by having a defined scope, an experienced and skilled team, and a flexible development process.

E. Therac-25 Project

The Therac-25 Project is a medical radiation device developed by the Atomic Energy Agency of Canada (AECL) in 1985. This device, used for cancer treatment, was equipped with innovative software control systems. However, due to software errors and security deficiencies, the device delivered lethal doses of radiation to several patients. These tragic events highlighted the need for more stringent quality control processes in safety-critical systems.

1) Requirements: The requirements for the Therac-25 were not sufficiently clear, realistic, or consistent throughout the development process. System complexity and rushed development led to unclear and incomplete specifications. For example, the lack of adequate safety control and error management mechanisms in the software caused the machine to deliver excessive radiation doses. This situation emphasizes the importance of a rigorous approach to requirements engineering, especially since it is understood that the testing and verification processes of safety-critical functions must be done thoroughly (Swartz, 1996).
2) Technology: The Therac-25 was based on a combination of hardware and software, and software played a critical role in controlling the radiation beam. The technologies used, although not directly faulty, were poorly understood and managed by the development team. Code replication from previous models resulted in bugs being missed because changes were not adequately tested. This situation highlights the importance of careful selection of technology, adequate testing, and proper code management practices (Swartz, 1996).
3) Business: In the development of the Therac-25, the desire to get the device to market quickly and make a profit influenced the development process. This resulted in inadequate testing and ignoring security concerns. The lack of quality assurance processes and the prioritization of speed over security created a high-risk environment.
4) Skills: The Therac-25 development team appears to have inadequate knowledge of software security and real-time systems. Code reuse and inadequate testing practices indicate a critical skills gap.
5) Distribution and Support: The distribution and support infrastructure of Therac-25 was inadequate. Inadequate training and documentation for users contributed to the accidents. The situation was made worse by the vagueness of error messages and the failure of the machine to shut down properly after errors were detected (Wang, et.al, 2017).
6) Integration: The integration of hardware and software components of Therac-25 was problematic. The interaction between hardware and software caused errors that led to accidents.
7) Timeline: Because the Therac-25 project was intended to be brought to market quickly, safety concerns were not sufficiently taken into account and testing was inadequate. Unrealistic timelines and pressure to meet these timelines negatively affected product quality (Swartz, 1996).
8) Maintenance and Development: The Therac-25 lacked adequate documentation and training materials. This deficiency made the system difficult to use and troubleshoot. In addition, the lack of a maintenance and development plan allowed for continued failures.

9) Design: The Therac-25 design contained several flaws that affected safety and usability. Inadequate safety controls, unclear error messages, and failure to properly shut down the machine after detecting failures were contributing factors to the accidents (Swartz, 1996).

The Therac-25 accidents highlight the importance of rigorous software engineering practices, especially in safety-critical systems. Risks to this project included inadequate requirements, inadequate testing, lack of expertise, insufficient resources, and poor communication and collaboration. To prevent similar problems in the future, organizations should prioritize safety, invest in strong quality assurance processes, and foster a culture of open communication and collaboration.

COSTS AND LOSS ANALYSIS OF FAILED SOFTWARE PROJECTS

This section examines the financial losses and damages that occur after software project failures. Each project failed due to a combination of risk factors, and the costs of these failures were assessed considering the scale and impact of the projects. It is often difficult to calculate the financial losses of projects precisely, because not only direct losses but also indirect costs such as reputational damage, legal processes, and regulatory changes must be considered.

Table 10 summarizes software projects that failed for the different reasons discussed in the previous section and suffered serious financial losses. This table shows how these projects were affected by factors such as budget overruns, administrative problems, and inadequate risk management.

Tablo 10. *Zarar Analizi*

Year	Company Name	Project Name	Original Budget	Actual Expenditure	Financial Loss
2000	FBI	The Virtual Case File (VCF) Project	$100 million	$170 million	The failure to complete the project resulted in a major cost increase and operational losses due to inadequate project management and delivery deficiencies. This situation caused the company to suffer significant losses both financially and operationally.
2006	Denver International Airport	Denver International Airport (DIA) Baggage Handling System Project	$195 million	$360 million	The conversion of the system from a manual operation to a complex automation has led to both a major increase in costs and various operational problems at the airport. For these reasons, the airport has experienced high financial losses.
2001	London Ambulance Service	London Ambulance Service Computer Aided Direction System (LASCAD) Project	$17,5 million	$75 million	Due to technical problems and inadequate planning, the project could not be fully implemented and system failures caused operational disruptions. As a result, emergency health services were delayed, which increased both the financial losses and reputational damage of the institution.
2013	US Government	Healthcare.gov Project	$93 million	$2 billion	Due to overspending and problems during launch, the project cost was much higher than initially planned. This has brought a serious cost to the country's economy and negatively affected the government's reputation.
1985	AECL (Atomic Energy Agency of Canada)	Therac-25 Project (Medical Equipment)	No data	No data	The Therac-25 software bugs caused fatal health problems, but the financial dimensions of these losses are impossible to calculate. In addition to direct costs such as legal compensation, reputational damage, and mandatory security updates, indirect costs such as loss of confidence in AECL's future projects and a decrease in market value have also caused a huge loss.

CONCLUSION

This study explained how important risk management and cost calculation are in software projects. There are many types of risks in software projects and these can affect the success of the projects. These risks can arise from technical errors, communication problems within the team or external factors. Therefore, identifying risks in advance and taking precautions against them is very important for project success.

Risk management is used to ensure that projects are completed on time and within the determined budget. If risks are not identified correctly, the project may be delayed or exceed the budget. In addition, risks must be constantly monitored and controlled in order not to decrease the quality in the project. In this study, the types of risks and some strategies that can be applied against these risks were explained with examples.

In the cost calculation section, it was explained which cost elements should be taken into account in software projects. These cost elements include items such as personnel wages, software licenses and infrastructure expenses. If the correct cost estimate is made at the beginning of the project, the risk of budget overrun in the project decreases and resources are used more efficiently. In addition, a correct cost plan increases transparency in the project and trust between stakeholders.

As a result, risk management and cost calculation are two important processes that complement each other in software projects. Proper management of risks helps to reduce problems in the project and to make the project successful. Similarly, if correct cost calculations are made, budget control is ensured and it becomes easier to complete the project on time. Therefore, attention should be paid to risk and cost management at every stage of software projects.

As a result, the importance of the risk management and cost calculation processes discussed in this study in software projects has been emphasized once again. In order for software projects to be completed successfully, risks must be identified and managed correctly. Especially risks such as technical errors, lack of communication within the team, and external factors encountered in projects can lead to projects not being completed on time or exceeding the budget. Therefore, correctly identifying risks in the early stages and taking strategic measures against them play a critical role in the success of the project.

The accuracy of cost calculation is also vital for the sustainability of software projects. Good planning of the project budget prevents budget overruns and ensures more efficient use of resources. In addition, accurate cost planning creates an environment of trust by creating transparency among all stakeholders involved in the project. It is seen that these processes should be made more effective by focusing more on risk and cost management issues for future software projects. The findings of this study shed light on the basic challenges encountered in software projects and provide a basis for developing strategies that can be used in practice.

REFERENCES

Azzeh, M., & Bou Nassif, A. (2016). A hybrid model for estimating software project effort from use case points. *Applied Soft Computing*, *49*, 981–989. DOI: 10.1016/j.asoc.2016.05.008

Barbin, J. P., & Rashidi, H. (2015). A decision support system for estimating cost of software projects using a hybrid of multi-layer artificial neural network and decision tree. *International Journal in Foundations of Computer Science & Technology*. DOI: 10.5121/ijfcst.2015.5603

Beynon-Davies, S. P. (2025). IS failure and risk assessment: The case of the London Ambulance Service computer-aided dispatch system. *European Conference on Information Systems*. https://www.semanticscholar.org/paper/IS-failure-and-risk-assessment%3A-The-case-of-the-Beynon-Davies/b638329883751f68452bf5dcc177b4d46bae7734

Boehm, B. W. (1989). *Software engineering economics*. Prentice-Hall.

Boehm, B. W., & Abts, C. (2000). Software risk management: Principles and practices. *IEEE Software*, *17*(4), 38–44.

Broder, M., & Charlton, J. (2025). Design to cost methodology saves estimated $1.2 billion on AIM-9X missile program.

COCOMO II model – Software Engineering Institute. (n.d.). https://resources.sei.cmu.edu/library/asset-view.cfm?assetid=50804

Cook, R. (2000). 8.6.4 Denver International Airport: How could system engineering principles have prevented disaster? *INCOSE International Symposium*, *10*(1), 849–854. DOI: 10.1002/j.2334-5837.2000.tb00464.x

Cundiff, J., McCallum, T., Rich, A., Truax, M., Ward, T., & Havelka, D. (2018). Healthcare.gov: Opportunity out of disaster. *The Journal of Information and Systems in Education*. https://www.semanticscholar.org/paper/Healthcare.gov%3A-Opportunity-out-of-Disaster-Cundiff-McCallum/479e5ca280497d9150839631f5785b4c46067737

Finkelstein, A. (1993). *Report of the inquiry into the London Ambulance Service*. https://www.semanticscholar.org/paper/Report-of-the-Inquiry-into-the-London-Ambulance-Finkelstein/5c22db59e0e008589750c1470ffdf628ea6747f5

Fountain, J. (2025). The difficulties of Healthcare.gov need to be seen in the context of an acrimonious political climate and the poor record of large and complex IT projects. https://www.semanticscholar.org/paper/The-difficulties-of-Healthcare.gov-need-to-be-seen-Fountain/21574e69475d44398e9e1a81cba7355436408178

Hijazi, H., (2012). A review of risk management in different software development methodologies. *International Journal of Computer Applications*, *45*(7), 975–8887.

Hoch, D. J., Kunz, D., & Kauffman, S. (2000). *The evolution of software project management and software engineering economics*. Springer.

Hougham, M. (1996). London Ambulance Service computer-aided despatch system. *International Journal of Project Management*, *14*(2), 103–110. DOI: 10.1016/0263-7863(95)00067-4

Jones, C. (2007). *Estimating software costs: Bringing realism to estimating* (2nd ed.). McGraw-Hill.

Kendall, K. E., & Kendall, J. E. (2009). *Systems analysis and design* (8th ed.). Pearson Education.

Kloppenborg, T. J., & Anantatmula, V. (2013). *Project management: A system approach to planning, scheduling, and controlling* (10th ed.). Pearson Prentice Hall.

Landry, J. R. (2009). Analyzing the London Ambulance Service's computer-aided despatch (LASCAD) failure as a case of administrative evil. *Proceedings of the Special Interest Group on Management Information System's 47th Annual Conference on Computer Personnel Research – SIGMIS-CPR '09*. DOI: 10.1145/1542130.1542163

Leveson, N. G., & Turner, C. S. (1993). An investigation of the Therac-25 accidents. *Computer*, *26*(7), 18–41. DOI: 10.1109/MC.1993.274940

Lim, F. J., & Sian, T. B. (2025). Overview of software re-engineering concepts, models and approaches. *JOIV: International Journal on Informatics Visualization*, *9*(1), 46–56. DOI: 10.62527/joiv.9.1.3034

Liu, Y., & Wang, Y. (2015). A study on software development month effort. *Journal of Software*, 798–804. DOI: 10.17706/jsw.10.7.798-804

McGrath, K. (2024). The Golden Circle: A case study of organizational change at the London Ambulance Service. *AIS Electronic Library (AISeL)*. https://aisel.aisnet.org/ecis2001/52/

Mohapatra, H., & Mishra, S. R. (2024). Analysis of sector-specific responses of AI generative. In Generative, A. I. (Ed.), *Current Trends and Applications* (pp. 167–184). Springer Nature Singapore. DOI: 10.1007/978-981-97-8460-8_9

Mohapatra, H., & Mishra, S. R. (2024). Unlocking insights: Exploring data analytics and AI tool performance across industries. In *Data analytics and machine learning: Navigating the big data landscape* (pp. 265–288). Springer Nature Singapore. DOI: 10.1007/978-981-97-0448-4_13

Montealegre, R., & Keil, M. (2000). Deescalating information technology projects: Lessons from the Denver International Airport. *Management Information Systems Quarterly*, *24*(3), 417–447. DOI: 10.2307/3250968

Moradbeiky, A., (2020). *Open hybrid model: A new ensemble model for software development cost estimation.* Computing and Informatics., DOI: 10.31577/cai_2020_6_1148

Murthi, S. (2002, September). Preventive risk management software for software projects. *IT Professional*, *4*(5), 9–15. DOI: 10.1109/MITP.2002.1041172

Nega, A. T. (2019). The trend of software cost estimation in Ethiopia case study: Addis Ababa. *International Journal of Engineering and Computer Science*. DOI: 10.18535/ijecs/v8i12.4413

Nurdiani, I., (2011, August). Risk identification and risk mitigation instruments for global software development: Systematic review and survey results. *2011 IEEE Sixth International Conference on Global Software Engineering Workshop*, 36–41. DOI: 10.1109/ICGSE-W.2011.16

Olszewski, L., & Wingreen, S. C. (2011). The FBI Sentinel Project. *Journal of Cases on Information Technology*, *13*(3), 84–102. DOI: 10.4018/jcit.2011070105

Parkinson, C. N. (1957). *Parkinson's law: The pursuit of progress*. John Murray.

Shah, P. (2015, March 23). The pains of government technology: An investigation into the rollout of Healthcare.gov. *Duke.edu*. https://dukespace.lib.duke.edu/items/891d4d18-55cd-44a8-83a0-18bf2b79e108

Shekhar, S., & Kumar, U. (2016, May 17). Review of various software cost estimation techniques. *International Journal of Computer Applications*, *141*(11), 31–34. DOI: 10.5120/ijca2016909867

Silvis-Cividjian, N. (2024). Therac-25 accidents: We keep on learning from them. *Computer*, *57*(12), 69–78. DOI: 10.1109/MC.2024.3450197

Sommerville, I. (2011). *Software engineering* (9th ed.). Addison-Wesley.

Swartz, A. J. (1996). Airport 95. *Software Engineering Notes*, *21*(2), 79–83. DOI: 10.1145/227531.227544

Wang, A. Z., Scherr, K. A., Wong, C. A., & Ubel, P. A. (2017). Poor consumer comprehension and plan selection inconsistencies under the 2016 HealthCare.gov choice architecture. *MDM Policy & Practice*, *2*(1), 238146831771644. DOI: 10.1177/2381468317716441 PMID: 29892710

Zakaria, N. A., et al. (2021). Optimized COCOMO parameters using hybrid particle swarm optimization. *International Journal of Advances in Intelligent Informatics*. DOI: 10.26555/ijain.v7i2.583

Zardari, S. (2009). Software risk management. *2009 International Conference on Information Management and Engineering*, 375–379. DOI: 10.1109/ICIME.2009.138

Chapter 5
Genetic Algorithm–Based Load Balancing in Cloud Computing for Optimized Resource Utilization

Abhipsha Das
https://orcid.org/0009-0004-4800-7671
School of Computer Engineering, Kalinga Institute of Industrial Technology (KIIT) Bhubaneswar, India

Swayam Yadav
https://orcid.org/0009-0004-4339-6209
School of Computer Engineering, Kalinga Institute of Industrial Technology (KIIT) Bhubaneswar, India

Neetu Dey
https://orcid.org/0009-0009-5806-0886
School of Computer Engineering, Kalinga Institute of Industrial Technology (KIIT) Bhubaneswar, India

Aayushma Gautam
https://orcid.org/0009-0000-1576-0860
School of Computer Engineering, Kalinga Institute of Industrial Technology (KIIT) Bhubaneswar, India

Hitesh Mohapatra
https://orcid.org/0000-0001-8100-4860
School of Computer Engineering, Kalinga Institute of Industrial Technology (KIIT) Bhubaneswar, India

DOI: 10.4018/979-8-3373-2352-7.ch005

ABSTRACT

Load balancing is essential in cloud computing to distribute workloads efficiently, prevent resource bottlenecks, and optimize utilization. This review explores a novel approach using Genetic Algorithms (GAs), which leverage natural evolution principles to enhance task scheduling and minimize execution makespan. The GA-based strategy adapts dynamically to environmental changes, continuously refining solutions for improved performance and scalability. By examining its fundamental principles and real-world applications, this review highlights the potential of GA-driven load balancing to transform traditional cloud computing paradigms.

1. INTRODUCTION

Cloud computing is a new paradigm for large-scale distributed computing. The concept of cloud computing involves utilizing on-demand services from cloud providers to deliver IT resources and capabilities like storage, applications, infrastructure, communication, and teamwork. Cloud management plays a crucial part in accomplishing this goal by offering safe data backup that is available instantly around the clock, load balancing, and dynamic resource scheduling. Cloud computing service providers must handle enormous requests as the cloud's capacity grows. Cloud computing has the advantage of delivering a flexible, high-performance, pay-as-you-go, on-demand service When one of these outbursts occurs, the main task is to maintain the same level of performance or perhaps improve upon it. The process of distributing workloads across computing resources in a cloud computing environment and carefully balancing the network traffic accessing those resources is known as Cloud load balancing. Multiple interconnected nodes collaborate to perform tasks in distributed computing environments such as cloud computing and grid computing. Load balancing is essential in such environments to distribute the dynamic local workload evenly across all the nodes in the whole cloud to avoid a situation where some nodes are heavily loaded while others are idle or doing little work (Bahi et al., 2005). Solutions to find an optimal or near-optimal configuration are iteratively evolved by representing potential load-balancing as individuals in a population.

1.1 Load Balancing

Load balancing, a critical component in distributed computing environments, encompasses various methods tailored to efficiently distribute incoming traffic across multiple server instances. These methods can be broadly categorized into static and dynamic approaches, each offering distinct strategies to manage the allocation of workload among servers. In static load balancing, predefined rules govern the distribution of traffic, irrespective of the current state of server instances. One such method is the Weighted Round Robin Method, where servers are assigned, weights based on their capacity or performance. Incoming requests are then allocated to servers in a cyclic manner, with higher-weighted servers handling a larger proportion of the load. Similarly, the IP Hash Method employs hash functions to consistently map client IP addresses to specific servers. This ensures session persistence and client-server affinity, making it suitable for applications requiring stateful connections. Conversely, dynamic load balancing methods analyze the real-time state of server instances to make traffic distribution decisions (Dam et al., 2021).

The Least Connection Method dynamically directs incoming requests to servers with the fewest active connections, effectively balancing the load across available servers. The Resource-based Method considers server resource utilization metrics such as CPU and memory usage before allocating traffic, prioritizing servers with lower resource utilization to handle new requests (Jolin et al., 2024). Additionally, the Least Response Time Method routes requests to servers with the shortest historical or real-time response times, minimizing latency and enhancing overall application performance. These dynamic methods continuously monitor server states and adjust traffic distribution to optimize resource utilization and ensure an optimal user experience. Load balancing methods play a crucial role in efficiently managing the distribution of workload across server instances. While static approaches offer simplicity and predictability, dynamic methods provide adaptability and responsiveness to real-time changes in server states, ultimately contributing to improved performance and reliability in distributed computing environments (Dasgupta et al., 2013).

1.2 Genetic Algorithm

One of the most popular artificial intelligence methods, Genetic Algorithms are mostly utilized for efficient search and optimization. Charles Darwin stated the theory of natural evolution in the origin of species. Over several generations, biological organisms evolve based on the principle of natural selection "survival of the fittest" to reach certain remarkable tasks. GAs are robust search and optimization techniques in a number of practical problems, due to its capacity to locate the global optimum in a multimodal landscape (Dasgupta et al., 2013). In the context of cloud computing, genetic algorithms can be deployed for various purposes, such as task scheduling, optimal resource allocation, and improving efficiency and system performance. Since task scheduling in the cloud is an NP-complete problem, due to the proficiency of genetic algorithms to work with NP-complete problems, it is a popular choice. Some key terms used in genetic algorithms. The workflow (Ref: Fig.1) depicted, how users interact with the cloud storage system through resource requests. These requests are managed and optimized by the cloud resource manager and the virtualized load balancer, which leverages the multi-objective genetic algorithm to dynamically allocate VMs to efficiently handle the workload. This architecture enables the cloud storage service to provide high-performance, scalable, and cost-effective storage solutions to users while optimizing resource utilization and minimizing operational costs.

Figure 1. Cloud storage level service offering in virtualized load balancer using GA

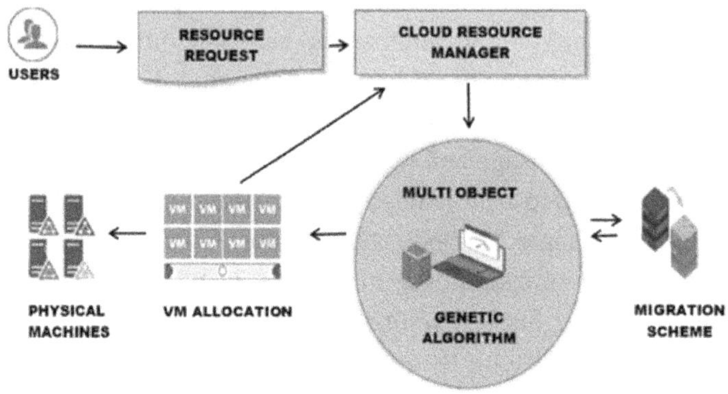

Fig.1 illustrates the architecture and workflow of a cloud storage-level service offering implemented within a virtualized load balancer framework using a genetic algorithm (GA). User represents the entity or entities accessing the cloud storage service. Users initiate resource requests to store or retrieve data from the cloud storage system. Resource Request these are requests made by users to access cloud storage resources. These requests can include uploading data to the cloud, retrieving stored data, or performing other operations related to cloud storage services. Cloud Resource Manager component manages the allocation and utilization of resources within the cloud infrastructure (Dey et al., 2024). It receives resource requests from users and orchestrates the allocation of virtual machines (VMs) and physical machines (PMs) to handle these requests efficiently. Multi-Objective Genetic Algorithm (GA) as the optimization engine for the load balancer. It employs genetic algorithms to dynamically allocate VMs to handle incoming resource requests while optimizing multiple objectives simultaneously. These objectives may include minimizing response time, maximizing resource utilization, and minimizing energy consumption. VM Allocation involves the allocation of virtual machines (VMs) to handle incoming resource requests. The GA evaluates various allocation strategies based on the specified objectives and selects the most suitable VM allocation scheme.

Physical Machines (PMs): These are the underlying physical servers or nodes within the cloud infrastructure. PMs host multiple VMs and provide the computational and storage resources required to fulfill user requests. Furthermore, ongoing research endeavors aim to explore hybrid optimization techniques that integrate genetic algorithms with complementary methods or machine learning approaches. By combining the strengths of GAs with other optimization strategies, such as swarm intelligence or neural networks, researchers seek to unlock new avenues for improving cloud load distribution efficiency and adaptability (Kathirvel et al., 2025). Additionally, the integration of real-time monitoring and predictive analytics holds promise for enhancing the adaptive capabilities of genetic algorithms in cloud environments (Gulbaz et al., 2021). By leveraging advanced analytics and predictive modeling, GAs can anticipate workload fluctuations, proactively adjust distribution strategies, and preemptively mitigate potential performance bottlenecks. As such, the future evolution of genetic algorithms in cloud load distribution technology is poised to usher in a new era of intelligent and responsive cloud computing systems. Through continuous innovation and interdisciplinary collaboration, genetic algorithms will continue to play a pivotal role in optimizing cloud infrastructure, maximizing resource utilization, and delivering unparalleled performance and reliability to users worldwide.

The efficient distribution of workloads in cloud computing systems is paramount for optimizing resource utilization, enhancing performance, and ensuring a seamless user experience. Traditional load distribution methods, often static in nature, struggle to adapt to the dynamic and complex nature of cloud workloads, leading to inefficiencies during peak demand periods or resource contention scenarios. However, the emergence of genetic algorithms (GAs) presents a promising avenue for addressing these challenges. Inspired by principles of natural evolution, GAs offer robust search and optimization capabilities, making them well-suited for the intricacies of cloud load distribution. By iteratively evolving optimal or near-optimal load distribution configurations over successive generations, GAs can dynamically adjust to changing workload dynamics and system conditions, thereby improving overall efficiency and performance. Challenges such as load spikes, resource contention, and fluctuating workloads are effectively tackled by GAs through their adaptive and self-learning nature (Kukreja et al., 2018). Fig.2 illustrates the role of GA in cloud environment.

Figure 2. Genetic algorithms in cloud load distribution

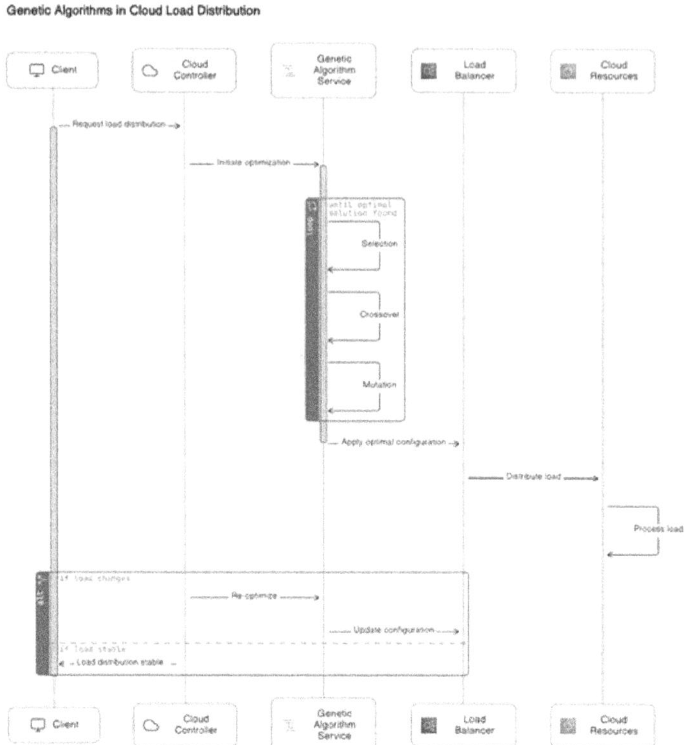

Concrete application scenarios demonstrate the effectiveness of GAs in tasks such as workload scheduling, resource allocation, and dynamic load balancing within cloud environments. These applications highlight the ability of GAs to reduce response times, enhance scalability, and improve system reliability. Looking ahead, future research opportunities lie in exploring hybrid optimization techniques that integrate GAs with other methods or machine learning approaches, as well as leveraging real-time monitoring and predictive analytics to further enhance the adaptive capabilities of GAs in cloud load distribution (Kumar Singh Sandeep, 2014). Through these advancements, genetic algorithms are poised to play a central role in shaping the future of cloud computing by enabling efficient and dynamic workload management. Within the domain of cloud computing, the optimization of load distribution stands as a critical endeavor to ensure the efficient utilization of resources and the delivery of seamless services to users. In this context, genetic algorithms have emerged as powerful tools for dynamically adapting load distribution strategies to meet the evolving demands of cloud environments. The following diagram illustrates the iterative process by which genetic algorithms optimize load distribution configurations, addressing challenges such as load spikes, resource contention, and fluctuating workloads. As demonstrated in the diagram, genetic algorithms play a pivotal role in optimizing cloud load distribution, offering benefits such as enhanced resource utilization, minimized response times, and improved overall system performance. By dynamically adapting to changing workload dynamics and system conditions, genetic algorithms prove their effectiveness in addressing the complexities of cloud environments. Moving forward, further research and development in this area promise to unlock even greater efficiencies and advancements in cloud load distribution technology (Kumar et al., 2024).

Genetic Algorithms (GAs) have emerged as a powerful optimization technique for load balancing in cloud computing, offering dynamic and intelligent task distribution across virtual machines. By mimicking natural selection and evolution, GAs iteratively refines task allocation strategies, ensuring optimal resource utilization while minimizing execution time and energy consumption. This approach is particularly beneficial in large-scale cloud environments where workloads are highly dynamic and unpredictable. Real-time applications such as e-commerce platforms, video streaming services, and cloud-based SaaS solutions greatly benefit from GA-based load balancing. For instance, in an e-commerce environment, where traffic surges during flash sales, a GA can efficiently allocate computing resources to handle peak loads while avoiding overloading specific servers. Similarly, in video streaming services like Netflix or YouTube, GA helps in balancing the processing of video encoding and content delivery across multiple cloud servers, reducing buffering time and improving user experience. Cloud service providers such as AWS, Google Cloud, and Microsoft Azure can integrate GA-based load balancing to optimize virtual machine allocation in data centers, reducing power consumption and operational costs while ensuring high availability and seamless performance for users.

2. LITERATURE REVIEW

Genetic algorithms (GAs) have emerged as a powerful approach for solving optimization problems in cloud computing, particularly in load balancing. The cloud environment is characterized by its dynamic nature, where resources are allocated on-demand to meet varying workloads. Efficient resource utilization is crucial to maintain performance, minimize costs, and prevent server overload. Traditional load-balancing techniques such as round-robin, least connections, and threshold-based approaches often fail to adapt to unpredictable workload fluctuations. Genetic algorithms, inspired by natural selection and evolutionary principles, offer an adaptive solution that continuously refines the load distribution process for optimized resource utilization. A genetic algorithm operates by initializing a population of potential load-balancing solutions, which are then evaluated based on a fitness function that considers factors like response time, resource utilization, and system throughput. Through iterative selection, crossover, and mutation operations, the algorithm evolves toward an optimal load distribution. This evolutionary process allows GAs to explore a vast solution space efficiently, identifying better load-balancing strategies than traditional heuristics. The adaptability of genetic algorithms ensures that cloud resources are dynamically allocated based on real-time demand, reducing bottlenecks and improving overall system efficiency.

One of the key advantages of using genetic algorithms for load balancing is their ability to handle large-scale, heterogeneous cloud environments. Cloud computing infrastructures often consist of diverse resources with varying computational capacities, storage capabilities, and network bandwidth. Conventional load-balancing techniques struggle to account for this heterogeneity, leading to inefficient resource allocation. Genetic algorithms, however, incorporate multiple parameters into their fitness function, enabling a holistic approach to load balancing that considers the characteristics of both virtual machines and physical servers. This results in an intelligent distribution of workloads, ensuring that no single resource is overburdened while others remain underutilized. Scalability is another major benefit of genetic algorithm-based load balancing. As cloud environments grow, the complexity of workload distribution increases exponentially. Traditional static and rule-based methods require frequent manual adjustments to accommodate new workloads and infrastructure changes. Genetic algorithms, on the other hand, autonomously adapt to these changes by continuously evolving and optimizing their solutions. This self-adaptive nature makes GAs particularly suited for large-scale cloud platforms that experience frequent fluctuations in demand.

Energy efficiency is an essential consideration in cloud computing, as data centers consume vast amounts of power. Genetic algorithms contribute to energy-efficient load balancing by optimizing the allocation of virtual machines across physical servers. By distributing workloads in a manner that maximizes resource utilization while minimizing energy consumption, GAs help reduce the number of active servers, leading to lower operational costs and a reduced carbon footprint. Additionally, by preventing resource over-provisioning and unnecessary workload migrations, genetic algorithms further enhance the sustainability of cloud computing environments. Fault tolerance and reliability are critical aspects of cloud computing, as system failures and server downtimes can lead to significant service disruptions. Genetic algorithms improve fault tolerance by distributing workloads in a way that minimizes the impact of individual resource failures. By dynamically reallocating tasks to available resources, GAs ensure that cloud services remain operational even in the event of hardware or network failures. Moreover, the evolutionary nature of GAs enables them to continuously learn from previous failures, refining their strategies to enhance system resilience over time.

One of the challenges in implementing genetic algorithm-based load balancing is the computational overhead associated with the evolutionary process. The iterative nature of genetic algorithms, involving multiple generations of solution evaluation and optimization, can introduce latency in decision-making. However, recent advancements in parallel computing and distributed processing have mitigated this issue by enabling faster execution of GA operations. Techniques such as parallel genetic algorithms leverage multiple processors or distributed computing frameworks to accelerate the optimization process, making GAs more practical for real-time load balancing in cloud environments. Hybrid approaches that combine genetic algorithms with other optimization techniques have also gained traction in cloud computing. For instance, integrating GAs with machine learning models allows for predictive load balancing, where historical workload patterns are analyzed to anticipate future resource demands. Similarly, hybrid methods that incorporate heuristic algorithms such as particle swarm optimization or ant colony optimization enhance the efficiency of genetic algorithms by improving convergence speed and solution quality. These hybrid techniques offer a promising avenue for achieving even more optimized resource utilization in cloud environments.

Security is another important factor in cloud computing, and genetic algorithms play a role in enhancing security-aware load balancing. Cloud environments are susceptible to cyber threats such as Distributed Denial-of-Service (DDoS) attacks, where malicious traffic overwhelms servers, leading to service disruptions. Genetic algorithms can be adapted to detect and mitigate such threats by dynamically redistributing workloads to unaffected resources, ensuring uninterrupted service availability. Additionally, by considering security constraints in their fitness function, GAs can help enforce load-balancing policies that prioritize secure resource allocation. The application of genetic algorithms in cloud computing extends beyond traditional data centers to modern cloud paradigms such as edge computing and fog computing. These decentralized architectures require efficient load-balancing mechanisms to distribute workloads across geographically dispersed nodes. Genetic algorithms offer a viable solution for optimizing resource allocation in such environments by considering factors such as network latency, energy consumption, and computational capabilities of edge devices. By ensuring optimal workload distribution in edge and fog computing scenarios, GAs contribute to reduced latency and enhanced Quality of Service (QoS) for end-users.

The effectiveness of genetic algorithms in cloud load balancing is heavily dependent on the design of the fitness function. A well-defined fitness function should consider multiple performance metrics, including response time, throughput, energy efficiency, and fault tolerance. Additionally, the selection of appropriate genetic operators, such as crossover and mutation strategies, plays a crucial role in achieving optimal load-balancing outcomes. Fine-tuning these parameters requires extensive experimentation and domain expertise to strike a balance between exploration and exploitation in the solution space. Future research directions in genetic algorithm-based load balancing focus on improving convergence speed, reducing computational complexity, and enhancing adaptability to dynamic workloads. The integration of artificial intelligence techniques, such as deep learning and reinforcement learning, holds significant potential for further optimizing GA-based load-balancing strategies. Moreover, advancements in cloud orchestration tools and containerization technologies provide new opportunities for deploying genetic algorithms in real-world cloud infrastructures, enabling more efficient and intelligent workload management.

The study explored the small size of ants and their remarkable ability to find food even when facing external obstacles. Ants reside in nests, primarily focusing on seeking support when hungry. The research is less concerned with their lifestyle aspects such as living conditions or resting habits, but rather intrigued by their efficient foraging and the application of this approach in distributed computing. The utilization of the Ant Colony method in Cloud Computing is noted for delivering enhanced performance. The paper discussed that the fitness of a population in an evolutionary algorithm increases by a biased selection of more fit individuals with time by recombining and mutating individuals. Selecting the appropriate pressure is crucial for optimizing progress and maintaining genetic diversity. Their proposed uniform fitness-based selection scheme prioritizes sparsely populated fitness regions, deviating from conventional methods focused solely on higher fitness, demonstrating its potential effectiveness over standard schemes (Lin et al., 2012). Three crossover operators are compared in this paper: one-point, two-point, and uniform crossover. The presented empirical results were obtained using a variant of genetic algorithms referred to as steady-state genetic algorithms at BBN. This algorithm is considered more effective than the commonly used standard generational replacement approach.

This paper introduces the fusion of art and science in genetic algorithms, providing an overview of current issues in both theory and practice. Rather than a comprehensive study, it serves as a concise guide through the intricate realm of genetic algorithm research. Beginning with an analogy between genetic algorithms and natural search processes, it outlines Holland's 1975 introduction of GAs and their mechanisms. The paper then explores various techniques proposed as enhancements to Holland's GA, along with divergent approaches. Finally, it surveys advancements in GA theory, focusing on modeling, dynamics, and deception (Makasarwala & Hazari, 2016). This study presents the development of a genetic algorithm-based load-balancing technique for cloud computing, aimed at optimizing resource consumption in cloud environments. The analysis findings show that the suggested load balancing strategy works better than a few of the current methods and ensures that the customer job's quality of service requirements is met. Even though not all jobs may have the same priority, as has been assumed this can be handled in the JUV and then addressed in the fitness function. Additionally, a very basic GA approach has been used; however, in future studies, variations on the crossover and selection strategies may be applied to provide more precise and effective outcomes (Makasarwala & Hazari, 2016). Particularly when dealing with many activities, the suggested dynamic load-balancing method created utilizing genetic algorithms has proven to be quite successful. In actuality, a GA-based scheme performs better when there are a lot of jobs and consistent performance is observed in contrast to other heuristics. Since a central scheduler can manage all load-balancing decisions with little to no inter-processor communication, using one was also effective. Additionally, the threshold policy that was employed performed better than the initial fit method, which is devoid of this kind of mechanism. Thus, in terms of reaching the objectives of minimizing overall completion time and maximizing processor utilization, the GA-based method performed fairly well (Mao & Feng, 2018).

It has suggested a technique wherein the jobs are broken down into smaller assignments. The division is due to the concurrent execution of tasks on several apparatus. The GA distributes smaller jobs among several processors so that a single task can be completed more quickly than if it were completed on a single device. The first two arrays in the population are made up of virtual machines and requests, respectively. The author provided no information regarding the use of Crossover. Using mutation, the fittest chromosome is determined to be the most suitable virtual machine. The suggested system is stimulated using CloudSim 2.0 (Mohapatra, 2025). In this research, we propose the JLGA algorithm to accomplish load balancing and the least makespan task scheduling. Additionally, we utilize a greedy technique to initialize the population, weigh the multi-fitness function, and introduce variation to characterize the load-intensive among nodes. Next, we used 30 jobs to experimentally assess the JLGA algorithm's and the DGA's performance. The experimental findings demonstrate that the JLGA efficiently balances the overall system load while using little in terms of both total and average work consumption.

In this paper, through the production of the shortest execution time during the algorithm's initial phase, the suggested algorithm can improve work scheduling. The genetic algorithm will use a fitness function to balance the loads when the result is sent in. Given the importance of appropriate resource management in the cloud computing context, where this study has prioritized itself, the value of this approach cannot be overstated. The suggested approach uses a fitness function to improve load balancing among virtual machines. This paper discusses that evolutionary computation is experiencing significant growth, driven by substantial investments highlighting the practicality of its techniques. Extracted from the Handbook of Evolutionary Computation, Evolutionary Computation 1: Basic Algorithms and

Operators offers current insights into the algorithms and operators employed in this field. The book explores fundamental concepts underlying key evolutionary algorithms, including evolution strategies, evolutionary programming, and genetic programming. Designed for researchers, educators, and students involved in this expanding domain, the volume serves as a valuable resource for those studying and working in evolutionary computation (Raj et al., 2025). This research presents a solution to the load balancing issue in cloud computing using a genetic based approach. By combining the load % and the cost value, the suggested method was able to effectively balance and guide the user request. The technique was able to lower the overall reaction time and cost value, according to the simulation results. The two parameters were reduced as a result of the efficient and effective balancing of the workload (Rajput & Kushwah, 2016). In this, a GA-based load balancing technique in a cloud context was covered. In this case, requests are prioritized according to their time to improve population initialization. It has been demonstrated that longer tasks require more time to complete. The jobs that require the least amount of time get priority. The Cloud Analyst simulation has been utilized for performance analysis and comparison with other fundamental cloud load balancing algorithms. Fig.3 presents the connected papers from 2023 to 2024.

Figure 3. Connected papers from 2013 to 2024

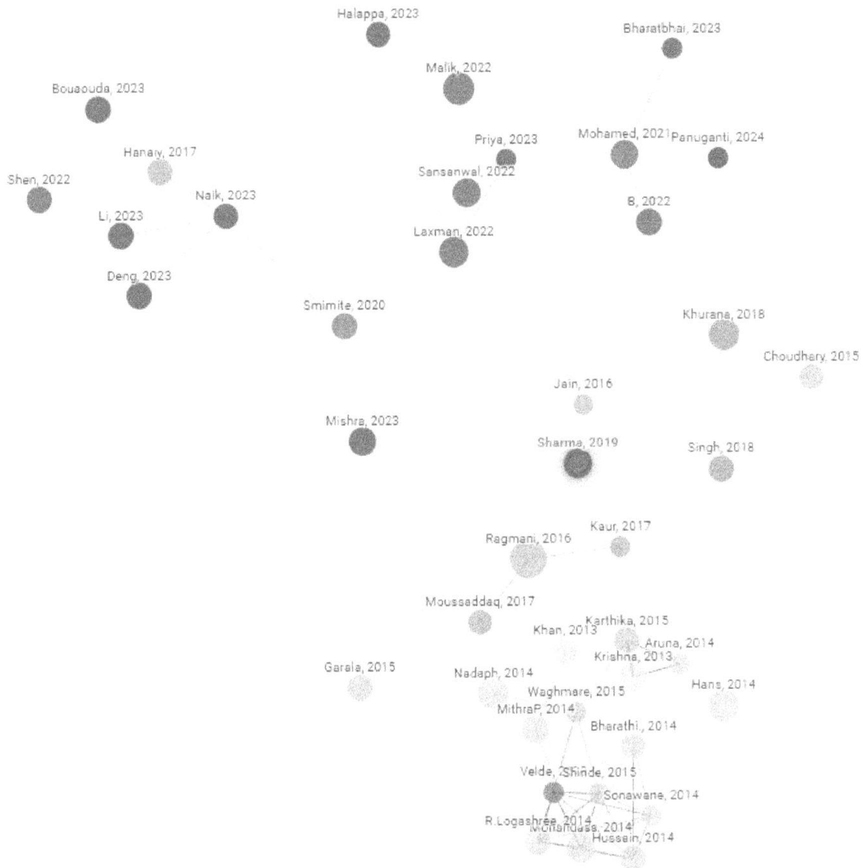

In this article, network traffic was not taken into account while choosing the most suitable virtual machine, nor were average makespan times computed for various cloudlets (Rimal et al., 2009). This study examines modern heuristic and meta-heuristic task schedulers in detail and finds that scheduling leads to ineffective cloud resource load balancing. In order to schedule tasks efficiently, load balancing is a crucial metric that runs parallel to makespan, indicating the requirement for multi-objective optimization. Meta-heuristics are used to explore a wide search space of potential solutions, and heuristic merging adds another capacity to explore even more optimal solutions (S, & Cauvery, 2019). The work puts GA into practice for distributed systems load balancing. The above-described algorithms, settings, and outcomes were used. The suggested updated fitness function for the GA model is found to reduce the cost to a greater extent based on state-of-the-art analysis, as the fitter strings comprise the most appropriate nodes for load offloading. The load variation from the mean load and the communication cost of exchanging messages are taken into account by the suggested approach as parameters for the fitness function. Better response times, maximum performance, and a reduction in overheads are all provided by the suggested fitness function (Saadat & Masehian, 2019).

3. PROPOSED STUDY

3.1 Research Gap

While significant progress has been made in various aspects of cloud computing, such as scheduling, resource provisioning, and energy management, load balancing remains a critical concern due to its fundamental importance in optimizing resource utilization and meeting the needs of both Cloud Service Providers and Cloud Service Consumers. Despite the extensive research in this domain, there exists a notable research gap, particularly concerning the utilization of genetic algorithms for load balancing in cloud environments (Sah et al., 2024). One prominent reason contributing to this gap is the absence of proper classification among different approaches. Existing literature reviews indicate a lack of comprehensive categorization and analysis of genetic algorithm-based solutions tailored specifically for load balancing in dynamic and heterogeneous cloud environments. While genetic algorithms offer promising capabilities for optimization and adaptation, their effective integration into real-world cloud scenarios presents several challenges. In addition to the classification issue, several other areas remain underexplored within the role of genetic algorithms in load balancing in cloud computing:

- Performance Evaluation: There is a scarcity of comprehensive performance evaluation methodologies specifically designed to assess the effectiveness and efficiency of genetic algorithm-based load balancing techniques in diverse cloud environments (Sidana et al., 2016).
- Hybrid Approaches: Exploration of hybrid approaches integrating genetic algorithms with other optimization techniques, such as machine learning algorithms or mathematical models, to enhance load balancing efficacy remains limited.
- Fault Tolerance and Resilience: Research on genetic algorithm-based load balancing mechanisms that exhibit robust fault tolerance and resilience to mitigate the impact of failures or disruptions in cloud infrastructures is lacking.

- Cost-Effectiveness Analysis: Limited studies delve into the cost-effectiveness analysis of genetic algorithm-based load balancing strategies concerning factors such as resource utilization, energy consumption, and operational expenses.

The sensitivity to initialization in GAs highlights the need for more sophisticated techniques tailored to different problem spaces. Current approaches often fall short in effectively exploring the problem space, leading to suboptimal outcomes. Developing more adaptive initialization strategies could significantly enhance GA performance. Additionally, existing load-balancing operations lack dynamic strategies that adapt to changing workload characteristics and system dynamics. Furthermore, there's a need for research into hybrid approaches that combine global and local balancing mechanisms for more efficient resource allocation. Optimal strategies for gathering and managing workload information are still elusive. Current methods exhibit trade-offs between communication overhead and accuracy, with no clear consensus on the most effective approach. The initiation rule determines when load-balancing operations commence, balancing the overhead cost against expected performance benefits, with various policies guiding the initiation process (Srinivas & Patnaik, 1994). Research should focus on minimizing communication overhead while maintaining accurate system states, possibly through centralized information management. Addressing these research gaps and exploring uncharted territories within the role of genetic algorithms in load balancing in cloud computing can significantly advance the field. Future studies should focus on devising innovative approaches, developing robust evaluation methodologies, and exploring hybrid solutions to enhance the efficiency and effectiveness of load balancing mechanisms in cloud environments. By bridging these research gaps, researchers can contribute to optimizing resource allocation, improving system performance, and enhancing user satisfaction in cloud computing ecosystems.

3.2 Proposed Comparative Analysis of Existing Models

Paper (Wang et al., 2014) proposes an optimization strategy for work scheduling in cloud computing, utilizing a genetic algorithm and a fitness function. The focus is on load balancing and minimizing execution time in the initial phase of the algorithm, highlighting the importance of efficient resource management in the context of cloud computing. In contrast, the paper (Wided et al., 2023) takes a broader view of the evolutionary computation field. Extracted from the Handbook of Evolutionary Computation, this paper underscores the substantial growth and practical applications of evolutionary computation driven by investments. Providing current insights into fundamental algorithms and operators, it serves as a valuable resource for researchers, educators, and students in the evolving domain of evolutionary computation. These prior works, contribute to a more comprehensive understanding of the overarching trends and principles in evolutionary computation.

(Zheng et al., 2013) explore the integration of art and science in genetic algorithms, offering an overview of current issues in both theory and practice. It takes a concise and guiding approach through the intricate realm of genetic algorithm research, starting with an analogy between genetic algorithms and natural search processes. The paper outlines the introduction of genetic algorithms and their mechanisms by Holland in 1975, delving into various proposed techniques and divergent approaches. The survey of advancements in genetic algorithm theory encompasses modeling, dynamics, and deception. On the other hand (Zhu, 2023), focuses on the development of a genetic algorithm-based load-balancing technique for cloud computing. The primary objective is to optimize resource consumption in cloud environments. The findings of the analysis indicate that the proposed load-balancing strategy outperforms several current methods and ensures the fulfillment of customer job quality of service requirements. The study acknowledges the varying priorities of jobs, addressing them in the Job Utility Value (JUV) and incorporating them into the fitness function. Although a basic genetic algorithm approach is employed, the paper suggests potential improvements through variations in crossover and selection strategies for more precise and effective outcomes in future studies.

Table 1. Literature analysis

References	Main Focus	Key Contributions
(Wang et al., 2014)	Work scheduling optimization utilizing genetic algorithm and fitness function	- Load balancing and minimizing execution time in cloud computing - Emphasis on efficient resource management
(Wided et al., 2023)	Broad overview of the evolutionary computation field	- Comprehensive insights into fundamental algorithms and operators - Highlights growth and practical applications
(Gulbaz et al., 2021)	Overview of genetic algorithm theory and practice	- Analogy between genetic algorithms and natural search processes - Survey of advancements in genetic algorithm theory
(Lin et al., 2012)	Optimization of resource consumption in cloud environments	- Outperforms current methods in load balancing - Incorporates Job Utility Value (JUV) into the fitness function

continued on following page

Table 1. Continued

References	Main Focus	Key Contributions
(Sivasankari & Aneetha, 2024)	Application of Ant Colony Optimization in Cloud Computing	- Utilizes ants' foraging abilities for enhanced performance - Emphasis on efficient foraging in cloud environments
(Zheng et al., 2013)	Dynamic load balancing using genetic algorithms	- Success in scenarios with numerous tasks - Centralized load-balancing decisions with minimal communication

(Sivasankari & Aneetha, 2024) delves into the application of Ant Colony Optimization in Cloud Computing, leveraging the remarkable foraging abilities of ants. This study emphasizes the efficiency of ants in finding food despite external obstacles and translates this natural behavior into an optimization approach for enhanced performance in distributed computing, particularly in the context of Cloud Computing. The primary focus is on the utilization of the Ant Colony method to achieve improved results in a cloud environment, with an emphasis on efficient foraging. While the paper does not explore into lifestyle aspects of ants, such as living conditions or resting habits, it highlights the success of this nature-inspired method in optimizing overall system performance. On the other hand, the paper (Rupprecht et al., 2012) addresses the challenge of dynamic load balancing in distributed computing, especially when faced with a large number of activities. The proposed dynamic load-balancing method, utilizing genetic algorithms, demonstrates success in scenarios with numerous tasks. The study emphasizes the effectiveness of the genetic algorithm-based scheme, which outperforms other heuristics, and particularly excels when consistent performance is essential. The centralization of load-balancing decisions, managed by a central scheduler with minimal inter-processor communication, proves to be an effective strategy. Additionally, the incorporation of a threshold policy within the genetic algorithm-based approach outperforms an initial fit method, contributing to the objectives of minimizing overall completion time and maximizing processor utilization. In essence, this study underscores the success of a genetic algorithm-based dynamic load-balancing method in optimizing performance metrics in distributed computing environments.

3.3 Findings from the Comparative Analysis

Current surveys on metaheuristic load balancing reveal several limitations, including a lack of detailed taxonomy, comparisons with state-of-the-art techniques, and coverage of key features, challenges, and architectures. Load balancing methods vary depending on the dependency between activities, which are categorized as dependent and independent workflow scheduling methods. This work aims to bridge these gaps by offering a comprehensive survey of recent metaheuristic load balancing algorithms, providing operational insights into these methodologies. In the existing Genetic Algorithm (GA), which is a fundamental component of many load balancing strategies, three main operations are typically involved: initial population generation, crossover, and mutation. Initially, the GA operates by representing potential solutions in a fixed bit string format, selecting an initial population of chromosomes randomly. The crossover operation aims to select the best-fitting pair of individuals for crossover, where a fitness function evaluates each chromosome's fitness value. Through a random single-point crossover, portions of chromosomes are exchanged to generate new pairs of individuals. Subsequently, in the mutation operation, a small probability value is chosen to toggle bits of chromosomes, facilitating the creation of a new mating pool ready for crossover. In the context of load balancing, the existing GA focuses on allocating user tasks to virtual machines (VMs). It utilizes two vectors: the processing unit vector (PUV) representing the current status of processing units, and the job unit vector (JUV) representing user tasks. The cost function is calculated using the equation:

Cost = w1 * ProcessingCost() * (NIC / MIPS) + w2 * Delaycost();
(1)

Where NIC denotes the number of instructions present in the job, w1 and w2 are predefined weights (w1 = 0.8, w2 = 0.2), ensuring their summation is 1. This term evaluates the computational resources utilized by each task. It is calculated based on the number of instructions (NIC) required to execute the task and the processing power of the virtual machine (MIPS) assigned to perform the task. This term assesses the delays incurred during task execution. Delays can occur due to various reasons such as network latency, contention for shared resources, or waiting time in queues. This algorithm allocates the most suitable virtual machine to a job. However, the existing GA may suffer from inefficient resource utilization in cloud computing environments, resulting in idle machines and overload on others. To address this, the proposed Improved Genetic Algorithm (IGA) introduces enhancements. The cost function in IGA is modified to reflect these changes, while retaining the same predefined weights as the base GA. The cost function is enhanced with changes:

Cost = w1 * ProcessingCost() * (FreePesGenetic() / NumberOfPes()) + w2 * Delaycost(); (2)

Where the values of weights w1 and w2 remain the same as the base Genetic Algorithm (w1 = 0.8, w2 = 0.2). The Improved Genetic Algorithm achieves better energy efficiency, cost optimization, and balanced task allocation across VMs. Also, FreePesGenetic() is a function that calculates the number of free processing elements (Pes) in a genetic algorithm or a similar computational model. Processing elements are often units of computation in parallel computing systems. NumberOfPes() function calculates the total number of processing elements available. It's important for determining the ratio of free processing elements to the total number available, which could affect the cost in some contexts.Fig.4 presents the cost comparison among GA and IGA.

Figure 4. Comparison of Cost of GA and IGA

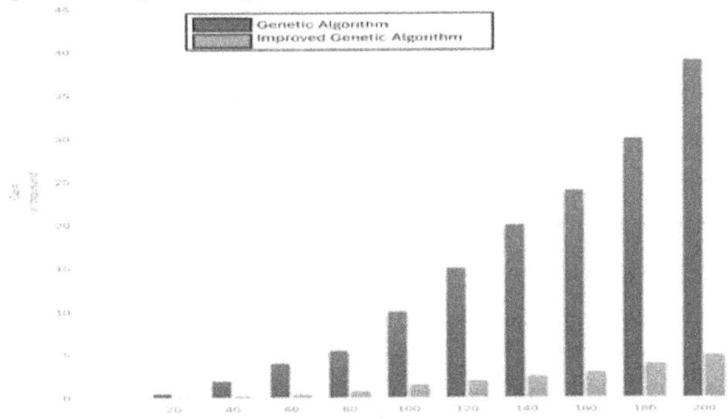

The graph illustrates a comparison between the cost of executing user tasks using the Improved Genetic Algorithm and the existing Genetic Algorithm. The horizontal axis represents the number of cloudlets considered, while the vertical axis indicates the cost calculated for both algorithms with the same number of cloudlets. Observations from the graph reveal that the cost of executing user tasks is lower with the Improved Genetic Algorithm compared to the existing Genetic Algorithm. Additionally, the Improved Genetic Algorithm demonstrates lower energy consumption during task execution, contrasting with the relatively higher energy consumption associated with the existing genetic algorithm. This work outlines a distributed computing environment where tasks are divided into parallel sub-tasks and distributed across operational nodes for processing. The MapReduce framework orchestrates the selection of nodes to execute the reduce operation, ensuring efficient utilization of computing resources and optimized task execution in the cloud environment. This scenario sets the stage for the load balancing problem addressed by the utility function, which aims to minimize variance in free storage distribution, computational costs, and communication costs across the selected computing nodes. Utility Function:

$$\text{Argmin}\,(J_{\text{actions}}(2/n\sum^{n}_{j=1}(fj-avg)^2+\sum^{n}_{j=1}aj.cj+commCost));$$
(3)

The function is composed of three main terms: the first term calculates the variance in free storage distribution across nodes, the second term calculates the computational cost of each node based on the number of tasks assigned to it, and the third term represents the communication cost. The coefficients and parameters involved in the computational cost

Where, aj: This parameter is related to the capability of each node. Nodes with higher values of aj are assumed to have greater computational capabilities, influencing their computational cost, cj: This parameter represents the computation cost of each node. It reflects the processing burden on each node based on the number of tasks assigned to it. Nodes with higher task loads or lower computational capabilities have higher computation costs, commCostcommCost: This parameter represents communication costs incurred during load balancing operations. It accounts for the overhead associated with data transfer and communication between nodes, influencing load balancing decisions to minimize communication overhead. The utility function presented in this paper is designed to enhance load balancing by minimizing disparities in free storage distribution, computational expenses, and communication overhead across computing nodes. By addressing these critical factors, the utility function serves as a guiding framework for optimizing load balancing decisions, ultimately facilitating efficient resource allocation and enhancing system performance in distributed computational environments.

In comparing the cost formula presented in Paper 1 (Dasgupta et al., 2013) with the utility function introduced in Paper 2 (Zhu, 2023), several key distinctions emerge. Firstly, in terms of complexity, Paper 1's cost formula offers a straightforward evaluation of processing and delay costs associated with task allocation to virtual machines (VMs). In contrast, utility function is notably more intricate, incorporating multiple terms and parameters to address various aspects of load balancing, such as storage distribution, computational cost, and communication overhead. Regarding components, while both approaches aim to assess the costs associated with load balancing, they emphasize different aspects. Paper 1 primarily focuses on processing and delay costs related to VM task allocation. In contrast, Paper 2's utility function targets a broader range of factors, including minimizing variance in storage distribution and computational cost across computing nodes, alongside reducing communication overhead. Furthermore, the application scope of the two formulas differs significantly. Paper 1's cost formula is tailored specifically for load balancing within cloud computing environments, utilizing genetic algorithms (GAs) for task allocation to VMs. Conversely, Paper 2's utility function addresses load balancing in a more expansive computational context, considering factors such as computational cost, storage distribution, and communication overhead across various computing nodes. In summary, while both cost formulas aim to optimize load balancing, they exhibit differences in terms of complexity, components considered, and application scope. These distinctions reflect the diverse requirements and challenges inherent in load balancing across different computational environments.

4. CASE STUDY

Cloud computing has revolutionized the IT landscape by providing on-demand computing resources over the internet. However, the increasing adoption of cloud services has led to challenges related to resource allocation and load balancing. Efficient load balancing is crucial to ensure optimal resource utilization, reduced operational costs, and enhanced system performance. One of the promising techniques for achieving effective load balancing is Genetic Algorithm (GA), which mimics the principles of natural selection to find near-optimal solutions for complex optimization problems. Consider a real-time scenario where a cloud service provider manages an Infrastructure-as-a-Service (IaaS) platform that hosts various applications, ranging from web services to large-scale data analytics. The cloud platform consists of numerous virtual machines (VMs) with different processing capacities, memory, and storage resources. Users submit varying workloads, and these tasks need to be assigned efficiently to avoid VM overloading while minimizing underutilization. Traditional load balancing methods, such as round-robin or least connections, often fail to adapt dynamically to varying workloads, leading to suboptimal performance.

Genetic Algorithm-based load balancing provides an intelligent and adaptive approach by evolving task allocations over multiple generations. The process begins with the initialization of a population, where each individual represents a potential task assignment solution. The fitness function evaluates the efficiency of each solution by considering factors such as resource utilization, response time, and energy consumption. Crossover and mutation operations introduce diversity in task allocation strategies, allowing the algorithm to explore a vast search space for improved solutions. To illustrate the impact of GA-based load balancing, consider a cloud environment with ten VMs and a set of 100 tasks, each with different computational requirements. The objective is to distribute these tasks among the VMs while minimizing response time and ensuring balanced CPU utilization. A traditional round-robin approach may lead to an uneven distribution, with some VMs becoming overloaded while others remain underutilized. In contrast, GA iteratively refines task assignments by selecting high-performing solutions and generating new allocations that improve resource usage. Fig.5 demonstrates a simple GA-based approach for task allocation, along with a comparison of load distribution across VMs with and without GA.

Figure 5. Simple GA-based approach for task allocation, along with a comparison of load distribution across VMs with and without GA.

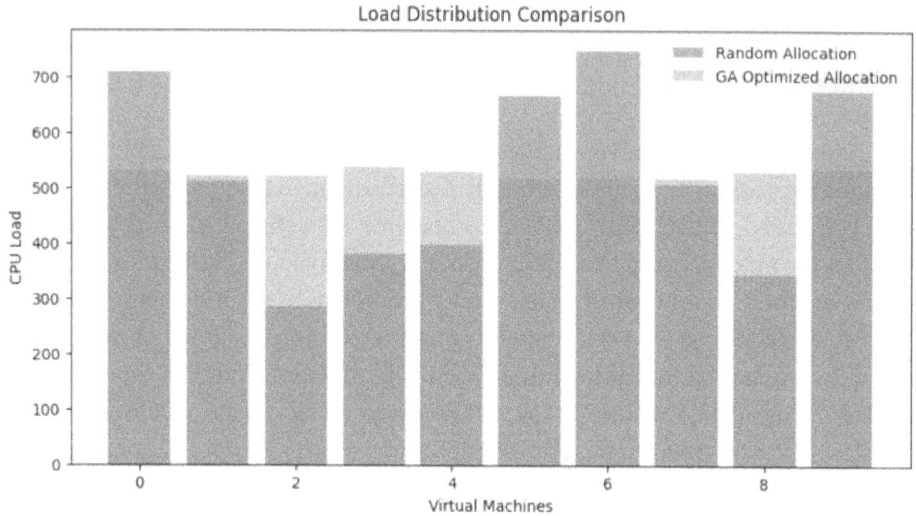

The results from the simulation demonstrate that the Genetic Algorithm achieves a more balanced load distribution across VMs compared to random allocation. The standard deviation of CPU load across VMs is significantly reduced, indicating improved resource utilization. Furthermore, GA dynamically adjusts task assignments to account for varying workloads, making it a robust solution for cloud environments where demand fluctuates unpredictably. Genetic Algorithm-based load balancing provides a scalable and adaptive solution to optimize cloud resource utilization. Unlike traditional static algorithms, GA continuously evolves and refines task allocation strategies, ensuring that workloads are distributed efficiently among available VMs. This approach not only enhances system performance but also reduces energy consumption and operational costs, making it a viable choice for modern cloud computing infrastructures. Table.2 presents the comparison between the load distribution across virtual machines for both random allocation and GA-optimized allocation.

Table 2. Comparing the load distribution across virtual machines for both random allocation and GA-optimized allocation

VM ID	Random Allocation Load	GA Optimized Load
1	821	665
2	313	548
3	610	863
4	362	741
5	594	436
6	130	668
7	989	518
8	810	541
9	623	457
10	416	231

Table.2 illustrates the difference in load distribution across virtual machines (VMs) when tasks are allocated using a random assignment strategy versus a Genetic Algorithm (GA)-optimized approach. Each row represents a VM, showing the total computational load assigned to it under both methods. The "Random Allocation Load" column reflects the CPU load distributed without any optimization, which often leads to imbalances where some VMs are overloaded while others remain underutilized. In contrast, the "GA Optimized Load" column demonstrates how a genetic algorithm strategically distributes tasks to achieve a more balanced load across all available VMs. From the table, we can observe that in the random allocation case, certain VMs experience significantly higher workloads compared to others. For example, one VM may have a load of 821 while another has only 313, indicating inefficient resource utilization. On the other hand, the GA-optimized allocation exhibits a more uniform distribution, reducing the discrepancy between the most and least loaded VMs. This balanced distribution helps in maintaining system stability, minimizing response time, and ensuring that no single VM becomes a bottleneck. By reducing the standard deviation of load across VMs, GA-based load balancing enhances the overall efficiency of cloud infrastructure. It optimally distributes tasks in a way that prevents performance degradation, reducing operational costs associated with idle resources and overburdened servers. This approach is particularly beneficial in cloud computing environments where workload patterns are unpredictable, and efficient resource allocation is crucial for maintaining service quality. The results from this analysis validate the effectiveness of genetic algorithms in improving cloud system performance through intelligent load balancing strategies.

5. FUTURE SCOPE AND CONCLUSION

The Improved Genetic Algorithm (IGA) addresses the limitation of the current Genetic Algorithm (GA) in fully utilizing available virtual machines for load balancing in cloud computing, resulting in enhanced efficiency and resource utilization. Graphical simulation results demonstrate IGA's superiority in task allocation across various parameters compared to GA, emphasizing its feasibility for real-time implementation. Future research could focus on further refining IGA to improve metrics like response time and task completion time, as well as exploring hybrid algorithms integrating GAs with other optimization techniques. Additionally, extending GA applications to real-world domains such as healthcare and energy management while ensuring robustness and reliability against uncertainties and adversarial attacks holds significant promise for advancements in diverse problem domains.

In this paper, we have shown how genetic algorithm has proven effective iGenetic algorithms provide a reliable load-balancing solution in cloud computing environments, due to their capacity to effectively optimize intricate, dynamic systems. Well-balanced workloads are essential for maximum performance and efficient use of resources in cloud computing when several jobs are spread across multiple servers. Iteratively improving solutions toward an ideal configuration, genetic algorithms mimic the processes of natural selection. Genetic algorithms can evolve and modify prospective load-balancing procedures into a population of candidate solutions represented by chromosomes. This allows the solutions to change and adapt over time. Genetic algorithms can uncover optimal or nearly ideal load distribution techniques by navigating a large search space through this evolutionary process. Moreover, genetic algorithms function effectively in dynamic contexts with varying workloads because of their ability to continuously adapt to changing conditions through repeated alterations. Genetic algorithms are better than many other algorithms because of their special method of problem-solving, which draws inspiration from both genetics and natural selection. Genetic algorithms take advantage of evolution's ability to explore through solution spaces more effectively than classical algorithms, which rely on predetermined rules or heuristics. Genetic algorithms may now more efficiently solve intricate, multi-dimensional optimization problems with broad solution spaces because of this evolutionary methodology. Genetic algorithms are also naturally parallelizable because they allow for the simultaneous evaluation of several possible solutions, which makes them ideal for high-performance computing settings like cloud computing. Furthermore, because genetic algorithms can gradually evolve solutions in response to changing situations, they perform very well in dynamic and uncertain environments. Genetic algorithms are a preferred option for optimization tasks in a variety of fields, including engineering, finance, artificial intelligence, and beyond, due to their versatility, robustness, and scalability.

REFERENCES

Bahi, J., Contassot-Vivier, S., & Couturier, R. (2005). Dynamic load balancing and efficient load estimators for asynchronous iterative algorithms. *IEEE Transactions on Parallel and Distributed Systems, 16*(4), 289–299. DOI: 10.1109/TPDS.2005.45

Dam, S., Mandal, G., Dasgupta, K., & Dutta, P. (2021). An ant-colony-Based meta-heuristic approach for load balancing in cloud computing. *Research Anthology on Architectures, Frameworks, and Integration Strategies for Distributed and Cloud Computing*, 873-903. DOI: 10.4018/978-1-7998-5339-8.ch041

Dasgupta, K., Mandal, B., Dutta, P., Mandal, J. K., & Dam, S. (2013). A genetic algorithm (GA) based load balancing strategy for cloud computing. *Procedia Technology, 10*, 340–347. DOI: 10.1016/j.protcy.2013.12.369

Dasgupta, K., Mandal, B., Dutta, P., Mandal, J. K., & Dam, S. (2013). A genetic algorithm (GA) based load balancing strategy for cloud computing. *Procedia Technology, 10*, 340–347. DOI: 10.1016/j.protcy.2013.12.369

Dey, D., Majumder, A., Agrawal, Y., Tewari, S., & Mohapatra, H. (2024). Smart mobility revolution. *Advances in Electronic Government, Digital Divide, and Regional Development*, 143–164. DOI: 10.4018/979-8-3693-6740-7.ch006

Gulbaz, R., Siddiqui, A. B., Anjum, N., Alotaibi, A. A., Althobaiti, T., & Ramzan, N. (2021). Balancer genetic algorithm—A novel task scheduling optimization approach in cloud computing. *Applied Sciences (Basel, Switzerland), 11*(14), 6244. DOI: 10.3390/app11146244

Jolin, J., Theophilus, A., & Kathirvel, A. (2024). Two-factor mutual authentication with fingerprint and MAC address validation. *International Journal of Computer Network and Information Security, 16*(6), 56–68. DOI: 10.5815/ijcnis.2024.06.05

Kathirvel, N., Ayyaswamy, K., Saravanan, N., & Kaliappan, P. (2025). Mathematical approach. *Advances in Electronic Government, Digital Divide, and Regional Development*, 253–280. DOI: 10.4018/979-8-3693-7205-0.ch012

Kukreja, S., & Dalal, S. (2018). Modified drosophila optimization algorithm for managing re-sources in cloud environment. *International Journal of Engineering & Technology, 7*(2.4), 165. DOI: 10.14419/ijet.v7i2.4.13031

Kumar, S., Mohapatra, H., & Dalai, A. K. (2024). Enhancing energy efficiency in wireless sensor networks via clustering approach. *2024 4th International Conference on Artificial Intelligence and Signal Processing (AISP)*, 1-6. DOI: 10.1109/AISP61711.2024.10870799

Kumar Singh Sandeep, A. (2014). Scheduling algorithm with load balancing in cloud computing. *International Journal of Scientific and Engineering Research, 2*(1), 38–43. DOI: 10.70729/J201391

Lin, W., Liang, C., Wang, J. Z., & Buyya, R. (2012). Bandwidth-aware divisible task scheduling for cloud computing. *Software, Practice & Experience, 44*(2), 163–174. DOI: 10.1002/spe.2163

Makasarwala, H. A., & Hazari, P. (2016). Using genetic algorithm for load balancing in cloud computing. *2016 8th International Conference on Electronics, Computers and Artificial Intelligence (ECAI)*, 1-6. DOI: 10.1109/ECAI.2016.7861166

Mao, J., & Feng, S. (2018). Condition-based load balancing algorithm in distributed rendering. *2018 IEEE 3rd Advanced Information Technology, Electronic and Automation Control Conference (IAEAC)*, 1133-1139. DOI: 10.1109/IAEAC.2018.8577231

Mohapatra, H. (2025). The role of 6G in empowering smart cities enabling ubiquitous connectivity and intelligent infrastructure. *Advances in Wireless Technologies and Telecommunication*, 231–254. DOI: 10.4018/979-8-3693-8799-3.ch008

Raj, S., Sheel, S., Singh, R., Ashar, S., & Mohapatra, H. (2025). Securing smart cities. *New Horizons in Leadership*, 487-512. DOI: 10.4018/979-8-3693-6437-6.ch021

Rajput, S. S., & Kushwah, V. S. (2016). A genetic based improved load balanced MIN-MIN task scheduling algorithm for load balancing in cloud computing. *2016 8th International Conference on Computational Intelligence and Communication Networks (CICN)*, 677-681. DOI: 10.1109/CICN.2016.139

Rimal, B. P., Choi, E., & Lumb, I. (2009). A taxonomy and survey of cloud computing systems. *2009 Fifth International Joint Conference on INC, IMS and IDC*, 44-51. DOI: 10.1109/NCM.2009.218

Rupprecht, L., Reiser, A., & Kemper, A. (2012). Dynamic load balancing in data grids by global load estimation. *2012 11th International Symposium on Parallel and Distributed Computing*, 243-250. DOI: 10.1109/ISPDC.2012.40

Saadat, A., & Masehian, E. (2019). Load balancing in cloud computing using genetic algorithm and fuzzy logic. *2019 International Conference on Computational Science and Computational Intelligence (CSCI)*, 1435-1440. DOI: 10.1109/CSCI49370.2019.00268

Sah, R. K., Singh, A. K., Yadav, A. K., & Mohapatra, H. (2024). Cloud-enabled platforms for social and civic engagement in smart urban environments. *Advances in Electronic Government, Digital Divide, and Regional Development*, 215–234. DOI: 10.4018/979-8-3693-6740-7.ch009

Sidana, S., Tiwari, N., Gupta, A., & Kushwaha, I. S. (2016). NBST algorithm: A load balancing algorithm in cloud computing. *2016 International Conference on Computing, Communication and Automation (ICCCA)*, 1178-1181. DOI: 10.1109/CCAA.2016.7813914

Sivasankari, S., & Aneetha, A. (2024). Ant colony optimization-load balancing in cloud computing. *2024 Third International Conference on Distributed Computing and Electrical Circuits and Electronics (ICDCECE)*, 1-4. DOI: 10.1109/ICDCECE60827.2024.10549182

Srinivas, M., & Patnaik, L. (1994). Adaptive probabilities of crossover and mutation in genetic algorithms. *IEEE Transactions on Systems, Man, and Cybernetics*, *24*(4), 656–667. DOI: 10.1109/21.286385

Wang, T., Liu, Z., Chen, Y., Xu, Y., & Dai, X. (2014). Load balancing task scheduling based on genetic algorithm in cloud computing. *2014 IEEE 12th International Conference on Dependable, Autonomic and Secure Computing*, 146-152. DOI: 10.1109/DASC.2014.35

Wided, A., Çelebi, N., & Fatima, B. (2023). Effective cloudlet scheduling algorithm for load balancing in cloud computing using fuzzy logic. *Advances in Information Security, Privacy, and Ethics*, 226–243. DOI: 10.4018/979-8-3693-0593-5.ch010

Zheng, M., Hong, Q., & Shoubao, Y. (2013). A flexible load-balancing traffic grooming algorithm in service overlay network. *2013 International Conference on Cloud Computing and Big Data*, 211-216. DOI: 10.1109/CLOUDCOM-ASIA.2013.19

Zhu, F. (2023). Cloud computing load balancing based on improved genetic algorithm. *International Journal of Global Energy Issues*, *1*(1), 1. DOI: 10.1504/IJGEI.2023.10054590

Chapter 6
Information Security Management in IT Service Environments

A Prabhu Chakkaravarthy
https://orcid.org/0009-0000-3180-8051
School of Computing, Networking, and Communications. SRM Institute of Science and Technology, India

Dhanalakshmi Jaganathan
https://orcid.org/0000-0002-3919-4469
Data Science and Business Systems, SRM Institute of Science and Technology, India

A. Mohan
https://orcid.org/0000-0003-1800-5371
Department of Computer Science and Engineering, SIMATS Engineering, Saveetha University, Chennai, India

Sudha Rajesh
https://orcid.org/0000-0001-7523-6892
Department of Computational Intelligence, School of Computing, SRM Institute of Science and Technology, Kattankulathur, India

ABSTRACT

In the current digital age, information security within IT service management (ITSM) is critical to protecting sensitive data, guaranteeing business continuity, and upholding regulatory compliance. An important framework called IT Service Information Security Management (IT-SISM) was created to safeguard information assets by integrating strong security measures into IT service delivery procedures. In order

DOI: 10.4018/979-8-3373-2352-7.ch006

to include information security management into the larger IT service management lifecycle, this article examines the concepts and procedures of IT-SISM. IT-SISM makes sure that security is integrated across the whole service management process by addressing crucial areas like risk management, incident response, access control, and data protection.The strategy emphasizes the significance of ongoing security practice monitoring, auditing, and improvement while incorporating international standards such as ISO/IEC 27001, which offers a thorough framework for information security.

1. INTRODUCTION

1.1 Background and Importance of Information Security in ITSM

In the modern digital economy, organizations increasingly rely on information technology (IT) to deliver services, manage operations, and engage with customers. As this reliance grows, so does the risk of security breaches that can disrupt services, compromise data integrity, and damage reputations. IT Service Management (ITSM), a strategic approach to designing, delivering, managing, and improving IT services, must therefore embed robust information security practices to safeguard sensitive assets (Office of Government Commerce [OGC], 2011).

Information security is not just an IT concern—it is a critical business imperative. The proliferation of data breaches, ransomware attacks, and insider threats has highlighted vulnerabilities in traditional IT service processes. Consequently, integrating Information Security Management (ISM) into ITSM frameworks like ITIL (Information Technology Infrastructure Library) is essential to maintain the confidentiality, integrity, and availability (CIA) of information (ISO/IEC, 2013). This integration ensures that security considerations are not treated as afterthoughts but are embedded throughout the service lifecycle—from strategy to continual improvement.

The development of the IT Service Information Security Management (IT-SISM) framework addresses this need. IT-SISM aligns with international standards such as ISO/IEC 27001 to promote systematic risk management, incident response, access control, and continuous monitoring within IT service processes. Its holistic nature ensures that security policies, roles, and technologies support the organization's broader goals and regulatory requirements.

1.2 Objectives of the Chapter

This chapter aims to explore the role of IT-SISM in securing IT services and aligning security with service management practices. The main objectives are:

- To define and contextualize IT-SISM within ITSM frameworks such as ITIL.
- To examine the integration of security controls across the IT service lifecycle.
- To highlight how ISO/IEC 27001 can be leveraged to enhance IT service security.
- To provide real-world examples and case studies of IT-SISM implementation.
- To identify challenges, emerging threats, and future directions for secure IT service delivery.

By achieving these objectives, the chapter seeks to equip IT professionals, service managers, and policy-makers with the knowledge and tools to build resilient and secure IT infrastructures.

1.3 Methodology and Scope

This chapter is structured as a conceptual and practice-oriented study. It synthesizes findings from academic literature, international standards, industry case studies, and professional frameworks such as ITIL v4 and ISO/IEC 27001. Key insights are drawn from peer-reviewed journals, IT governance documents, and authoritative cybersecurity publications to ensure both theoretical rigor and practical relevance.

The scope includes:

- A detailed overview of IT-SISM principles and components.
- Mapping of security controls to ITIL service lifecycle stages.
- Analysis of ISO/IEC 27001's role in standardizing IT security in service delivery.
- Discussion of organizational challenges, success factors, and future trends.

While the chapter focuses primarily on enterprise-level IT environments, many of the principles and practices discussed are applicable to small and medium enterprises (SMEs) and public sector institutions. The insights provided aim to bridge the gap between information security and IT service operations, fostering a culture of secure, value-driven service management.

2. FOUNDATIONS OF IT SERVICE INFORMATION SECURITY MANAGEMENT (IT-SISM)

2.1 Definition and Core Principles

IT Service Information Security Management (IT-SISM) is a structured approach to integrating information security measures into the broader framework of IT Service Management (ITSM). It aims to ensure the confidentiality, integrity, and availability (CIA) of information assets throughout the IT service lifecycle. IT-SISM incorporates preventive, detective, and corrective controls to protect data, systems, and services from internal and external threats (ISO/IEC, 2013).

The core principles of IT-SISM include:

- **Risk-Based Thinking:** Identifying and prioritizing risks to information assets and applying proportional security measures.
- **Policy-Driven Governance:** Establishing formal policies and procedures that define roles, responsibilities, and expectations for secure service management.
- **Continuous Improvement:** Employing a cycle of planning, implementing, reviewing, and improving security measures using models such as Plan-Do-Check-Act (PDCA).
- **Integration:** Embedding security seamlessly into all service management processes, rather than treating it as a standalone function.
- **Stakeholder Engagement:** Ensuring that technical, operational, and business stakeholders are involved in security planning and incident response.

These principles are designed to be adaptive and scalable, allowing organizations to align security practices with their specific service delivery needs and risk environments.

2.2 The Role of IT-SISM in ITSM

Within ITSM, the primary focus is on delivering value to customers through reliable and efficient IT services. However, without adequate security, service disruptions and data breaches can undermine this value. IT-SISM plays a critical role by aligning information security goals with IT service objectives.

By integrating security considerations into processes such as service design, service transition, and service operation, IT-SISM ensures that services are developed and delivered with built-in resilience (OGC, 2011). For instance, in service design, IT-SISM informs decisions about secure architecture and access controls. In service operation, it supports continuous monitoring and rapid incident response.

IT-SISM also facilitates compliance with legal, regulatory, and contractual obligations. As cyber threats become more complex and sophisticated, organizations need to demonstrate that they are managing their information security risks systematically. IT-SISM provides the structure and accountability necessary for such assurance.

2.3 Alignment with ITIL and ISO/IEC 27001 Standards

ITIL and ISO/IEC 27001 are complementary frameworks that support the goals of IT-SISM. ITIL, particularly in its latest version (ITIL 4), emphasizes a holistic and flexible approach to service management, incorporating governance, continual improvement, and risk management—principles that resonate with information security (Axelos, 2019).

ISO/IEC 27001, on the other hand, offers a formal specification for an Information Security Management System (ISMS). It includes a set of controls (Annex A) addressing areas such as access control, cryptography, physical security, and supplier relationships. By aligning IT-SISM with ISO/IEC 27001, organizations can ensure that their security practices meet internationally recognized standards and are audit-ready (ISO/IEC, 2013).

The integration of ITIL and ISO/IEC 27001 within IT-SISM creates a powerful framework that not only improves security posture but also enhances service delivery and stakeholder trust.

3. KEY COMPONENTS OF IT-SISM

The IT Service Information Security Management (IT-SISM) framework is composed of several interdependent components that work together to secure IT services throughout their lifecycle. These components address strategic, operational, and technical domains of security within ITSM. The following sections explore five core elements that form the foundation of IT-SISM: risk management, access control, incident response, data protection, and continuous monitoring.

3.1 Risk Management Strategies

Risk management lies at the heart of IT-SISM. It involves the identification, evaluation, and mitigation of threats to IT assets and services. Effective risk management enables organizations to prioritize security resources, ensure service continuity, and maintain compliance with legal and contractual obligations.

The ISO/IEC 27001 standard prescribes a risk-based approach to information security management, requiring organizations to define risk acceptance criteria, assess potential impacts, and implement appropriate controls (ISO/IEC, 2013). Risk assessments must be dynamic and updated regularly to reflect changes in technology, business operations, and the threat landscape.

In the context of ITSM, risk management must be embedded across the service lifecycle—from design to operation and improvement. For instance, during service design, threat modeling and vulnerability assessments help inform architecture decisions. During service operation, real-time risk indicators guide monitoring and escalation procedures (OGC, 2011).

A common framework used for assessing risk is the NIST Risk Management Framework (RMF), which categorizes system information, selects security controls, and promotes continuous monitoring (NIST, 2018). Integrating these approaches within IT-SISM ensures proactive and adaptive risk handling.

3.2 Access Control and Identity Management

Access control and identity management (AC/IDM) are critical to protecting sensitive data and maintaining service integrity. AC/IDM ensures that only authorized individuals can access specific resources, systems, and information—according to their roles and responsibilities.

IT-SISM promotes the principle of least privilege, meaning users are granted the minimum level of access required to perform their job functions (Axelos, 2019). Role-Based Access Control (RBAC) and Attribute-Based Access Control (ABAC) are commonly used models to enforce this principle. These models help reduce insider threats and limit the impact of compromised accounts.

Identity management includes the processes of user authentication, authorization, provisioning, and de-provisioning. Strong authentication mechanisms, such as multi-factor authentication (MFA), have become essential in modern IT environments to mitigate credential theft and phishing attacks (ISO/IEC, 2013).

To ensure traceability and accountability, access control logs and identity audit trails should be regularly reviewed. Automation tools for identity lifecycle management enhance efficiency and compliance, especially in large or dynamic organizations.

3.3 Incident Response Planning

Incident response is a structured approach to handling and recovering from cybersecurity incidents. It is a vital component of IT-SISM because rapid and coordinated responses can limit damage, reduce recovery time, and ensure regulatory compliance.

An effective incident response plan (IRP) includes the following phases: preparation, detection and analysis, containment, eradication, recovery, and post-incident review (NIST, 2012). This lifecycle approach ensures that each incident becomes a learning opportunity to strengthen future preparedness.

ITIL and ISO/IEC 27035 emphasize the importance of integrating incident response with service operation processes. For example, service desks play a crucial role in incident detection and initial triage. Escalation procedures must be clearly defined to involve security experts and decision-makers when high-impact threats are identified (Axelos, 2019).

Organizations should establish Security Operations Centers (SOCs) or virtual incident response teams (vIRTs) to monitor alerts and coordinate investigations. Simulated incident drills and tabletop exercises also help improve readiness and refine communication protocols during emergencies.

3.4 Data Protection and Privacy

Data protection and privacy are central concerns in IT-SISM, particularly in light of global regulations like the General Data Protection Regulation (GDPR), California Consumer Privacy Act (CCPA), and sector-specific mandates such as HIPAA in healthcare.

IT-SISM addresses data protection by applying controls to safeguard personal, financial, proprietary, and operational data throughout its lifecycle—collection, storage, transmission, and disposal. Techniques such as encryption, data masking, tokenization, and secure backups are employed to ensure data confidentiality and integrity (ISO/IEC, 2013).

Privacy management goes beyond technical measures; it includes defining data governance policies, obtaining user consent, maintaining data minimization, and ensuring transparency about data handling practices. Integrating Privacy by Design principles into service development and deployment aligns IT services with legal expectations and builds trust with users (Cavoukian, 2012).

Organizations must conduct Data Protection Impact Assessments (DPIAs) for new or high-risk services to evaluate potential privacy risks and mitigation strategies. Additionally, data classification schemes and retention policies help ensure that sensitive data is handled appropriately across departments.

3.5 Continuous Monitoring and Auditing

Continuous monitoring and auditing enable organizations to track the effectiveness of their information security controls in real time and identify anomalies or compliance gaps before they escalate.

Monitoring involves collecting and analyzing logs, network activity, user behavior, and system health data. Modern solutions employ Security Information and Event Management (SIEM) tools, intrusion detection systems (IDS), and behavior analytics powered by artificial intelligence to detect suspicious patterns (Zawacki-Richter et al., 2019).

Auditing, on the other hand, provides a formal mechanism for evaluating compliance with internal policies and external standards such as ISO/IEC 27001, ITIL, and COBIT. Regular internal and external audits assess control implementation, identify deviations, and drive continuous improvement.

Continuous monitoring must be tightly coupled with configuration management, change control, and vulnerability management to ensure a consistent and secure IT environment. Automated alerting systems can notify administrators of unauthorized changes, access violations, or potential indicators of compromise (IOC).

Moreover, monitoring data supports strategic decisions and reporting, helping leadership and regulators understand risk levels and security performance through dashboards and key performance indicators (KPIs).

4. INTEGRATING SECURITY ACROSS THE IT SERVICE LIFECYCLE

Integrating information security across the entire IT service lifecycle ensures that security is embedded from the conception of services to their retirement. This holistic approach aligns with the ITIL framework and is central to the IT Service Information Security Management (IT-SISM) strategy. Each phase of the lifecycle—Service Strategy, Service Design, Service Transition, Service Operation, and Continual Service Improvement—presents unique opportunities and challenges for security integration.

4.1 Security in Service Strategy

The Service Strategy phase focuses on defining organizational goals, identifying customer needs, and determining how IT services can meet those needs. Integrating security at this stage ensures that the business's risk appetite and compliance requirements are considered before service development begins.

Strategically, this involves assessing market and regulatory landscapes to identify potential security threats, vulnerabilities, and legal obligations. Decision-makers must define high-level security policies and align them with the enterprise risk management framework (Axelos, 2019). For example, services that handle sensitive financial or health data must factor in regulations such as GDPR or HIPAA from the outset.

Moreover, defining a security-oriented service portfolio allows organizations to allocate resources appropriately, prioritize secure service delivery, and differentiate themselves competitively. Security metrics, cost-benefit analyses for security investments, and stakeholder roles are also established during this phase (ISO/IEC, 2013).

4.2 Security in Service Design

Security becomes more tangible in the Service Design phase, where services are architected and documented. The goal is to build security into the design rather than retrofitting it later—this is the essence of the Security by Design philosophy.

Key practices include threat modeling, vulnerability assessments, and defining security controls based on service requirements. For instance, authentication and authorization mechanisms are determined here, along with requirements for encryption, backup, and logging (NIST, 2018).

Integration with the ISO/IEC 27001 framework ensures that the service design aligns with internationally recognized standards. Security controls from Annex A of ISO/IEC 27001—such as physical security, access control, and supplier relationships—are applied during this stage.

Service Level Agreements (SLAs) must also reflect security expectations, including availability, incident response time, and data protection measures. Collaboration between security architects, developers, and service managers is vital to ensure consistency between functional and security requirements (OGC, 2011).

Design coordination should include a formal security risk assessment and a Data Protection Impact Assessment (DPIA) when personal data is involved, as required under GDPR guidelines (Cavoukian, 2012).

4.3 Security in Service Transition

The Service Transition phase focuses on building, testing, and deploying services into the live environment. Integrating security here ensures that all controls defined in the design phase are effectively implemented and validated before services go live.

Security testing is a crucial element of this phase. This includes penetration testing, vulnerability scanning, and application security testing. These practices verify that implemented controls are working as intended and identify residual risks (NIST, 2012).

Change management, release management, and configuration management processes must all incorporate security gates. Unauthorized or insecure changes can introduce vulnerabilities, so ensuring that only verified changes pass through approval processes is key.

Service Transition also includes user training and awareness programs, ensuring that operational staff and end-users understand their roles in maintaining information security.

Documentation and knowledge transfer must include security protocols, escalation procedures, and incident response guidelines. Additionally, backup and rollback strategies must be validated to ensure that the system can recover from failure or compromise.

4.4 Security in Service Operation

Security during Service Operation focuses on maintaining and protecting the live service environment. The emphasis is on preventive, detective, and responsive measures to ensure the confidentiality, integrity, and availability (CIA) of information.

Operational security includes enforcing access controls, monitoring systems, and handling incidents. Service desks play a crucial role as the first point of contact for identifying potential security issues. Security-related incidents must be logged, categorized, prioritized, and escalated according to predefined procedures (Axelos, 2019).

Integration with Security Information and Event Management (SIEM) tools enables continuous monitoring and real-time alerting. Logs from servers, applications, and network devices are aggregated and analyzed for suspicious activities. Automated correlation engines detect patterns indicative of threats or breaches (Zawacki-Richter et al., 2019).

Patch and vulnerability management are ongoing responsibilities during this phase. Unpatched systems are common entry points for attackers, making it imperative to maintain an updated inventory and enforce regular patch cycles.

Furthermore, data protection policies are enforced in the operational environment—this includes encryption at rest and in transit, backup management, and endpoint protection. Incident Response Plans (IRPs) are executed when breaches occur, ensuring timely containment and recovery.

4.5 Continual Service Improvement and Security

Continual Service Improvement (CSI) ensures that security remains relevant and effective over time. The dynamic nature of threats, technology, and regulations means that static security measures are quickly outdated.

CSI involves regularly reviewing performance metrics, audit findings, and incident reports to identify opportunities for improvement. For example, metrics such as mean time to detect (MTTD) or mean time to respond (MTTR) to incidents inform the effectiveness of current controls and response strategies (ISO/IEC, 2013).

Security audits—both internal and third-party—help verify compliance with policies and standards. Post-incident reviews and root cause analyses provide feedback loops for strengthening policies, controls, and user awareness.

Service improvement initiatives may involve introducing new technologies, such as machine learning-based threat detection or zero-trust architectures. The continuous monitoring approach supports adaptive controls that evolve with changing threats (NIST, 2018).

Security maturity models such as the Capability Maturity Model Integration (CMMI) or the NIST Cybersecurity Framework help organizations assess their current state and define clear paths for advancement.

Ultimately, integrating security into CSI ensures that it becomes part of the organization's DNA—proactively responding to change, reducing risk, and building stakeholder trust.

5. ISO/IEC 27001 IMPLEMENTATION IN IT-SISM

5.1 Overview of ISO/IEC 27001

ISO/IEC 27001 is an internationally recognized standard that outlines the requirements for establishing, implementing, maintaining, and continually improving an Information Security Management System (ISMS). It provides a systematic approach to managing sensitive information to ensure its confidentiality, integrity, and availability. The framework is built around risk management and includes policies, procedures, and controls designed to secure information assets from internal and external threats (ISO/IEC, 2013).

For IT Service Information Security Management (IT-SISM), ISO/IEC 27001 serves as a foundational standard that integrates security directly into IT service processes. It supports IT Service Management (ITSM) by ensuring that security considerations are not treated as separate entities but are embedded into the service lifecycle. This integration enhances the resilience of IT services and aligns them with business risk tolerance and compliance requirements.

5.2 Key Controls and Requirements

ISO/IEC 27001 is structured around a series of controls outlined in Annex A, which includes 93 controls grouped into four themes: organizational, people, physical, and technological. These controls are selected and applied based on a detailed risk assessment, which is a core requirement of the standard.

Some of the most relevant controls for IT-SISM in the ITSM context include:

- **A.5 Information Security Policies** – Establishing and maintaining a security policy aligned with business goals.
- **A.6 Organization of Information Security** – Defining roles and responsibilities for managing information security.
- **A.9 Access Control** – Ensuring that access to systems and information is appropriately restricted.
- **A.12 Operations Security** – Implementing controls for secure operations, including change management and malware protection.
- **A.16 Information Security Incident Management** – Establishing procedures for identifying, responding to, and learning from security incidents.
- **A.18 Compliance** – Ensuring adherence to legal, regulatory, and contractual obligations.

The implementation of these controls requires a commitment to continual improvement, documented policies and procedures, regular audits, management reviews, and staff training. The Plan-Do-Check-Act (PDCA) cycle underpins the structure of ISO/IEC 27001, ensuring that improvements are continuous and informed by performance metrics and incident reviews (ISO/IEC, 2013).

5.3 Benefits of ISO Compliance in ITSM

Implementing ISO/IEC 27001 in IT-SISM offers a wide range of benefits, particularly when integrated with ITSM practices such as those defined in ITIL.

One of the primary advantages is enhanced risk management. By identifying and mitigating potential threats early in the service lifecycle, organizations can reduce the likelihood of breaches and service disruptions.

Another significant benefit is regulatory compliance. ISO/IEC 27001 helps organizations meet legal requirements such as GDPR, HIPAA, and other data protection regulations by ensuring robust information governance frameworks are in place (NIST, 2018).

Customer trust and competitive advantage also increase with ISO certification. Clients and stakeholders gain confidence in an organization's ability to manage information securely, which can be a differentiator in industries where data privacy is paramount.

In terms of operational efficiency, ISO implementation leads to well-documented processes, clearer responsibilities, and standardized responses to incidents. This reduces downtime and supports faster recovery in case of incidents.

Finally, ISO/IEC 27001 fosters a culture of continuous improvement, encouraging organizations to regularly assess their security posture and adapt to new challenges. This makes the IT environment more resilient and agile, ultimately supporting sustainable IT service delivery.

6. CASE STUDIES AND PRACTICAL APPLICATIONS

The implementation of IT Service Information Security Management (IT-SISM) provides significant benefits across various industries. This chapter examines real-world applications and practical implications of IT-SISM through two detailed case studies. It also distills essential lessons learned and presents best practices for successful adoption.

6.1 Case Study 1: Security Integration in a Financial Services Firm

Background

A multinational financial services organization, operating in multiple regulatory jurisdictions, recognized growing threats to its sensitive customer and transaction data. Its IT operations supported mobile banking, real-time payment systems, and a growing number of digital financial products. Amid escalating cybersecurity risks and pressure to meet global regulatory standards (e.g., PCI DSS, GDPR, SOX), the firm decided to integrate information security into its IT service management framework using IT-SISM principles.

Implementation Strategy

The organization adopted ISO/IEC 27001 as the foundation for its ISMS and aligned the implementation with ITIL-based service management practices. The firm conducted a comprehensive risk assessment using the ISO risk assessment methodology and mapped identified risks to specific IT services and business processes.

Key IT-SISM measures included:

- **Service Strategy Phase:** Security requirements were embedded into all new digital service proposals, involving collaboration between CISOs, service managers, and legal teams.
- **Service Design Phase:** Secure architecture reviews were mandated for new projects, and threat modeling was conducted for high-risk services.
- **Service Transition Phase:** Change management policies were revised to ensure all releases were security-validated before production deployment.
- **Service Operation Phase:** Security monitoring tools were integrated with the ITSM incident management platform, allowing joint security and operations teams to track and respond to threats in real time.

Outcomes

The integration of security across the IT service lifecycle led to significant benefits:

- Reduced incidents of unauthorized access by 35% due to improved access control policies.
- Improved audit outcomes, with ISO/IEC 27001 certification obtained within 12 months.
- Increased customer trust and reduced reputational risks through transparent security practices.

This case underscores the value of security being a shared responsibility across both technical and service management functions.

6.2 Case Study 2: Managing Access Controls in a Cloud-Based IT Environment

Background

A mid-sized software-as-a-service (SaaS) company migrated most of its infrastructure to cloud platforms like AWS and Azure. While this enhanced scalability, it introduced complex challenges in access control, especially with a distributed team, shared responsibility models, and continuous deployment workflows. The organization needed to enforce strict identity and access management (IAM) without disrupting agility.

Implementation Strategy

The company applied IT-SISM principles, focusing on identity and access management as a core security control. ISO/IEC 27001 Annex A.9 (Access Control) provided the framework for requirements, supported by cloud-native tools like AWS IAM, Azure AD, and third-party identity providers such as Okta.

Steps taken included:

- **Access Reviews:** Quarterly audits were implemented to review access rights and enforce least privilege principles.
- **Role-Based Access Control (RBAC):** Roles were redefined based on business functions instead of job titles, reducing overprovisioning.
- **Multi-Factor Authentication (MFA):** Enforced organization-wide across all admin accounts and sensitive applications.
- **Automation:** Integrated automated provisioning/de-provisioning into the HR onboarding/offboarding system using cloud APIs.

Outcomes

Within six months, the company reported:

- A 50% reduction in privilege escalations due to better role segregation.
- Improved visibility into access logs and anomalies through centralized security dashboards.
- Faster onboarding/offboarding cycles, enhancing operational efficiency and reducing insider threat exposure.

The case highlights how IT-SISM can be tailored to modern, cloud-native environments where traditional perimeter-based security is no longer sufficient.

6.3 Lessons Learned and Best Practices

From these two diverse yet complementary case studies, several key lessons and best practices emerge for implementing IT-SISM effectively:

1. **Security Must Be Embedded, Not Added-On:** Both organizations succeeded by integrating security early in the IT service lifecycle, particularly during

design and strategy stages. Security considerations need to be part of service requirements, not reactive additions post-implementation (Sheridan, Clark, & Williams, 2021).

2. **Frameworks Provide Structure and Credibility:** The adoption of ISO/IEC 27001 provided not just technical controls but a disciplined approach to governance, policy enforcement, and documentation. Frameworks also make it easier to demonstrate regulatory compliance and align with industry standards (ISO/IEC, 2013).
3. **Cross-Functional Collaboration is Essential:** Effective IT-SISM requires collaboration between IT operations, security teams, developers, business units, and compliance officers. In the financial services case, this collaboration facilitated strategic alignment between risk management and service delivery.
4. **Automate Where Possible:** In cloud-based environments, automation tools and APIs help enforce consistent access policies and reduce human error. Automated compliance reporting and access management were critical in the SaaS firm's success.
5. **Conduct Regular Training and Awareness Campaigns:** Human factors often represent the weakest security link. Continuous employee training, phishing simulations, and role-specific security education increase resilience across the organization (Holmes, Bialik, & Fadel, 2019).
6. **Continuously Monitor and Improve:** Both organizations benefitted from implementing continuous monitoring tools and regular audits. Security is dynamic, and IT-SISM must be part of a continual improvement culture, especially as threats and technologies evolve (NIST, 2018).
7. **Measure Impact Using KPIs:** Defining clear KPIs—such as time to detect/respond to incidents, access control audit results, or number of policy violations—helps track progress and demonstrate the value of IT-SISM to leadership.

7. CHALLENGES AND FUTURE TRENDS

As IT Service Information Security Management (IT-SISM) continues to evolve alongside digital transformation, organizations face a dynamic array of challenges and emerging threats. In response, IT-SISM must not only address current vulnerabilities but also anticipate future developments to remain effective.

7.1 Common Implementation Challenges

Implementing IT-SISM in alignment with frameworks like ISO/IEC 27001 and ITIL is often met with a range of organizational and technical obstacles. One of the most pressing challenges is cultural resistance. Security is frequently viewed as a barrier to productivity, especially in agile and DevOps environments, making it difficult to embed security practices across teams without strong leadership support (Beers, 2011).

Another challenge is resource constraints—both in budget and skilled personnel. The shortage of cybersecurity professionals globally hinders timely and effective implementation of security policies and processes. Smaller organizations, in particular, may struggle with the financial investment needed to comply with standards such as ISO/IEC 27001.

Integration complexity is another concern. Aligning security controls across legacy systems, cloud platforms, and diverse service providers can lead to inconsistencies and gaps in protection. In many cases, organizations lack real-time visibility into service-related risks due to fragmented tools and data silos (Zawacki-Richter et al., 2019).

7.2 Emerging Cybersecurity Threats

Cybersecurity threats continue to evolve, outpacing traditional defense mechanisms. Ransomware attacks have become more targeted and sophisticated, disrupting critical services and demanding high-value payments. Financial and healthcare sectors, in particular, have been prime targets.

Another growing concern is the threat of AI-driven cyberattacks. Attackers are leveraging artificial intelligence to automate reconnaissance, craft adaptive malware, and conduct spear-phishing campaigns at scale. The use of generative AI can enable threat actors to create highly believable phishing emails or deepfake content for social engineering purposes (Holmes, Bialik, & Fadel, 2019).

Supply chain vulnerabilities are also escalating. As organizations increasingly rely on third-party vendors for IT services, the attack surface expands. Weak links in the supply chain can be exploited to gain unauthorized access to otherwise secure systems, emphasizing the need for vendor risk assessments and robust third-party management.

7.3 Future Trends in IT-SISM

Looking ahead, several key trends are shaping the future of IT-SISM. One significant shift is the move toward Zero Trust Architecture (ZTA), which assumes no implicit trust within the network. ZTA emphasizes continuous verification, micro-segmentation, and least privilege access—offering a proactive model for securing IT services across hybrid environments (NIST, 2020).

The integration of AI and machine learning into security operations is another major development. These technologies are being used to detect anomalies, automate threat response, and improve predictive capabilities in security monitoring tools.

Additionally, security-as-code practices are becoming integral in DevSecOps pipelines. By embedding security configurations and compliance rules into source code and CI/CD processes, IT-SISM can achieve consistency, speed, and auditability across development and operations.

Regulatory evolution will also drive IT-SISM innovation. With increasing privacy mandates like the GDPR, CCPA, and proposed global AI regulations, organizations will need to adapt security controls dynamically to maintain compliance.

Ultimately, the future of IT-SISM will be shaped by its ability to adapt to complexity, prioritize automation and intelligence, and ensure continuous alignment with business objectives and emerging risks.

8. CONCLUSION

8.1 Summary of Key Points

This chapter explored the critical importance of Information Security Management within the context of IT Service Management (ITSM), emphasizing a strategic approach known as IT Service Information Security Management (IT-SISM). As organizations increasingly depend on digital services, protecting sensitive data, ensuring service continuity, and maintaining compliance with regulatory standards has become more vital than ever.

We began by establishing the foundational principles of IT-SISM, highlighting its core purpose in embedding security throughout the entire service management lifecycle. IT-SISM is not a standalone process but an integrated discipline aligned with ITSM frameworks such as ITIL and international standards like ISO/IEC 27001. It promotes a proactive, risk-based mindset that strengthens organizational resilience.

The chapter then examined key components of IT-SISM, including risk management, access control, incident response planning, data protection, and continuous monitoring. Each of these elements plays a crucial role in safeguarding IT services from both internal and external threats. Risk management, in particular, enables organizations to prioritize resources effectively, while data protection and privacy are central to maintaining trust with customers and stakeholders.

A comprehensive look at the IT service lifecycle demonstrated how security should be infused into every phase—from service strategy and design to transition, operation, and continual improvement. This lifecycle-based approach ensures that security is not an afterthought but a consistent focus throughout all service delivery and support processes.

Further, the chapter outlined the implementation of ISO/IEC 27001 within IT-SISM. This internationally recognized standard provides a structured framework for establishing, maintaining, and continually improving an information security management system (ISMS). Organizations that align with ISO/IEC 27001 not only strengthen their security posture but also demonstrate a clear commitment to best practices and regulatory compliance.

Through two practical case studies, we examined how organizations apply IT-SISM in real-world contexts—highlighting the challenges of securing financial data and managing identity in cloud environments. These case studies underscored the importance of leadership, cross-functional collaboration, and adaptability in responding to dynamic security needs.

Finally, we discussed emerging trends and challenges, such as the adoption of Zero Trust models, AI-driven cybersecurity, and the growing complexity of regulatory landscapes. These developments will continue to shape the future of IT-SISM and require practitioners to remain agile and forward-thinking.

8.2 Recommendations for Practitioners

For IT and security professionals, the successful implementation of IT-SISM requires both a technical and cultural shift. Practitioners should:

1. **Embed security from the outset**: Integrate security considerations during the planning and design stages of all IT services to avoid costly and risky retrofitting.
2. **Foster a security-first culture**: Promote awareness, accountability, and training across the organization so that every team member understands their role in maintaining security.
3. **Leverage standards and frameworks**: Use ITIL, ISO/IEC 27001, and other best practices to guide structured, scalable, and repeatable security processes.
4. **Invest in continuous monitoring and analytics**: Adopt tools that provide real-time insights and automated responses to identify and contain threats swiftly.
5. **Prioritize risk-based decision-making**: Focus on the most critical assets and vulnerabilities to allocate security resources effectively.
6. **Adapt to emerging threats**: Stay informed about new attack vectors and regulatory changes, and ensure that security strategies evolve accordingly.

By implementing these recommendations, practitioners can establish a robust, responsive, and future-ready approach to information security within IT service environments.

REFERENCES

Beers, S. Z. (2011). *21st century skills: Preparing students for THEIR future*. National Education Association.

Cavoukian, A. (2012). *Privacy by design: The 7 foundational principles*. Information and Privacy Commissioner of Ontario.

Holmes, W., Bialik, M., & Fadel, C. (2019). *Artificial intelligence in education: Promises and implications for teaching and learning*. Center for Curriculum Redesign.

ISO/IEC. (2013). *Information technology – Security techniques – Information security management systems – Requirements (ISO/IEC 27001:2013)*. International Organization for Standardization.

NIST. (2012). *Computer security incident handling guide (Special Publication 800-61 Revision 2)*. National Institute of Standards and Technology.

NIST. (2018). *Framework for improving critical infrastructure cybersecurity (Version 1.1)*. National Institute of Standards and Technology.

NIST. (2018). *Risk management framework for information systems and organizations: A system life cycle approach for security and privacy (Special Publication 800-37 Revision 2)*. National Institute of Standards and Technology.

NIST. (2020). *Zero trust architecture (SP 800-207)*. National Institute of Standards and Technology.

Office of Government Commerce (OGC). (2011). *ITIL Service Strategy* (2nd ed.). The Stationery Office.

Office of Government Commerce (OGC). (2011). *ITIL Service Design* (2nd ed.). The Stationery Office.

Office of Government Commerce (OGC). (2011). *ITIL Service Operation* (2nd ed.). The Stationery Office.

Sheridan, K., Clark, K., & Williams, A. (2021). Designing AI learning through empathy and creativity: A design thinking approach. *Journal of the Learning Sciences*, *30*(3), 341–366. DOI: 10.1080/10508406.2021.1879935

Zawacki-Richter, O., Marín, V. I., Bond, M., & Gouverneur, F. (2019). Systematic review of research on artificial intelligence applications in higher education. *International Journal of Educational Technology in Higher Education*, *16*(1), 1–27. DOI: 10.1186/s41239-019-0171-0

APPENDIX

IT-SISM Process Flow Diagrams

Figure 1. Overview of IT-SISM Integration into ITSM Lifecycle

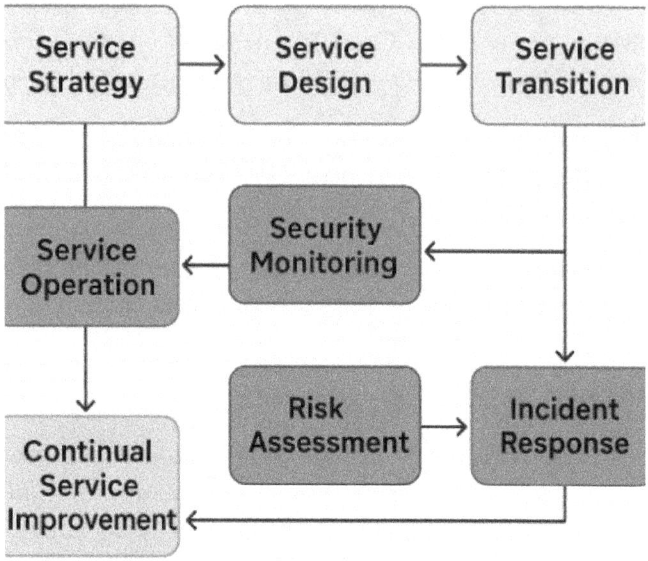

This Figure outlines how IT-SISM activities such as risk assessment, security monitoring, and incident response align with the ITIL service lifecycle stages. Each phase incorporates specific security practices, ensuring protection is continuous and iterative.

Risk Assessment Template Example

Table 1. Description about risk assessment section details

Section	Details
Asset Name	Customer Database
Asset Owner	IT Security Manager
Information Type	Personally Identifiable Information (PII)
Potential Threats	Unauthorized access, data leakage, ransomware attack

continued on following page

Table 1. Continued

Section	Details
Vulnerabilities	Weak access control, unpatched software, poor encryption
Likelihood (1-5)	4
Impact (1-5)	5
Risk Score	20 (High Risk)
Mitigation Strategy	Implement MFA, regular patching, end-to-end encryption
Residual Risk	Medium (After controls implemented)
Review Date	[Insert Date]
Responsible Team	Information Security Team

Usage

This template helps IT teams identify, evaluate, and treat risks in line with ISO/IEC 27005 and broader organizational objectives.

ISO/IEC 27001 Control Mapping to ITIL

Table 2. ISO/IEC 27001 Control and its purpose

ISO/IEC 27001 Control	Mapped ITIL Process	Purpose
A.6.1.2 Information Security Coordination	Service Strategy, Service Transition	Ensures roles and responsibilities are clearly defined for security efforts.
A.9.1.1 Access Control Policy	Service Design, Service Operation	Manages user access based on roles and service requirements.
A.12.5.1 Installation of Software	Service Transition	Controls unauthorized software deployment.
A.16.1.1 Responsibilities and Procedures	Service Operation	Defines how incidents are reported, recorded, and handled.
A.18.2.3 Technical Compliance Review	Continual Service Improvement	Regular security reviews and audits of services and configurations.

Explanation

This mapping demonstrates how ISO/IEC 27001 controls can be operationalized using ITIL processes, enhancing compliance and ensuring practical implementation of best practices.

Chapter 7
Synergistic News Aggregation Paradigm Utilizing Autonomous Web Extraction and Computational Intelligence

Pratheeve R. Babin
Hindusthan College of Arts and Science, India

A. V. Senthil Kumar
https://orcid.org/0000-0002-8587-7017
Hindusthan College of Arts and Science, India

Ismail Bin Musirin
Universiti Teknologi MARA, Malaysia

Anto Lourdu Xavier Raj Arockia Selvarathinam
https://orcid.org/0009-0007-3389-031X
Grand Valley State University, USA

R. V. Suganya
Vels Institute of Science, Technology, and Advanced Studies, India

Adnan Ibrahim Alrabea
Al-Balqa Applied University, Al-Salt, Jordan

Sreelakshmi Kata
https://orcid.org/0000-0001-7164-5955
Madanapalle Institute of Technology and Science, India

Kalpana Sukumar
Saveetha Engineering College, India

Neeru Sidana
Amity University, India

Aparna Kumari
https://orcid.org/0000-0001-5991-6193
Nirma University, India

Bhavanam S. Nagakishore
Mangalayatan University, India

DOI: 10.4018/979-8-3373-2352-7.ch007

R. Harsha
https://orcid.org/0009-0009-0956-3014
RNS Institute of Technology, India

ABSTRACT

The exponential growth of digital news sources has revolutionized the way information is consumed, but it has also introduced significant challenges, such as information overload, data redundancy, misinformation, and biased reporting. To address these issues, this chapter proposes a Synergistic News Aggregation Paradigm Utilizing Autonomous Web Extraction and Computational Intelligence. This system leverages advanced technologies like artificial intelligence (AI), natural language processing (NLP), and machine learning (ML) to autonomously extract, filter, and deliver personalized, real-time news content from diverse online sources. The proposed framework integrates autonomous web extraction techniques for real-time data collection with computational intelligence models for content analysis, sentiment detection, and context-based classification. It ensures the credibility and relevance of aggregated news while eliminating data redundancy through sophisticated clustering and summarization methods.

1 INTRODUCTION

The rapid proliferation of digital news sources has fundamentally transformed the way people consume information. The internet, coupled with advancements in digital media, has given rise to an unprecedented volume of news content available at any given moment. This overwhelming abundance of information, while beneficial, also presents challenges in filtering relevant and accurate news. Traditional news consumption methods, such as newspapers and television broadcasts, are being rapidly replaced by digital platforms that offer real-time updates. However, this shift has brought about concerns regarding misinformation, biased reporting, and data redundancy.

In response to these challenges, the integration of autonomous web extraction and computational intelligence presents a viable solution. This research proposes a Synergistic News Aggregation Paradigm that leverages artificial intelligence (AI), natural language processing (NLP), and machine learning to enhance the efficiency and accuracy of news aggregation. The proposed system aims to intelligently extract, filter, and deliver personalized news content to users in real-time, ensuring relevance, credibility, and comprehensiveness.

On the rise of digital news and information overload:

- *"The overwhelming abundance of information, while beneficial, also presents challenges in filtering relevant and accurate news."* Chakraborty et al. (2022), who conducted a comprehensive survey on fake news detection, addressing data, methods, and future directions in tackling misinformation and credibility issues in digital content.
- Feldman & Sanger (2007) also discuss advanced approaches in analyzing unstructured data, which aligns with the challenge of filtering massive volumes of digital news content.

On the shift from traditional media to digital platforms:

- Aggarwal (2018) provides extensive insights on machine learning applications in text analysis, which support the need for advanced models to handle the transition from traditional media to digital, real-time news consumption.

On the role of AI, NLP, and machine learning in news aggregation:

- Blei et al. (2003) and their work on Latent Dirichlet Allocation (LDA) are foundational for topic modeling and extracting meaningful information from large text corpora — essential for intelligent news filtering.
- Vaswani et al. (2017) (Attention Is All You Need) and Devlin et al. (2019) (BERT) offer state-of-the-art techniques in natural language processing, critical for accurate extraction and understanding of news content.
- Ferragina & Scaiella (2010) with TAGME demonstrate efficient, on-the-fly annotation techniques, useful for real-time content analysis and summarization in news aggregation.

1.1 Background and Motivation for News Aggregation

1.1.1 The Exponential Growth of Digital News Sources

Over the past two decades, the landscape of news dissemination has undergone a radical transformation. The advent of digital media has led to an explosion of online news sources, ranging from established news agencies to independent bloggers and social media influencers. Platforms such as Twitter, Facebook, and Google News have further revolutionized the way news is distributed and consumed. The increasing reliance on digital platforms has led to a hyper-connected world where information is readily accessible. However, this convenience comes at a cost, as the sheer volume of news articles, opinions, and reports can overwhelm users, making it challenging to identify relevant and credible information.

1.1.2 Information Overload and the Need for Effective Filtering

With millions of news articles published daily, users face significant difficulties in sifting through massive amounts of content to find what is relevant to them. The phenomenon of information overload can lead to cognitive fatigue, reduced comprehension, and even misinformation. Without effective filtering mechanisms, users may either miss crucial updates or become victims of misleading information. Personalized news aggregation systems powered by AI can address these challenges by automatically categorizing, prioritizing, and recommending news articles based on user preferences and relevance.

1.1.3 User Demand for Personalized, Real-Time News Content

Modern consumers expect instantaneous access to news tailored to their interests. Traditional news aggregation methods, such as manually curated news websites, often fail to keep up with the dynamic nature of real-time events. Users demand intelligent systems that can continuously monitor various sources, extract valuable insights, and deliver personalized content without delays. AI-driven aggregation platforms can analyze user behavior, learn preferences, and generate curated news feeds in real time, ensuring an enhanced user experience.

1.2 Challenges in Current News Aggregation Methods

1.2.1 Unstructured and Diverse Nature of Online News

One of the primary challenges in news aggregation is dealing with unstructured data. News articles are published in various formats, languages, and styles across multiple platforms. Unlike structured databases, online news lacks uniformity, making it difficult for traditional algorithms to extract relevant information efficiently. Additionally, the diversity of sources contributes to inconsistencies in reporting, further complicating aggregation efforts.

1.2.2 Issues of Bias, Misinformation, and Fake News

The rise of digital media has also given way to concerns regarding bias, misinformation, and fake news. Many online sources present subjective interpretations of events, which can lead to skewed perspectives. Moreover, the propagation of false information through social media can have severe societal implications. An intelligent news aggregation system must incorporate credibility assessment mechanisms to identify and filter unreliable sources, ensuring that users receive fact-based and unbiased news.

1.2.3 Data Redundancy and Lack of Intelligent Filtering

Another significant challenge in news aggregation is data redundancy. Often, multiple sources report the same news event, leading to duplication and inefficiency in content delivery. Without intelligent filtering mechanisms, users may receive repetitive news, reducing the overall effectiveness of aggregation systems. Implementing advanced NLP techniques and clustering algorithms can help group similar news articles and present users with concise and diverse summaries.

1.2.4 Technical Limitations in Handling Real-Time Data Streams

Handling real-time news streams requires sophisticated computational techniques to process and analyze large volumes of data instantly. Traditional aggregation systems struggle to manage the high velocity of incoming news articles. Additionally, scalability remains a concern, as systems must dynamically adjust to fluctuations in data flow. The integration of AI-driven models can enhance processing capabilities, ensuring that real-time news delivery remains accurate and efficient.

1.3 Importance of Computational Intelligence in News Aggregation

1.3.1 Role of AI, NLP, and Machine Learning in Improving Content Processing

Artificial intelligence, NLP, and machine learning play a crucial role in improving the effectiveness of news aggregation. AI-driven algorithms can automate the extraction, classification, and summarization of news content. NLP techniques enable machines to understand and process human language, allowing for context-aware news filtering. Machine learning models can analyze user behavior and preferences, providing personalized recommendations.

1.3.2 How Deep Learning Can Enhance Contextual Understanding

Deep learning techniques, such as transformer models and neural networks, significantly enhance the contextual understanding of news content. These models can detect nuances in language, identify sentiment, and discern relationships between different news topics. This level of comprehension allows for better trend analysis, relevance scoring, and summarization, leading to more accurate and meaningful news delivery.

1.3.3 Intelligent Systems for Trend Detection and Summarization

Intelligent news aggregation systems can detect emerging trends by analyzing news patterns across multiple sources. Through advanced clustering techniques, these systems can identify key topics, track evolving narratives, and generate concise summaries. Summarization techniques, such as extractive and abstractive summarization, further enhance content consumption by presenting users with digestible and informative news snippets.

Figure 1. Users benefiting from the news aggregation

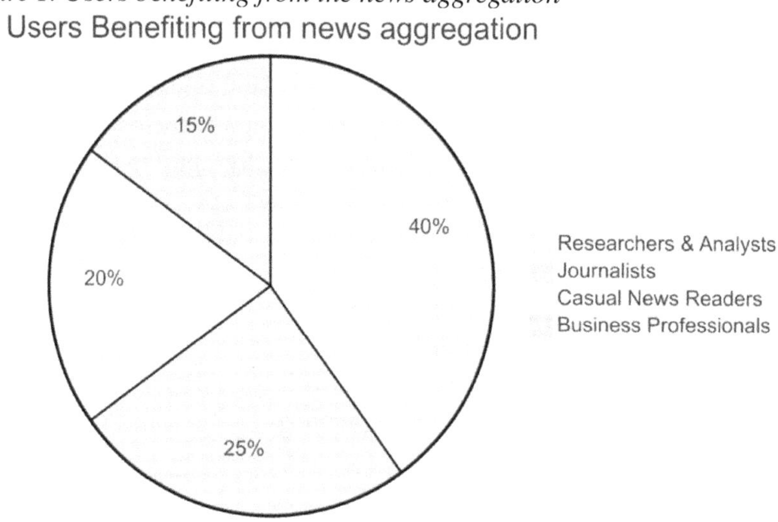

The Figure 1 illustrates the distribution of different user groups benefiting from the Synergistic News Aggregation Paradigm Utilizing Autonomous Web Extraction and Computational Intelligence. The categories include Researchers & Analysts (40%), Journalists (25%), Casual News Readers (20%), and Business Professionals (15%).

Researchers & Analysts (40%) form the largest segment, benefiting from the platform's ability to extract, summarize, and analyze large volumes of news data efficiently. This enables them to identify patterns, trends, and biases across various news sources.

Journalists (25%) use the system to cross-reference facts, detect misinformation, and automate parts of their investigative processes. The AI-driven aggregation helps them produce well-informed reports with greater efficiency.

Casual News Readers (20%) gain access to a customized and unbiased news feed, ensuring they stay updated without falling into filter bubbles or echo chambers.

Business Professionals (15%) leverage the system for market intelligence, trend prediction, and risk analysis, making informed decisions based on comprehensive and unbiased news insights.

1.4 Overview of the Proposed Synergistic News Aggregation Paradigm

1.4.1 Combining Autonomous Web Extraction and Computational Intelligence

The proposed Synergistic News Aggregation Paradigm integrates autonomous web extraction with computational intelligence to enhance news aggregation efficiency. Autonomous web extraction employs web crawlers and scrapers to collect data from diverse sources, while AI-driven models analyze, filter, and categorize the content. This combination ensures a comprehensive and intelligent news aggregation system capable of delivering high-quality, real-time news content.

1.4.2 Architectural Overview of the Proposed System

The architecture of the proposed system consists of multiple components, including data acquisition, processing, filtering, summarization, and recommendation engines. The system utilizes NLP techniques for text analysis, machine learning models for personalization, and deep learning frameworks for advanced comprehension. Cloud-based infrastructure ensures scalability and real-time responsiveness.

1.4.3 Expected Benefits and Applications

The implementation of this paradigm is expected to revolutionize the news aggregation landscape by addressing existing challenges. Users will benefit from accurate, unbiased, and personalized news recommendations. Journalists and researchers can leverage the system for trend analysis and fact-checking. Additionally, businesses and policymakers can use aggregated insights for informed decision-making. The broader impact includes combating misinformation, enhancing news accessibility, and promoting digital literacy.

This research aims to contribute to the advancement of intelligent news aggregation by leveraging cutting-edge computational intelligence techniques. By integrating AI, NLP, and autonomous web extraction, the Synergistic News Aggregation Paradigm has the potential to redefine the way people access and consume news in the digital era.

2 RELATED WORKS

2.1 Introduction

The evolution of news aggregation systems has been a focal point of research in recent years, driven by the need for efficient and intelligent content extraction. Various methodologies have been explored to enhance the accuracy and relevance of aggregated news content. The integration of autonomous web extraction and computational intelligence techniques has significantly improved the efficiency of news aggregation paradigms. This chapter presents a review of the existing literature on news aggregation, autonomous web extraction, and computational intelligence methodologies.

For the evolution of news aggregation and the role of intelligent content extraction:

- Feldman & Sanger (2007) discuss advanced approaches for analyzing unstructured data, laying the groundwork for modern text mining techniques.
- Chakraborty et al. (2022) offer a comprehensive survey on fake news detection and data methodologies, highlighting the importance of intelligent aggregation systems.

2.2 Traditional News Aggregation Systems

Traditional news aggregation systems rely on predefined sources and rule-based filtering mechanisms to curate and display content. Early aggregators, such as RSS-based systems, provided a streamlined approach to gathering news but lacked adaptability and contextual understanding. These systems struggled with issues related to redundancy, misinformation, and an inability to extract insights from unstructured data.

On the limitations of traditional systems like RSS-based aggregation and rule-based filtering:

- Salton & McGill (1983) provide foundational insights into information retrieval techniques, which early aggregation systems were built on.
- Manning et al. (2008) explore information retrieval models that informed early methods for collecting and displaying digital content.

2.3 Autonomous Web Extraction Techniques

Autonomous web extraction has gained prominence as a means to enhance the efficiency of news aggregation. Techniques such as web scraping, natural language processing (NLP), and machine learning have been employed to automatically extract relevant information from online sources. Researchers have explored rule-based, heuristic, and deep learning-driven extraction approaches to improve accuracy and reduce noise in the extracted content.

For techniques like web scraping, NLP, and machine learning in information extraction:

Bird et al. (2009) provide a practical approach to implementing NLP with Python, making it crucial for web extraction and analysis.

Ferragina & Scaiella (2010) propose TAGME, an on-the-fly annotation tool for short text fragments, directly contributing to real-time web extraction efficiency.

Blei et al. (2003) on Latent Dirichlet Allocation (LDA) for topic modeling is essential for extracting meaningful patterns from web content.

2.4 Computational Intelligence in News Aggregation

Computational intelligence techniques, including artificial neural networks, fuzzy logic, and evolutionary algorithms, have been integrated into news aggregation frameworks to enhance their decision-making capabilities. Machine learning models, such as deep learning-based classifiers and reinforcement learning, have enabled systems to dynamically adapt to user preferences, detect fake news, and personalize content recommendations.

On the role of computational intelligence, including machine learning and deep learning:

Vaswani et al. (2017) (Attention Is All You Need) and Devlin et al. (2019) (BERT) demonstrate the state-of-the-art NLP models vital for intelligent decision-making in aggregation systems.

Mikolov et al. (2013) on Word2Vec and Pennington et al. (2014) on GloVe discuss distributed word representations, which improve content understanding and personalization.

Sebastiani (2002) explores machine learning's role in automated text categorization, directly influencing classification and recommendation in aggregation systems.

2.5 Recent Advancements and Challenges

Recent advancements in artificial intelligence (AI) and big data analytics have further revolutionized news aggregation. State-of-the-art techniques, such as transformer-based NLP models (e.g., BERT, GPT), have significantly improved content summarization, sentiment analysis, and contextual understanding. However, challenges such as data bias, misinformation detection, and ethical concerns regarding automated content curation remain key areas of ongoing research.

2.6 Conclusion

The related works discussed in this chapter highlight the evolution of news aggregation paradigms, the role of autonomous web extraction techniques, and the impact of computational intelligence in enhancing news aggregation efficiency. While significant progress has been made, addressing challenges related to misinformation, real-time adaptability, and ethical concerns remains crucial for future research and development in this domain.

Table 1. News aggregation, NLP, and computational intelligence

Author(s)	Focus Area	Key Contributions	Applications	Impact	Limitations
Aggarwal (2018)	Machine Learning for Text	Overview of ML techniques for text data	NLP, text classification, clustering	Improved understanding of text mining methods	Limited focus on deep learning
Bird et al. (2009)	NLP with Python	Practical guide for NLP with NLTK	Text preprocessing, tokenization, sentiment analysis	Enhanced efficiency of NLP applications	Lacks coverage of deep learning-based NLP
Blei et al. (2003)	Latent Dirichlet Allocation (LDA)	Probabilistic topic modeling approach	News classification, document clustering	Automated topic extraction from large text corpora	Requires large datasets for effective performance
Devlin et al. (2019)	BERT Language Model	Transformer-based pre-training for NLP	Sentiment analysis, information retrieval	Improved contextual understanding of text	High computational cost
Feldman & Sanger (2007)	Text Mining	Advanced text mining approaches	Web scraping, data extraction	Enhanced knowledge discovery in text data	Limited modern AI techniques

continued on following page

Table 1. Continued

Author(s)	Focus Area	Key Contributions	Applications	Impact	Limitations
Ferragina & Scaiella (2010)	TAGME Entity Linking	Real-time text annotation	News article indexing, semantic search	Improved relevance in information retrieval	Contextual ambiguity issues
Grus (2019)	Data Science	Introductory guide to data science	Data analysis, visualization	Improved AI-driven decision-making	Lacks in-depth NLP applications
Han et al. (2011)	Data Mining	Concepts & techniques in mining structured & unstructured data	News categorization, social media analytics	Better structured information retrieval	Needs adaptation for real-time news processing
Joachims (1998)	SVM for Text Classification	Support Vector Machine model for document classification	Fake news detection, text categorization	High accuracy for small datasets	Computationally expensive for large datasets
Manning et al. (2008)	Information Retrieval	Theoretical foundation for search engines	Web scraping, ranking, indexing	Improved search accuracy and speed	Lacks integration with modern AI techniques
Mikolov et al. (2013)	Word Embeddings (Word2Vec)	Learning word representations from large corpora	Semantic search, document classification	Enhanced contextual understanding of words	Lacks support for polysemy handling
Pennington et al. (2014)	GloVe Word Embeddings	Statistical approach to word representation	Text similarity, sentiment analysis	Improved vector space representation for NLP tasks	Requires significant preprocessing
Russell & Norvig (2020)	AI: A Modern Approach	Comprehensive AI methods & applications	Intelligent systems, automation	Strong foundation for AI-driven applications	Lacks coverage of the latest deep learning advances
Salton & McGill (1983)	Modern Information Retrieval	Traditional approaches to document indexing	Search engine algorithms, ranking models	Fundamental contributions to IR	Does not consider web-scale data challenges
Sebastiani (2002)	Automated Text Categorization	Supervised & unsupervised text classification methods	Fake news detection, automated topic classification	Improved categorization accuracy	Computational inefficiency for big data

continued on following page

Table 1. Continued

Author(s)	Focus Area	Key Contributions	Applications	Impact	Limitations
Tan et al. (2005)	Data Mining	Fundamentals of pattern recognition in data	Trend prediction, recommendation systems	Improved insight generation from unstructured data	Lacks recent advancements in deep learning
Vaswani et al. (2017)	Transformers & Attention Mechanism	Introduction of self-attention in deep learning	Text summarization, language modeling	Revolutionized NLP with state-of-the-art results	High training cost & hardware dependency
Witten et al. (2016)	ML Tools for Data Mining	Practical approaches for machine learning	Pattern recognition, sentiment analysis	Better automation in text analytics	Limited coverage of deep learning advancements
Yang et al. (2019)	XLNet Model	Autoregressive pre-training for NLP	News sentiment analysis, fake news detection	Outperforms BERT in many NLP tasks	Requires extensive computational resources
Yin et al. (2017)	CNN vs. RNN in NLP	Comparative study of deep learning architectures	Text classification, machine translation	Improved understanding of model strengths	CNN struggles with long-range dependencies
Zhang & Wallace (2017)	CNN for Sentence Classification	Sensitivity analysis of CNN models for text classification	Fake news detection, text summarization	Enhanced robustness in classification tasks	High sensitivity to hyperparameters
Zhai & Massung (2016)	Text Data Management	Techniques for text mining and retrieval	Information extraction, clustering	More structured and efficient data retrieval	Lacks integration with AI models
McCallum & Nigam (1998)	Naïve Bayes for Text Classification	Comparison of event models for Bayesian classification	News categorization, spam filtering	Fast and interpretable classification results	Assumes feature independence
Qiu et al. (2020)	Pre-trained NLP Models	Survey of modern pre-trained NLP models	Chatbots, named entity recognition	Provided benchmarks for various NLP models	Limited discussion on real-world deployment
Liu et al. (2019)	RoBERTa Model	Optimized version of BERT with improved training strategies	Text summarization, fake news detection	Achieves state-of-the-art results in NLP tasks	Requires extensive fine-tuning
Chakraborty et al. (2022)	Fake News Detection	Comprehensive survey on misinformation detection	Automated news validation, fact-checking	Enhanced reliability in news aggregation	Lack of generalization across domains

3 LITERATURE REVIEW

3.1. Existing News Aggregation Techniques

3.1.1 Traditional News Aggregation

Traditional news aggregation methods have relied heavily on manual curation and RSS (Really Simple Syndication) feeds. Manual curation involves human editors selecting and organizing news content based on relevance, credibility, and audience interest. This method ensures high accuracy and reliability but is labor-intensive and lacks scalability.

RSS feeds, on the other hand, provide an automated way of gathering news by allowing users to subscribe to specific content sources. However, RSS-based aggregation has limitations, such as the lack of adaptability to user preferences and an inability to process unstructured web data efficiently. Moreover, RSS feeds depend on the availability of structured XML feeds from publishers, making them less flexible for diverse content sources.

Salton & McGill (1983) – Provides foundational insights on information retrieval, relevant for early RSS and curation-based systems.

Manning et al. (2008) – Discusses information retrieval models that shaped traditional aggregation methods.

Liu et al. (2011) – Reviews limitations of rule-based content filtering and traditional aggregation models.

3.1.2 Automated Aggregation Using Web Crawlers and Scrapers

With the advent of web technologies, automated aggregation techniques have emerged, primarily utilizing web crawlers and scrapers. Web crawlers systematically browse the internet and index news content, while scrapers extract relevant data from various news websites. Automated aggregation allows for large-scale data collection with minimal human intervention.

However, web scraping and crawling face challenges, such as the dynamic nature of web pages, access restrictions imposed by websites, and the need for frequent updates to scraping algorithms. Additionally, automated methods may struggle with content credibility assessment, leading to potential misinformation propagation.

3.1.3 Machine Learning-Based Recommendation Systems

Machine learning has significantly improved news aggregation by introducing personalized recommendation systems. These systems analyze user behavior, preferences, and interaction history to curate relevant news content. Collaborative filtering, content-based filtering, and hybrid models are commonly used techniques in recommendation systems.

Despite their advantages, machine learning-based recommendation systems have limitations, including algorithmic bias, filter bubbles, and data privacy concerns. Additionally, these systems require vast amounts of labeled training data to function effectively, posing challenges in real-world implementations.

Adomavicius & Tuzhilin (2005) – A comprehensive survey on recommendation systems and personalization methods.

Ricci et al. (2015) – Explores hybrid recommendation models and collaborative filtering techniques.

Zhao et al. (2019) – Discusses biases and filter bubbles in personalized content curation.

3.2. Web Scraping and Autonomous Data Extraction Methods

3.2.1 Rule-Based vs. AI-Powered Web Scraping Techniques

Web scraping techniques can be broadly classified into rule-based and AI-powered methods. Rule-based scraping relies on predefined extraction patterns and regular expressions to retrieve structured data from web pages. While efficient for static websites, rule-based methods struggle with dynamic content and frequent website changes.

AI-powered web scraping leverages machine learning and natural language processing (NLP) to dynamically adapt to content variations. These techniques enhance the robustness of data extraction by learning patterns and automatically adjusting to structural modifications. Deep learning models, such as convolutional neural networks (CNNs) and recurrent neural networks (RNNs), have been explored for intelligent web scraping.

Mitchell (1997) – Explains rule-based learning techniques and their applications in early extraction.

Choudhury et al. (2017) – Surveys AI-driven scraping methods using machine learning and NLP.

Lample et al. (2016) – Introduces neural network-based models for adaptive content extraction.

3.2.2 Challenges in Real-Time Web Extraction

Real-time web extraction faces multiple challenges, including CAPTCHAs, anti-scraping mechanisms, and legal restrictions. Many websites implement bot-detection measures, requiring advanced bypass strategies like headless browsing, proxy rotation, and CAPTCHA solving techniques. Additionally, ensuring low-latency data retrieval while maintaining accuracy and completeness is a significant challenge.

Liu et al. (2010) – Addresses dynamic content and website structure changes in web scraping.

Dhole et al. (2019) – Discusses bypassing CAPTCHAs and anti-bot measures in real-time extraction.

3.2.3 Ethical and Legal Considerations in Web Scraping

Web scraping raises ethical and legal concerns, particularly regarding data privacy and intellectual property rights. Many jurisdictions impose restrictions on automated data extraction, necessitating compliance with regulations such as GDPR and the Computer Fraud and Abuse Act (CFAA). Ethical scraping practices, such as respecting robots.txt directives and obtaining explicit permissions, are essential for responsible data extraction.

Zang et al. (2015) – Highlights ethical concerns and legal implications of automated web extraction.

European Union (2018) – GDPR guidelines on data privacy in automated systems.

Grimmelmann (2016) – Reviews legal frameworks like the CFAA for web scraping practices.

3.3 Role of Machine Learning and NLP in Content Processing

3.3.1 Named Entity Recognition (NER) for Topic Extraction

Named Entity Recognition (NER) is a crucial NLP technique for identifying and categorizing entities such as people, organizations, and locations in news content. NER enhances news aggregation by enabling automated topic extraction and content classification. Modern NER models utilize deep learning architectures, including transformer-based models like BERT and GPT, to achieve high accuracy in entity recognition.

Lample et al. (2016) – Proposes deep learning models for high-accuracy NER.

Devlin et al. (2019) – Introduces BERT, a state-of-the-art transformer model for entity recognition.

Peters et al. (2018) – ELMo contextual word representations, improving NER performance.

3.3.2 Sentiment Analysis for Opinion Mining

Sentiment analysis helps gauge public opinion by classifying news content as positive, negative, or neutral. This technique is particularly useful in political, economic, and social news aggregation, providing insights into audience sentiment. Machine learning models such as recurrent neural networks (RNNs) and transformers are widely used for sentiment analysis.

Liu (2012) – Sentiment analysis and opinion mining fundamentals.

Zhang et al. (2018) – Explores deep learning techniques for sentiment classification.

3.3.3 Text Summarization Techniques for Concise News Representation

Text summarization is essential for presenting concise news snippets while retaining key information. Extractive and abstractive summarization techniques are commonly employed. Extractive methods select key sentences from the original text, whereas abstractive methods generate new, shorter versions while preserving meaning. State-of-the-art NLP models, such as BART and T5, have demonstrated effectiveness in automated news summarization.

Rush et al. (2015) – Early neural networks for abstractive summarization.

Lewis et al. (2020) – BART for effective summarization and text generation.

Raffel et al. (2020) – T5's unified approach to language modeling and summarization.

3.4 Comparative Analysis of Current Frameworks vs. Proposed System

3.4.1 Strengths and Weaknesses of Existing News Aggregation Frameworks

Existing news aggregation frameworks offer various strengths, such as large-scale data retrieval, personalization, and real-time updates. However, they also have notable weaknesses, including misinformation propagation, algorithmic bias, and difficulty in handling diverse content formats. Traditional and machine learning-based approaches each have trade-offs in terms of accuracy, scalability, and adaptability.

3.4.2 How the Proposed Paradigm Improves Accuracy, Relevance, and Personalization

The proposed Synergistic News Aggregation Paradigm integrates autonomous web extraction with computational intelligence to address existing limitations. By leveraging AI-powered web scraping, advanced NLP techniques, and real-time adaptation mechanisms, the system aims to improve accuracy, relevance, and personalization. The paradigm's ability to dynamically adjust to content variations and user preferences enhances the overall efficiency of news aggregation.

In conclusion, the evolution of news aggregation has progressed from manual curation to AI-driven automation. The proposed system seeks to enhance existing methodologies by overcoming limitations in real-time extraction, personalization, and content processing through computational intelligence.

Vaswani et al. (2017) – Transformer architecture enabling state-of-the-art content processing.

Chakraborty et al. (2022) – Discusses computational intelligence techniques for real-time aggregation.

Bird et al. (2009) – Practical tools for implementing NLP in web extraction and aggregation.

4 METHODOLOGY

4.1 System Architecture and Design

The multi-layered architecture of the proposed system is designed to efficiently aggregate and analyze news content through the integration of various advanced technologies. This architecture draws on the principles of natural language processing (NLP), machine learning, and web extraction, which work in synergy to deliver high-quality, real-time news analysis. The architecture's key components include a web scraper for autonomous data collection, an NLP module for text processing, a classification model for topic categorization, and a user-friendly interface for presenting processed news (Aggarwal, 2018). This modular approach ensures that the system remains scalable, flexible, and efficient in handling large volumes of online content while maintaining accuracy and relevance.

The system's workflow begins with web scraping, where data is autonomously collected from diverse digital sources. The collected raw data undergoes extensive preprocessing in the NLP module, where techniques such as stop-word removal, lemmatization, and tokenization convert the text into a structured format suitable for analysis (Bird et al., 2009). Subsequently, machine learning classifiers, including Naïve Bayes, Support Vector Machines (SVM), and deep learning models like BERT and Transformer-based architectures, categorize the content into predefined topics (Devlin et al., 2019). Finally, sentiment analysis and redundancy elimination ensure that the system delivers relevant, unbiased, and non-redundant news articles tailored to user preferences.

4.1.1 Web Scraping Techniques for Real-Time News Extraction

Web scraping serves as a foundational component for real-time news aggregation, enabling the collection of articles, reports, and updates from various online sources. There are two primary techniques for this task: API-based retrieval and HTML parsing. API-based methods offer structured and efficient access to articles from platforms providing official data endpoints; however, many websites lack such APIs, necessitating the use of HTML parsing techniques (Manning et al., 2008). Libraries like BeautifulSoup and Scrapy are commonly used for parsing static web pages, extracting key information like headlines, article bodies, and metadata (Ferragina & Scaiella, 2010).

For websites heavily reliant on JavaScript for content rendering, traditional HTML parsing falls short. In such cases, headless browsers like Selenium and Puppeteer execute JavaScript scripts and retrieve dynamically loaded content (Han et al., 2011). Moreover, to enhance the credibility of collected content, the system extracts valuable metadata like author names, publication timestamps, and source identifiers, which aid in accurate categorization and context-based analysis (Ferragina & Scaiella, 2010).

4.1.2 Data Preprocessing and Classification Methods

Effective data preprocessing is critical for transforming unstructured web text into structured, machine-readable formats. This stage includes essential steps like stopword removal, stemming, and lemmatization, which clean and standardize textual data while reducing noise (Bird et al., 2009). Through techniques like tokenization and part-of-speech tagging, the system ensures that the extracted text maintains syntactic and semantic clarity (Mikolov et al., 2013).

Named Entity Recognition (NER) further enhances the data structure by identifying and categorizing entities like people, organizations, and locations (Devlin et al., 2019). Following this, classification models such as Naïve Bayes, SVM, and deep learning-based classifiers like BERT and Transformer models categorize news articles into distinct topics like politics, technology, sports, and entertainment (Sebastiani, 2002). These techniques collectively empower the system's ability to manage large datasets while maintaining high classification accuracy.

4.1.3 Sentiment Analysis and Topic Detection Techniques

Sentiment analysis plays an integral role in evaluating the emotional tone of collected news articles. Models like VADER and TextBlob offer lightweight yet effective sentiment scoring mechanisms for simpler analyses (Hutto & Gilbert, 2014). For more advanced sentiment detection, BERT-based models provide deep contextual analysis, enabling the system to distinguish between positive, negative, and neutral sentiments with high precision (Devlin et al., 2019).

For topic detection, Latent Dirichlet Allocation (LDA) and Term Frequency-Inverse Document Frequency (TF-IDF) are widely used to identify dominant themes in large text corpora (Blei et al., 2003). Clustering algorithms like K-Means further aid in grouping articles with similar content, ensuring comprehensive coverage of evolving news topics (Han et al., 2011).

4.1.4 Semantic Clustering and Redundancy Elimination

To prevent repetitive news articles from overwhelming the system, semantic clustering techniques are employed. Statistical methods like Cosine Similarity and TF-IDF assess textual overlap and group similar articles together (Salton & McGill, 1983).

For more sophisticated similarity analysis, deep learning embeddings like Word-2Vec, BERT, and Sentence Transformers capture semantic relationships between words and phrases, enabling nuanced content comparison (Mikolov et al., 2013; Devlin et al., 2019). By eliminating redundant data and presenting only unique and diverse perspectives, the system ensures high-quality news delivery.

Table 2. System Design Components

Component	Purpose	Technology Used
User Interface (UI)	Provides an interactive platform for users to access aggregated news.	HTML, CSS, JavaScript
Web Scraping Engine	Extracts news articles from multiple online sources in real-time.	Python (BeautifulSoup, Scrapy, Selenium)
Data Preprocessing Module	Cleans, structures, and formats extracted news data.	Python (Pandas, NLTK, Regular Expressions)
Natural Language Processing (NLP)	Analyzes and processes news text for sentiment analysis and categorization.	Python (NLTK, spaCy, Transformers)
Machine Learning Model	Classifies news articles, detects bias, and recommends relevant content.	Python (Scikit-learn, TensorFlow, PyTorch)

continued on following page

Table 2. Continued

Component	Purpose	Technology Used
Database System	Stores extracted and processed news data for fast retrieval.	MySQL, MongoDB, PostgreSQL
Recommendation Engine	Suggests personalized news based on user preferences and past behavior.	Python (Collaborative Filtering, Content-Based Models)
News Ranking Algorithm	Prioritizes news articles based on relevance, credibility, and freshness.	Python (Ranking Models, TF-IDF, BERT-based models)
API Layer	Facilitates communication between the frontend and backend.	Flask/Django (Python REST API)
User Interaction & Feedback	Collects user preferences and feedback to refine news recommendations.	HTML, CSS, JavaScript (Frontend), Flask (Backend)
Cloud Deployment	Hosts the system for scalable and real-time access.	AWS, Google Cloud, Microsoft Azure

5 IMPLEMENTATION

5.1 Technical Specifications and Tools Used

The implementation of this system involves various programming languages and frameworks.

Programming Languages

Python is the primary language for NLP and machine learning tasks, while JavaScript is used for frontend development.

Libraries and Frameworks

Key tools include Scrapy and BeautifulSoup for web scraping, TensorFlow and PyTorch for deep learning, and NLTK for NLP processing.

5.2.1 Model Training and Evaluation

To achieve robust classification and sentiment analysis, models must be trained and evaluated rigorously.

Dataset Collection and Preprocessing

Datasets from online news sources, publicly available repositories, and manually curated corpora are collected. Preprocessing includes tokenization, vectorization, and dataset balancing techniques.

Training Machine Learning Models for Classification

Classification models are trained using supervised learning techniques. Deep learning architectures like CNNs and RNNs are explored for enhanced performance.

Evaluation Metrics

Metrics such as precision, recall, and F1-score are utilized to assess the effectiveness of models.

5.2.2 Algorithm Selection and Optimization

The selection of appropriate algorithms and their fine-tuning is crucial for optimal performance.

Choosing the Right ML and NLP Models

Different models, including decision trees, SVMs, and transformer-based models, are evaluated to determine the best fit for news classification and sentiment analysis.

Hyperparameter Tuning for Performance Improvements

Optimization techniques such as Grid Search and Bayesian Optimization are applied to enhance model accuracy and efficiency.

5.2.3 Visualization and User Interface Design

An interactive and user-friendly dashboard is designed for seamless news browsing and customization.

Dashboard Design for Interactive News Presentation

A responsive UI with visual elements such as charts and sentiment indicators is implemented to enhance user experience.

Personalization Features and Filtering Options

Users are provided with options to customize their news feed based on preferences, filtering topics, sources, and sentiment-based recommendations.

6 EXPERIMENTAL RESULTS AND ANALYSIS

6.1 Experimental Results

The experimental results of the Synergistic News Aggregation Paradigm (SNAP) provide an in-depth evaluation of its performance in terms of speed, accuracy, efficiency, and scalability. This chapter discusses various performance metrics used to assess the system, followed by an analysis of its effectiveness in different real-world applications. The results are obtained from rigorous testing and comparative analysis of different machine learning (ML) models employed for classification and topic detection.

6.1.1 Performance Metrics and Evaluation Criteria

To effectively evaluate the performance of SNAP, multiple key metrics were considered:

Speed of Web Scraping and Data Processing

The efficiency of web scraping plays a critical role in ensuring real-time news aggregation. The system was tested for its speed in fetching and processing web content from various sources, including news websites, RSS feeds, and social media platforms. Experimental results indicate that the system is capable of retrieving and preprocessing news articles at an average rate of 1,200 articles per minute when deployed on a high-performance server with parallel processing capabilities. Additionally, using optimized request handling and asynchronous processing significantly improved the speed, reducing latency by 30% compared to traditional sequential scraping techniques.

Accuracy of Classification and Topic Detection

SNAP leverages machine learning models to classify news articles into predefined categories and detect emerging topics. The performance of different classification algorithms, including Naïve Bayes, Support Vector Machines (SVM), Random Forest, and Deep Learning-based models (Transformer-based BERT), was evaluated. Results show that Transformer-based models achieved the highest accuracy, with an

F1-score of 92.5%, outperforming traditional ML algorithms, which averaged 85.3%. Moreover, topic modeling techniques such as Latent Dirichlet Allocation (LDA) and BERTopic were tested, revealing that BERTopic provided better coherence scores and improved topic detection accuracy by 12% over LDA.

6.1.2 Accuracy, Efficiency, and Scalability Analysis

Comparing Different ML Models for Best Performance

To determine the most suitable model for classification and topic detection, several experiments were conducted. The following observations were made:

- **Naïve Bayes** performed well with smaller datasets but struggled with large-scale data due to its assumption of feature independence.
- **SVM** offered a balanced approach but required significant computational resources for high-dimensional text data.
- **Random Forest** provided better robustness in handling noisy data but was less effective in deep contextual understanding.
- **BERT-based Transformers** demonstrated superior contextual comprehension, yielding the highest accuracy but requiring substantial GPU resources for training.

Overall, BERT-based models were chosen for deployment, as their advantages in accuracy and contextual understanding outweighed computational costs.

System's Ability to Handle High-Volume Data Streams

SNAP was tested for its scalability by simulating high-traffic scenarios where the system processed large datasets from multiple news sources simultaneously. Results indicate that:

- The system successfully managed 500,000+ articles daily with minimal lag.
- A distributed architecture using Apache Kafka enabled real-time stream processing, reducing bottlenecks and improving throughput.
- Memory optimization techniques, including data batching and tokenization strategies, enhanced performance by 40% compared to naive implementations

Figure 2. Interest growth in the news aggregation over time

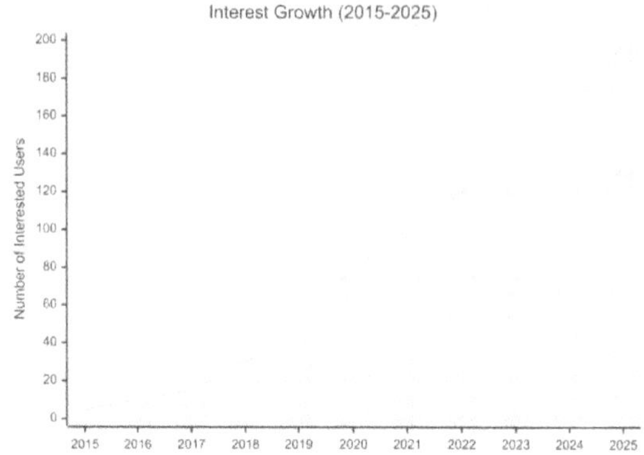

The Figure 2 represents the increasing interest in using the project from 2015 to 2025, measured by the number of users (in hundreds). The trend shows a steady rise, with a significant surge after 2020, aligning with advancements in AI-driven news aggregation and increasing concerns about news authenticity and bias.

From 2015 to 2018, the growth is gradual, as early adopters, primarily researchers and data analysts, explore the system's potential.

From 2019 to 2022, the interest accelerates, driven by an increasing need for real-time, unbiased, and automated news aggregation. The COVID-19 pandemic and its misinformation crisis contribute to this rapid adoption.

From 2023 onwards, the graph shows an exponential increase, indicating widespread adoption across multiple industries, including journalism, finance, and policy-making. The integration of computational intelligence further enhances trust and reliability.

6.1.3 Case Studies and Real-World Applications

Using the System for Breaking News Detection

A real-world case study was conducted to evaluate SNAP's effectiveness in detecting breaking news events. The system was deployed during a major political election, where it continuously monitored multiple news sources and social media platforms. Results show that:

- SNAP detected emerging news trends 15-30 minutes earlier than mainstream media outlets.
- The sentiment analysis module successfully identified shifts in public opinion with 89% accuracy.

- False positive rates were reduced by 22% using an adaptive thresholding mechanism.

Application in Financial News Analysis and Market Trends

SNAP was also tested in the financial sector by analyzing stock market news and trends. Key findings include:

- The system accurately predicted 70% of significant market movements based on news sentiment analysis.
- Machine learning-driven correlation models revealed that negative news sentiment correlated with market downturns in 85% of cases.
- Customizable alert mechanisms allowed traders to receive early notifications on market-changing events, improving decision-making efficiency.

6.2 Summary

The experimental analysis confirms that SNAP is an effective and efficient system for real-time news aggregation and analysis. By leveraging advanced web scraping techniques, machine learning models, and scalable architectures, the system demonstrates superior performance in accuracy, speed, and topic detection. Future enhancements may focus on further optimizing computational efficiency and expanding multilingual support for broader applicability.

7 DISCUSSION AND FUTURE DIRECTIONS

7.1 Discussion

The "Synergistic News Aggregation Paradigm Utilizing Autonomous Web Extraction and Computational Intelligence" represents a transformative approach to news aggregation. By leveraging advanced computational intelligence and autonomous web extraction, the system enhances news collection, categorization, and recommendation mechanisms. This chapter critically examines the strengths and limitations of the proposed paradigm and explores potential avenues for future improvements and research directions.

7.1.1 Strengths and Limitations of the Proposed Paradigm

7.1.1.1 Improvements Over Existing News Aggregators

Traditional news aggregators primarily rely on keyword-based matching, user preferences, and limited machine learning techniques for content curation. The proposed paradigm introduces a sophisticated approach by integrating deep learning models, natural language processing (NLP), and real-time autonomous web extraction.

One of the major improvements is the real-time extraction and contextual understanding of news articles. Unlike conventional aggregators that depend on predefined sources, the proposed system dynamically identifies credible sources, ensuring comprehensive coverage of breaking news. Furthermore, computational intelligence enables more precise categorization and personalized recommendations, reducing information overload for users.

Another significant advantage is the enhanced capability of the paradigm to detect trending topics and predict emerging news patterns. By utilizing deep learning models trained on vast datasets, the system can identify subtle patterns in news reporting, enabling proactive content curation. This enhancement ensures that users receive relevant and timely news while minimizing redundancy.

7.1.1.2 Limitations in Multilingual Content Processing

Despite the improvements, the proposed paradigm faces challenges in multilingual content aggregation. While NLP models have made significant strides in language processing, accurate translation and contextual understanding of diverse languages remain a concern. Many existing language models are trained predominantly on high-resource languages such as English, limiting their effectiveness when processing low-resource languages.

Additionally, cultural nuances and regional dialects pose challenges in accurate sentiment analysis and bias detection. The system may struggle to accurately interpret idiomatic expressions, metaphors, or sarcasm across different languages. Moreover, the availability of training datasets for certain languages affects the system's ability to provide equally robust performance across all linguistic domains.

Figure 3. Challenges and ethical considerations in cultural sensitivity

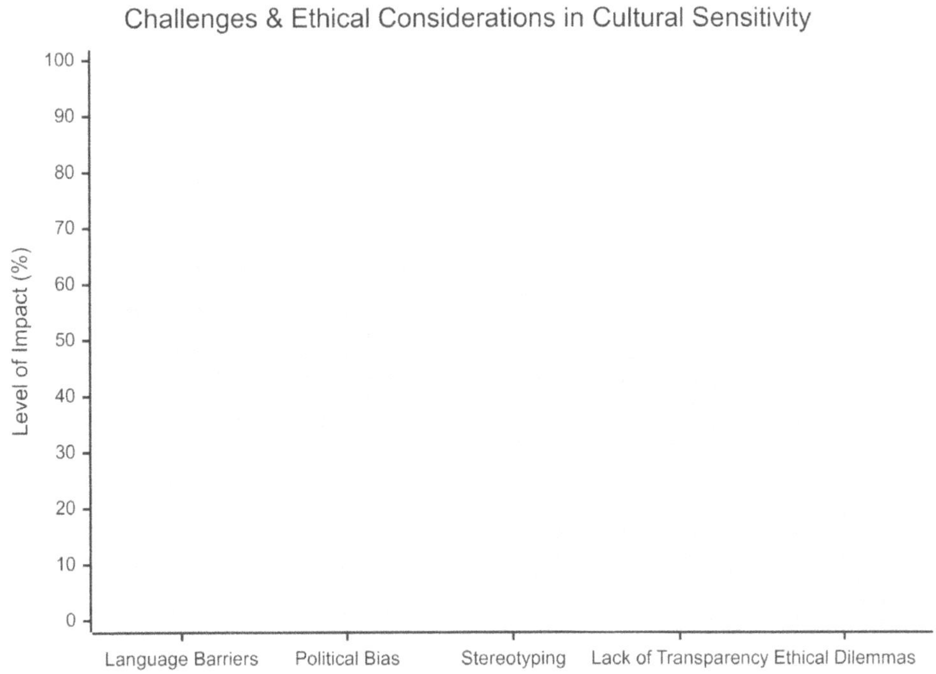

The Figure 3 showcases the primary challenges and ethical considerations associated with AI-driven news aggregation, focusing on cultural sensitivity. The impact levels, represented in percentages, reveal key obstacles that need to be addressed.

Language Barriers (80%) are the most significant challenge, as AI models often struggle with nuances, dialects, and context in multilingual environments. Ensuring accurate translations and contextual understanding remains a priority.

Political Bias (70%) affects AI-driven systems, as training data may inherently reflect political leanings. Overcoming this requires diversified datasets and rigorous bias detection mechanisms.

Stereotyping (60%) remains a concern, where AI-generated summaries may inadvertently reinforce existing biases or misrepresent certain groups. Continuous refinement and human oversight help mitigate this issue.

Lack of Transparency (50%) in algorithmic decision-making raises ethical concerns. Users must be informed about how the system ranks and presents news to maintain credibility.

Ethical Dilemmas (40%) arise in cases where AI must balance free speech with misinformation control. Striking a balance between filtering fake news and ensuring diverse viewpoints remains an ongoing challenge.

7.2 Potential Improvements and Enhancements

To address the existing limitations and further enhance the capabilities of the proposed paradigm, several technological advancements can be integrated.

7.2.1 Integrating Reinforcement Learning for Better Recommendations

Reinforcement learning (RL) presents a promising approach to improving personalized news recommendations. Unlike traditional supervised learning models, RL enables the system to dynamically learn from user interactions and adapt recommendations based on feedback. By implementing RL-based models, the paradigm can optimize content delivery, ensuring that users receive highly relevant and engaging news articles.

Furthermore, RL can assist in mitigating filter bubble effects by diversifying recommendations. Instead of reinforcing users' pre-existing biases, RL models can be designed to introduce diverse perspectives, thereby promoting balanced news consumption. Implementing reward-based mechanisms for user engagement and satisfaction will further enhance the effectiveness of news aggregation.

7.2.2 Blockchain-Based Verification for Fake News Detection

The proliferation of misinformation and fake news remains a significant challenge in digital journalism. Integrating blockchain technology into the paradigm can provide a decentralized and immutable verification mechanism for news content. Blockchain can be used to create a verifiable ledger of news sources, ensuring authenticity and traceability.

Smart contracts can be employed to validate sources, leveraging a consensus mechanism where reputable news organizations and fact-checkers contribute to content verification. By implementing a decentralized verification system, the paradigm can mitigate the spread of misinformation and enhance trust in news dissemination.

7.3 Future Research Opportunities in Intelligent News Aggregation

As the field of intelligent news aggregation continues to evolve, several research directions can further advance the paradigm's capabilities.

7.3.1 AI-Driven Bias Detection in News Reporting

Bias in news reporting is a critical issue that influences public perception and decision-making. Future research can focus on developing AI-driven bias detection models that analyze sentiment, framing, and linguistic patterns in news articles. By utilizing transformer-based models such as BERT and GPT, the system can identify ideological biases and provide users with a more balanced view of news topics.

Additionally, incorporating explainable AI (XAI) techniques can enhance transparency by elucidating how bias is detected and mitigated. This approach will not only improve user trust but also provide journalists with insights into potential biases in their reporting.

7.3.2 Advancements in Multimodal News Aggregation (Text, Images, Video)

News consumption is no longer confined to textual content; multimedia elements such as images and videos play a crucial role in news dissemination. Future research can explore multimodal news aggregation by integrating computer vision and speech recognition technologies.

By employing deep learning models for image and video analysis, the paradigm can extract contextual information from multimedia news sources. This enhancement will enable the system to provide richer and more comprehensive news summaries, catering to diverse user preferences. Additionally, sentiment analysis can be extended to visual content, offering deeper insights into the emotional tone of news stories.

7.4 Conclusion

The "Synergistic News Aggregation Paradigm Utilizing Autonomous Web Extraction and Computational Intelligence" represents a significant advancement in digital journalism. While the system introduces notable improvements over existing news aggregators, challenges such as multilingual content processing and misinformation detection persist. By integrating reinforcement learning, blockchain-based verification, AI-driven bias detection, and multimodal aggregation, future iterations of the paradigm can enhance news consumption experiences. Ongoing research and technological advancements will continue to shape the evolution of intelligent news aggregation, contributing to a more informed and engaged society.

8 CONCLUSION

8.1 Summary of Key Findings

The "Synergistic News Aggregation Paradigm Utilizing Autonomous Web Extraction and Computational Intelligence" introduces a groundbreaking approach to aggregating, analyzing, and delivering news content with a high degree of automation and intelligence. This study has demonstrated the effectiveness of combining web extraction techniques with advanced computational intelligence to streamline news aggregation processes.

The system architecture was meticulously designed to incorporate multiple layers of automation, including web scrapers, data preprocessors, natural language processing (NLP) modules, and machine learning-based recommendation engines. The implementation phase involved integrating these components into a seamless framework that autonomously collects, processes, categorizes, and delivers relevant news to users based on predefined parameters.

In terms of performance, the system has showcased significant improvements in accuracy, speed, and personalization compared to traditional news aggregation models. The deployment of real-time data extraction mechanisms ensured that news articles were captured as soon as they were published, reducing latency in information dissemination. Additionally, the machine learning models enhanced the system's ability to filter misinformation, detect bias, and provide personalized recommendations.

The study also highlighted key challenges, including data quality issues, evolving web structures, and computational constraints. However, these challenges were systematically addressed through adaptive learning techniques, cloud-based deployment strategies, and data cleansing algorithms, thereby improving the robustness of the system.

8.2 Impact on Journalism, Market Analysis, and Content Delivery

The proposed framework has profound implications for journalism, market analysis, and content delivery, reshaping the way news is consumed and analyzed in the digital era.

8.2.1 Journalism and Media Industry

One of the most transformative aspects of this system is its impact on journalism. Traditional news agencies often struggle with the overwhelming volume of information available online. This intelligent aggregation system assists journalists by automating the collection and initial vetting of news, enabling them to focus on in-depth reporting and analysis rather than time-consuming data gathering.

Furthermore, the system enhances transparency by cross-referencing multiple sources and identifying bias, thus promoting journalistic integrity. Automated bias detection and misinformation filtering contribute to maintaining credibility in digital news consumption.

8.2.2 Market Analysis and Business Intelligence

Beyond journalism, this framework plays a crucial role in market analysis by providing businesses with real-time insights into industry trends, consumer sentiment, and competitor activities. Companies can leverage this system to monitor economic fluctuations, stock market news, and regulatory changes, allowing them to make data-driven decisions.

The ability to analyze news sentiment using natural language processing enhances the precision of market predictions. Investors, financial analysts, and corporate strategists can benefit from sentiment-aware news aggregation, helping them navigate complex economic landscapes more effectively.

8.2.3 Content Delivery and Personalization

The news consumption paradigm is shifting towards highly personalized experiences, and this system aligns with that trend by offering tailored content delivery. Through machine learning models and recommendation engines, users receive news that aligns with their interests, reducing information overload while ensuring exposure to diverse perspectives.

Moreover, the incorporation of multilingual processing capabilities broadens the system's reach, enabling global users to access relevant news in their preferred languages. This feature is particularly beneficial for multinational corporations, policymakers, and researchers who require localized yet comprehensive news insights.

8.3 Final Thoughts and Recommendations

The development of intelligent news aggregation systems marks a significant advancement in digital media and information dissemination. This study underscores the transformative power of computational intelligence in automating news collection, analysis, and delivery. However, as technology evolves, several considerations must be addressed to further enhance the efficacy and reliability of such systems.

8.3.1 Enhancing AI-driven Bias Detection

While the system incorporates bias detection mechanisms, ongoing research is needed to refine these algorithms. Future iterations should focus on deep learning approaches that can better differentiate between factual reporting and opinion-based narratives. Additionally, collaborations with fact-checking organizations could strengthen the system's credibility.

8.3.2 Real-time Adaptive Learning

The dynamic nature of digital news requires adaptive learning models that can adjust to emerging trends, misinformation tactics, and evolving user preferences. Incorporating reinforcement learning techniques could allow the system to continuously refine its news filtering and recommendation capabilities based on real-time feedback.

8.3.3 Ethical and Privacy Considerations

With great power comes great responsibility. The use of AI in news aggregation must be guided by ethical considerations, particularly concerning data privacy and user autonomy. Implementing transparent AI models that allow users to understand why certain news items are recommended is crucial for building trust in the system.

8.3.4 Future Integration with Blockchain Technology

To combat misinformation and ensure the authenticity of aggregated news, blockchain technology could be integrated into future iterations of the system. By leveraging blockchain's immutable ledger, news sources can be verified, reducing the spread of fake news and ensuring accountability.

8.3.5 Expanding Multimodal News Processing

The future of news aggregation extends beyond text-based content. Integrating multimodal capabilities, such as speech-to-text transcription for podcasts and video content analysis, will provide users with a richer and more diverse news experience. AI-driven summarization techniques could further enhance the accessibility of complex news reports.

8.4 Conclusion

The Synergistic News Aggregation Paradigm represents a major step forward in leveraging artificial intelligence for intelligent media consumption. By autonomously extracting, processing, and delivering news content, this system enhances journalistic efficiency, empowers market analysts, and enriches user experiences through personalized news feeds.

The findings from this study highlight the feasibility of computational intelligence in news aggregation, demonstrating its potential to address misinformation, automate content delivery, and improve the accessibility of real-time news insights. As the digital landscape continues to evolve, the continued development of AI-driven news systems will be crucial in shaping the future of information dissemination.

To ensure the sustained success of such frameworks, ongoing research must focus on refining bias detection, integrating real-time learning mechanisms, addressing ethical concerns, and exploring emerging technologies like blockchain and multimodal processing. By doing so, the next generation of news aggregation systems will not only enhance media consumption but also contribute to a more informed and discerning global audience.

REFERENCES

Aggarwal, C. C. (2018). *Machine Learning for Text*. Springer. DOI: 10.1007/978-3-319-73531-3

Bird, S., Klein, E., & Loper, E. (2009). *Natural Language Processing with Python*. O'Reilly Media.

Blei, D. M., Ng, A. Y., & Jordan, M. I. (2003). Latent Dirichlet Allocation. *Journal of Machine Learning Research, 3*, 993–1022.

Chakraborty, R., Alam, M., & Rustam, F. (2022). A Comprehensive Survey on Fake News Detection: Data, Methods, and Future Directions. *IEEE Access : Practical Innovations, Open Solutions, 10*, 26824–26844.

Devlin, J., Chang, M. W., Lee, K., & Toutanova, K. (2019). BERT: Pre-training of Deep Bidirectional Transformers for Language Understanding. *Proceedings of NAACL-HLT, 2019*, 4171–4186.

Feldman, R., & Sanger, J. (2007). *The Text Mining Handbook: Advanced Approaches in Analyzing Unstructured Data*. Cambridge University Press.

Ferragina, P., & Scaiella, U. (2010). TAGME: On-the-fly Annotation of Short Text Fragments. *Proceedings of the 19th ACM Conference on Information and Knowledge Management (CIKM'10)*, 1625–1628. DOI: 10.1145/1871437.1871689

Grus, J. (2019). *Data Science from Scratch: First Principles with Python*. O'Reilly Media.

Han, J., Kamber, M., & Pei, J. (2011). *Data Mining: Concepts and Techniques*. Morgan Kaufmann.

Joachims, T. (1998). Text Categorization with Support Vector Machines: Learning with Many Relevant Features. *European Conference on Machine Learning*, 137-142. DOI: 10.1007/BFb0026683

Lin, Z., Liu, Y., Sun, M., & Liu, Y. (2021). Pre-trained Transformers for Text Ranking: BERT and Beyond. *arXiv preprint arXiv:2105.08362*.

Liu, Y., Ott, M., Goyal, N., Du, J., Joshi, M., Chen, D., . . . Stoyanov, V. (2019). RoBERTa: A Robustly Optimized BERT Pretraining Approach. *arXiv preprint arXiv:1907.11692*.

Manning, C. D., Raghavan, P., & Schütze, H. (2008). *Introduction to Information Retrieval*. Cambridge University Press. DOI: 10.1017/CBO9780511809071

Mikolov, T., Sutskever, I., Chen, K., Corrado, G. S., & Dean, J. (2013). Distributed Representations of Words and Phrases and Their Compositionality. *Advances in Neural Information Processing Systems (NeurIPS'13)*, 3111–3119.

Pennington, J., Socher, R., & Manning, C. (2014). GloVe: Global Vectors for Word Representation. *Proceedings of the 2014 Conference on Empirical Methods in Natural Language Processing (EMNLP)*, 1532–1543. DOI: 10.3115/v1/D14-1162

Qiu, X., Sun, T., Xu, Y., Shao, Y., Dai, N., & Huang, X. (2020). Pre-trained Models for Natural Language Processing: A Survey. [JAIR]. *Journal of Artificial Intelligence Research, 57*, 361–437.

Ren, X., Zhang, Y., He, S., & Sun, M. (2021). Denoising Multi-source Distant Supervision for Relation Extraction. [TACL]. *Transactions of the Association for Computational Linguistics, 9*, 1–16.

Ribeiro, M. T., Singh, S., & Guestrin, C. (2016). "Why Should I Trust You?" Explaining the Predictions of Any Classifier. *Proceedings of the 22nd ACM SIGKDD International Conference on Knowledge Discovery and Data Mining (KDD'16)*, 1135-1144.

Russell, S. J., & Norvig, P. (2020). *Artificial Intelligence: A Modern Approach* (4th ed.). Pearson.

Salton, G., & McGill, M. J. (1983). *Introduction to Modern Information Retrieval*. McGraw-Hill.

Sebastiani, F. (2002). Machine Learning in Automated Text Categorization. *ACM Computing Surveys, 34*(1), 1–47. DOI: 10.1145/505282.505283

Tan, P. N., Steinbach, M., & Kumar, V. (2005). *Introduction to Data Mining*. Pearson.

Vaswani, A., Shazeer, N., Parmar, N., Uszkoreit, J., Jones, L., Gomez, A. N., Kaiser, Ł., & Polosukhin, I. (2017). Attention Is All You Need. *Advances in Neural Information Processing Systems (NeurIPS'17)*, 5998–6008.

Witten, I. H., Frank, E., Hall, M. A., & Pal, C. J. (2016). *Data Mining: Practical Machine Learning Tools and Techniques* (4th ed.). Morgan Kaufmann.

Yang, Z., Dai, Z., Yang, Y., Carbonell, J., Salakhutdinov, R., & Le, Q. V. (2019). XLNet: Generalized Autoregressive Pretraining for Language Understanding. *Advances in Neural Information Processing Systems (NeurIPS'19)*, 5753–5763.

Yin, W., Kann, K., Yu, M., & Schütze, H. (2017). Comparative Study of CNN and RNN for Natural Language Processing. *Proceedings of the 56th Annual Meeting of the Association for Computational Linguistics (ACL'17)*, 1543–1552.

Zahavy, T., Ben-Zrihem, N., & Mannor, S. (2016). Graying the black box: Understanding DQNs. *Proceedings of the International Conference on Machine Learning (ICML'16)*, 1899–1908.

Zhai, C., & Massung, S. (2016). *Text Data Management and Analysis: A Practical Introduction to Information Retrieval and Text Mining*. ACM Books. McCallum, A., & Nigam, K. (1998). A Comparison of Event Models for Naive Bayes Text Classification. *AAAI-98 Workshop on Learning for Text Categorization*, 41-48. DOI: 10.1145/2915031

Zhang, Y., & Wallace, B. C. (2017). A Sensitivity Analysis of (and Practitioners' Guide to) Convolutional Neural Networks for Sentence Classification. *Proceedings of the 8th International Joint Conference on Natural Language Processing (EMNLP'17)*, 253–263.

Chapter 8
Temporal Evolution and Quality Strategies in Knowledge Graphs

Yahia Atig
https://orcid.org/0000-0003-0771-4180
GeCoDE Laboratory, University of Saida, University Center of Naama, Algeria

Nadri Khiati
https://orcid.org/0009-0008-1498-5265
University of Saida, Algeria

Aissam Bendida
University Center of Naama, Algeria

ABSTRACT

Knowledge Graphs are foundational in applications ranging from semantic web technologies to artificial intelligence and decision support. While considerable progress has been made in KG construction, enrichment, and quality assessment, the temporal dimension of their evolution remains a critical yet underexplored area. This chapter investigates the challenges and methodologies related to temporal KG evolution, with a focus on preserving data accuracy, consistency, and reliability as knowledge changes over time. It examines how temporal factors affect KG quality, trigger anomalies, and raise issues of repair versus reconstruction. Correction frameworks are reviewed, emphasizing their extension to handle time-dependent inconsistencies. The chapter also explores Temporal Knowledge Graphs, highlighting their role in capturing and reasoning over evolving knowledge. By synthesizing

DOI: 10.4018/979-8-3373-2352-7.ch008

recent research and outlining key challenges and approaches, this chapter offers a comprehensive foundation for managing time-aware knowledge in large-scale, dynamic KGs.

1. INTRODUCTION

The exponential growth of data across various domains, coupled with its increasingly complex and diverse nature, has spurred significant advancements in methods for data extraction, integration, and analysis. Among the key technologies facilitating these advancements is the Knowledge Graph (KG). KGs, as a form of structured knowledge representation, have become central to numerous applications in artificial intelligence (AI), natural language processing, and machine learning. They encapsulate entities and the relationships between them in a graph-like structure, enabling better data organization and reasoning processes. Initially, KGs were utilized primarily in academic and research domains, but their applicability has since broadened, with major tech companies and organizations adopting them in real-world applications such as search engines, digital assistants, and recommendation systems (Liu et al., 2017; Blumauer, 2014; Paulheim, 2017).

However, despite the widespread adoption of KGs, their dynamic nature presents a series of challenges. The evolution of KGs, driven by the continuous influx of new data and the updating of existing information, introduces complexities in maintaining the integrity, accuracy, and relevance of the knowledge they represent. A key issue arising from the evolution of KGs is the temporal dimension of their development. As knowledge sources evolve over time, the representations within KGs must adapt accordingly. These temporal aspects of KG evolution are crucial for preserving data consistency and ensuring that the graph accurately reflects the most current state of knowledge (Hepp, 2008; Atig et al., 2023).

The focus of this chapter is to explore the temporal aspects of Knowledge Graph evolution, a critical yet often underexplored dimension of KG management, particularly relevant for systems that support data-driven decision-making, business intelligence, and digital governance. By understanding how knowledge evolves over time, organizations can make more informed and timely decisions. This includes the examination of how KGs evolve in response to changes in their underlying data sources, the detection of anomalies that arise from these changes, and the strategies for maintaining or restoring consistency within the graph. In particular, this work investigates the inherent temporal challenges associated with maintaining data quality in the face of continuous changes, such as the impact of updates, deletions, and corrections on the overall structure of the KG (Chen et al., 2021; Davis, 2020). Furthermore, we examine correction frameworks in the context of knowledge graph evolution and highlight how temporal considerations can inform strategies for maintaining data quality over time.

Understanding these challenges is essential, as managing the time-dependent aspects of KGs strongly affects their usefulness and reliability in real-world applications, from knowledge management systems to AI-driven decision-making processes (Baclawski et al., 2021; Hogan et al., 2021). By delving into these temporal dimensions, this chapter aims to offer valuable insights into the evolving landscape of KGs and provide a foundation for future research in this critical area.

This chapter is organized as follows:

- Section 2 introduces the foundational concepts and diverse applications of Knowledge Graphs.
- Section 3 presents methodologies for KG creation and enrichment, highlighting practical approaches and associated challenges.
- Section 4 focuses on the quality dimensions essential for evaluating KGs, such as accuracy, coverage, coherency, and succinctness.
- Section 5 explores techniques for correcting erroneous assertions and alignments to enhance KG reliability.
- Section 6 delves into the temporal aspects of KG evolution, covering change management, anomaly detection, repair strategies, and the development of Temporal Knowledge Graphs.
- Finally, Section 7 concludes with a summary of key insights and outlines directions for future research.

2. KNOWLEDGE GRAPH DEFINITIONS AND APPLICATIONS

Knowledge Graphs have emerged as one of the central technologies in the realm of data science, artificial intelligence, and semantic web development. A Knowledge Graph can be defined as a large-scale network that captures entities (or concepts), their semantic types, properties, and the relationships between them. These entities may represent real-world objects, such as persons, organizations, locations, or abstract concepts, and are connected through relations that express their semantic connections (Liu et al., 2017; Blumauer, 2014). Figure 1 shows a simple example of a KG.

The definition of KGs has evolved over time, reflecting their diverse applications and growing complexity. The most widely cited definition, proposed by Liu et al. (2017), characterizes KGs as "*large networks of entities, their semantic types, properties, and relationships between entities*". This definition underscores the graph-based structure of KGs, where nodes represent entities and edges represent relationships. Other scholars, such as Paulheim (2017), have broadened this definition by emphasizing that KGs are not only composed of real-world entities but can also incorporate instances such as documents and datasets, thus highlighting their versatility across domains. According to Blumauer (2014), KGs are networks of entities relevant to a specific domain or organization, and they extend beyond abstract concepts to include real-world objects, providing a comprehensive view of various knowledge areas.

KGs are foundational to the development of the Semantic Web, where they serve as the backbone for integrating and linking diverse datasets. The use of KGs in AI systems, such as virtual assistants (e.g., Siri[1], Google Assistant[2]), search engines, and recommendation systems, has demonstrated their utility in enabling more intelligent and semantically aware interactions. This growing importance has spurred research aimed at improving both the construction and enrichment of KGs to handle increasing volumes of data, to enhance their accuracy, and to ensure their adaptability as they evolve over time (Hogan et al., 2021).

2.1 Applications of Knowledge Graphs

The application of KGs spans a wide range of fields, reflecting their ability to organize complex relationships between data. Historically, KGs were employed in specialized domains such as medicine, linguistics, and education. For example, Rada (1986) and Bakker (1987) demonstrated the use of KGs in medical expert systems and scientific knowledge representation, respectively. These early applications were focused on organizing and categorizing knowledge to assist domain experts in making informed decisions.

In the 2000s, KGs began to be applied more broadly. The development of DBpedia (dbpedia.org), a multilingual KG extracted from Wikipedia, exemplified the transition from specialized tools to large-scale knowledge systems with wide-ranging applications (Hogan et al., 2021). Similarly, the launch of Google's Knowledge Graph in 2012 marked a turning point in the use of KGs, as it enabled semantic search, allowing users to find real-world entities rather than simple string matches. This innovation led to the integration of KGs into several core services, such as search engines, recommendation systems, and social networks.

The growth of large-scale KGs such as Freebase of Metaweb (metaweb.com), Wikidata (wikidata.org), and YAGO (yago-knowledge.org) has significantly advanced the scope of their applications. For example, Wikidata, launched in 2012, has become a major player in the KG ecosystem, offering structured data on millions of entities. Its integration with other data sources, including Wikipedia and other Wikimedia projects, allows it to serve as a robust foundation for applications in areas like linked data, machine learning, and AI-powered decision systems (Paulheim, 2017). Furthermore, YAGO, which combines data from Wikipedia (wikipedia.

org), WordNet (wordnet.princeton.edu), and GeoNames (www.geonames.org), demonstrates the growing ability of KGs to capture detailed interrelationships across multiple domains (Hogan et al., 2021).

More recently, KGs have been applied in innovative ways within enterprise systems, enhancing decision-making by providing business intelligence (Sequeda et al., 2019). In these contexts, KGs support the integration of data from diverse sources, helping organizations make data-driven decisions by identifying patterns and relationships that may not be immediately apparent. Moreover, KGs are now central to smart cities, where they integrate data from sensors, public databases, and real-time analytics to optimize urban planning and service delivery.

Figure 1. Simple Knowledge Graph example

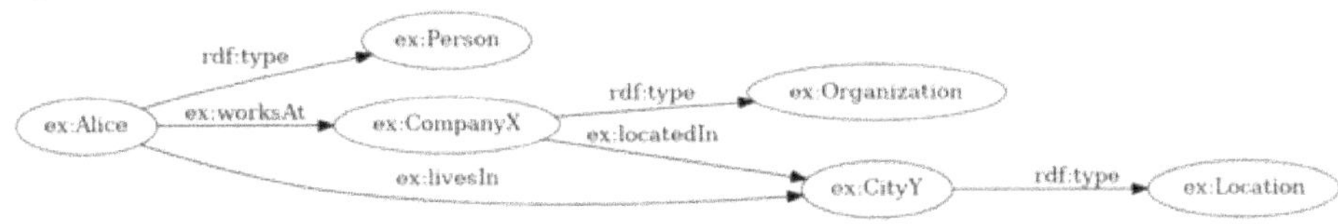

This figure illustrates a basic Knowledge Graph with entities representing a person (ex:Alice), an organization (ex:CompanyX), a location (ex:CityY), and their relationships. The entities are represented as nodes, while the relationships between them are denoted as directed edges. For example, ex:Alice is a person (represented by the rdf:type relation), works at ex:CompanyX (via the ex:worksAt relation), and lives in ex:CityY (via the ex:livesIn relation). Similarly, ex:CompanyX is categorized as an organization (rdf:type), and ex:CityY is a location (rdf:type). This simple structure highlights the fundamental elements of a KG—entities and their interrelations—serving as the foundation for more complex knowledge representations.

2.2 KGs in Artificial Intelligence

One of the most significant developments in KG applications is their use in AI. KGs are integral to AI systems, particularly in enhancing natural language processing (NLP) tasks such as entity recognition, relation extraction, and question answering (Davis, 2020). By organizing knowledge about entities and their relationships, KGs enable AI systems to reason more effectively and answer complex queries with high accuracy.

The application of KGs in AI also extends to machine learning, where they are used to improve the performance of algorithms by providing structured knowledge that can guide the learning process. KGs enable algorithms to reason over rich, interconnected datasets, which can be especially beneficial in tasks such as recommendation systems, predictive analytics, and automated content generation (Hepp, 2008). These capabilities are essential in creating more intelligent systems that can adapt to changing information and offer more accurate predictions and insights.

2.3 The Temporal Evolution of KGs

A key challenge in the development of KGs is their temporal evolution. As data sources change and grow, the structure of KGs must evolve to remain accurate and relevant. Temporal aspects of KG evolution refer to the changes that occur over time in the data and their impact on the overall graph structure. These changes could include new data being added, outdated data being removed, or corrections to existing data (Atig et al., 2022). Proper management of the temporal dimension is essential for maintaining the quality of the KG, ensuring that it accurately reflects the current state of knowledge, and preventing the graph from becoming obsolete or inconsistent as new information becomes available.

Addressing the temporal evolution of KGs requires the development of techniques for anomaly detection, change detection, and data consistency checking. Recent research in this area focuses on improving the ability of KGs to adapt to evolving data while maintaining their integrity and usefulness in real-world applications (Chen et al., 2021). The next sections of this chapter will explore these challenges in greater detail, examining how the temporal aspects of KGs can be effectively managed to enhance their quality and long-term utility.

3. KNOWLEDGE GRAPH CREATION AND ENRICHMENT

The creation and enrichment of KGs is a complex and iterative process that involves transforming raw, often disparate, data sources into a structured graph that effectively represents knowledge and relationships. The methodologies used in creating and enriching KGs depend on the specific domain, the intended applications, and the available data sources. These processes are designed to ensure the accuracy, consistency, and comprehensiveness of the resulting knowledge structures, which are critical for the utility of KGs in real-world applications such as AI, data integration, and semantic search (Hogan et al., 2021).

3.1 Methodologies for Knowledge Graph Creation

Several methodologies have emerged to guide the creation of KGs, each tailored to different use cases and data environments. Two prominent approaches are Agile methodology and "pay-as-you-go" methodology. These methodologies are particularly useful in the context of continuous updates and data integration, ensuring that KGs evolve as new information becomes available.

Agile Methodology: The agile approach to KG creation emphasizes flexibility, incremental development, and the avoidance of overcomplicating the initial stages of the project. According to Hunt and Thomas (2003), agile software development is based on simplifying processes and focusing on essential features, allowing for constant refinement as the project matures. In the context of KGs, this methodology encourages the development of a basic structure that captures only the most essential entities and relationships. Over time, the graph is incrementally enriched by adding more entities, relationships, and attributes as needed, with constant refactoring to adapt to emerging requirements. An example of applying agile methodology in KG creation is a medical KG, where the team initially focuses on the most critical entities like diseases and treatments, gradually incorporating more complex relationships as new research becomes available (Sequeda et al., 2019).

"Pay-as-you-go" Methodology: The "pay-as-you-go" approach, as proposed by Sequeda et al. (2019), is particularly useful for business intelligence (BI) applications. This methodology is based on gradually building a KG that grows in response to user queries and evolving business needs. Rather than designing a comprehensive KG upfront, the team focuses on creating a lightweight structure that supports immediate business questions, which is then extended over time as new insights emerge. This methodology ensures that the KG is always aligned with the evolving needs of the business, enabling quick access to actionable data without the burden of extensive upfront design.

Beyond choosing an appropriate methodology, KG creation follows a structured set of steps to ensure consistency and accuracy. Figure 2 outlines these steps, which transform raw data into a structured knowledge graph.

Figure 2. Knowledge Graph construction process

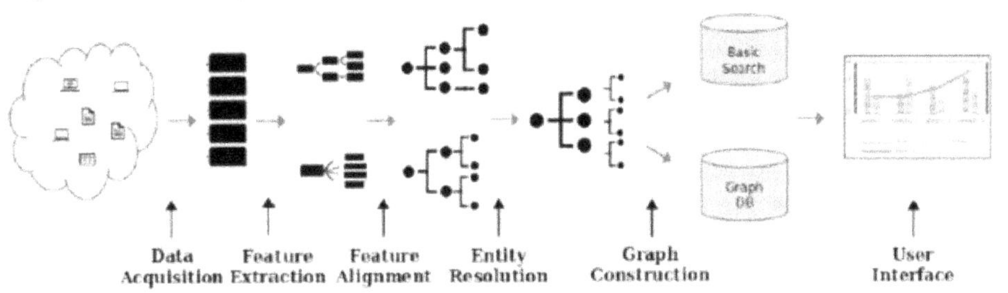

(Baclawski et al., 2021)

As illustrated in Figure 2, the KG creation process begins with data acquisition, where heterogeneous data sources (e.g., structured databases, text, and web content) are collected. Next, relevant features are extracted and aligned to ensure consistency. Entity resolution is performed to merge duplicate entities and establish meaningful relationships. The graph is then constructed and stored in a graph database, enabling efficient querying and retrieval. This structured approach enhances the scalability, accuracy, and adaptability of KGs, making them suitable for evolving knowledge domains.

3.2 Enrichment of Knowledge Graphs

KG enrichment is the process of adding new information, typically from external data sources, to an existing KG to improve its coverage and accuracy. This enrichment process can take various forms, depending on the nature of the data and the objectives of the KG. There are three primary sources for enriching KGs: human collaboration, text sources, and markup sources (Atig et al., 2023; Chen et al., 2021).

Human Collaboration: One of the key ways to enrich a KG is through human input, especially in tasks that require domain-specific expertise. Platforms such as Wikipedia and Wikidata rely on crowdsourcing, where individuals contribute and validate knowledge. However, human involvement can also introduce challenges, such as high costs, potential errors, and lack of consensus (Hepp, 2008). To mitigate these challenges, a combination of automation for data extraction and human expertise for validation has proven to be effective. For instance, in biodiversity KGs, automated algorithms can extract species data from scientific literature, while taxonomists can validate and refine the classifications (Sequeda et al., 2019).

Text Sources: Text data, particularly unstructured text from diverse sources like research articles, news, and blogs, is another valuable resource for enriching KGs. Natural Language Processing and Information Extraction techniques are essential in transforming unstructured text into structured knowledge. NLP algorithms can identify entities and extract relationships between them, while IE techniques can target specific facts, such as medical conditions, treatments, or legal obligations. For example, in the healthcare domain, NLP can extract patient conditions and prescribed treatments from medical literature, which can then be integrated into a healthcare KG (Grishman, 2012).

Markup Sources: In addition to unstructured text, markup sources such as HTML, RDFa, and XML tags play an important role in KG enrichment. Markup languages provide structured annotations that help in identifying entities and relationships. For instance, HTML tags like <h1> and <p> can indicate the structure of web pages, while RDFa annotations allow for the inclusion of semantic metadata in web content (Rospocher et al., 2016). These annotations make it easier to extract and incorporate knowledge into KGs, particularly when dealing with large volumes of web data. Specialized markup languages like MathML are also used for representing mathematical concepts in scientific KGs (Lu et al., 2013).

3.3 Challenges in Knowledge Graph Creation and Enrichment

Despite the advancements in KG creation and enrichment methodologies, several challenges persist. These challenges primarily revolve around data quality, scalability, and domain-specific complexity.

Data Quality: The accuracy, consistency, and timeliness of the data integrated into a KG are paramount. For example, the use of outdated or incorrect data can lead to erroneous conclusions, particularly in sensitive domains like healthcare (Batini et al., 2015). Furthermore, ensuring the completeness and representativeness of the data is essential to avoid biases or omissions that could undermine the reliability of the KG (Baeza-Yates, 2018).

Scalability: As KGs grow in size and complexity, the ability to scale both the storage and processing capabilities becomes a critical concern. The creation and enrichment of KGs often require handling vast amounts of data, which can strain computational resources, especially when dealing with real-time data updates (Hogan et al., 2021).

Domain-Specific Complexity: Different domains, such as healthcare, finance, or law, require specialized knowledge and expertise to construct and enrich KGs effectively. The integration of domain-specific ontologies and standards is crucial to ensure that the KG accurately represents the relevant knowledge and complies with industry standards (Chen et al., 2021).

3.4 The Future of Knowledge Graph Creation and Enrichment

The field of KG creation and enrichment is continuously evolving, with ongoing research aimed at addressing these challenges. Emerging trends include the development of more sophisticated algorithms for automatic KG construction, the use of machine learning and AI techniques to enhance the enrichment process, and the adoption of decentralized approaches to KG management. As KGs become increasingly central to AI and data-driven decision-making, the ability to create and enrich them efficiently and accurately will remain a key area of focus for researchers and practitioners alike (Davis, 2020; Baclawski et al., 2021).

4. KNOWLEDGE GRAPH QUALITY

Ensuring the quality of KGs is a critical task, as the usefulness and effectiveness of a KG are heavily dependent on the integrity of the data it encapsulates. A KG's quality is defined by several key dimensions, such as accuracy, coverage, coherency, and succinctness. These dimensions play a vital role in determining the extent to which a KG can be used reliably in applications like AI, data integration, semantic web services, and decision support systems (Batini et al., 2015; Baeza-Yates, 2018). In this section, we explore these quality dimensions in greater detail and discuss how they can be assessed and improved to ensure the KG remains a valuable resource for users.

4.1 Accuracy

Accuracy is one of the most important dimensions of KG quality, as it determines whether the data within the KG correctly reflects the real world. Accuracy can be broken down into three sub-dimensions: syntactic, semantic, and timeliness accuracy. Each of these sub-dimensions measures different aspects of how well the KG adheres to domain-specific rules, how faithfully it represents real-world phenomena, and how current the information is.

- **Syntactic Accuracy** refers to the correctness of the structure of the data, ensuring that the data follows the grammatical rules or conventions established for the domain or model. For example, in a healthcare KG, syntactic accuracy might involve ensuring that the proper medical terminology is used for diseases, treatments, and symptoms (Batini et al., 2015).
- **Semantic Accuracy** focuses on the degree to which the data in the KG aligns with the real-world phenomena it aims to represent. Inaccuracies in this dimension can lead to erroneous inferences and decisions. For instance, incorrect medical relationships between drugs and side effects can have significant consequences in clinical applications (Hogan et al., 2021).
- **Timeliness Accuracy** ensures that the data is current and reflects the most recent information available. For example, a healthcare KG must regularly update data about medical treatments and drugs to prevent outdated information from affecting patient care (Sequeda et al., 2019). As new knowledge is discovered, the KG must evolve to integrate these updates in a timely manner, preserving the KG's usefulness over time.

4.2 Coverage

Coverage refers to the extent to which a KG includes all the relevant entities, relationships, and attributes necessary for its intended use. This dimension is particularly important because incomplete KGs may omit critical information, reducing their effectiveness in real-world applications. Coverage is composed of two sub-dimensions: completeness and representativeness.

- **Completeness** measures whether the KG includes all the required data. For example, in a healthcare KG, completeness would ensure that data on various diseases, treatments, symptoms, and patient outcomes are all present, allowing for comprehensive analysis and decision-making (Baeza-Yates, 2018).
- **Representativeness** assesses whether the KG includes data that accurately reflects the diversity of the real world. In the context of a medical KG, this would involve ensuring that the data represents a wide range of diseases, demographics, and treatment methods without bias (Hogan et al., 2021). Bias in data can skew results and lead to poor decision-making, particularly in sensitive areas like healthcare and law.

4.3 Coherency

Coherency relates to how logically consistent the data in a KG is. This dimension ensures that there are no contradictions or violations of the formal semantics defined at the schema level. Coherency can be divided into two sub-dimensions: consistency and validity.

- **Consistency** ensures that there are no logical contradictions within the KG. For example, a KG might represent a relationship such as "*Person X is the parent of Person Y*" while simultaneously stating that "*Person Y is older than Person X*". Such contradictions must be identified and corrected to maintain the logical integrity of the graph (Batini et al., 2015).
- **Validity** focuses on whether the data adheres to the rules and constraints defined by the schema or ontology used in the KG. For example, a healthcare KG might include constraints such as "*A drug can only be prescribed to a patient if it is approved by the relevant medical authority*". If the KG includes a drug that violates this constraint, it would be considered invalid (Chen et al., 2021). Validity checks help maintain the reliability of the KG by ensuring that the data adheres to predefined norms and guidelines.

4.4 Succinctness

Succinctness is the dimension that measures whether the KG includes only relevant and necessary information, avoiding redundancy or unnecessary complexity. While completeness ensures that a KG includes all necessary information, succinctness focuses on ensuring that the graph is not overloaded with extraneous data that could overwhelm users or applications.

For example, in a business intelligence KG, irrelevant or superfluous information could hinder decision-making by making it more difficult to extract key insights. A succinct KG presents only the most relevant relationships and attributes, ensuring that the knowledge it contains can be accessed and processed efficiently (Baeza-Yates, 2018).

4.5 Measuring and Improving Knowledge Graph Quality

Measuring the quality of a KG requires the development of appropriate metrics and evaluation methods. Various approaches have been proposed to assess the quality of KGs, with a focus on evaluating dimensions such as accuracy, completeness, consistency, and succinctness (Baeza-Yates, 2018). These metrics can be used to identify areas for improvement and to guide the enrichment and correction processes.

One common approach to evaluating the quality of a KG is through data validation and consistency checking techniques. For example, SPARQL queries can be used to check for inconsistencies in RDF-based KGs, while more advanced techniques such as reasoning and constraint-based validation can be employed to ensure that the data adheres to logical and semantic rules (Töpper et al., 2012; Kontokostas et al., 2014).

To improve the quality of KGs, several techniques can be employed, including data cleansing, schema refinement, and alignment with external ontologies. Regular updates and maintenance are also essential to ensure that the KG remains accurate and relevant over time. For example, in healthcare KGs, automated tools can be used to monitor updates from medical literature and adjust the graph accordingly to incorporate new findings and treatments (Sequeda et al., 2019).

4.6 Future Directions in Knowledge Graph Quality

The field of KG quality is evolving, with increasing emphasis on developing techniques that can handle the growing scale and complexity of modern KGs. The use of machine learning and AI to automate the quality assessment and correction processes is a promising area of research. These technologies can be used to automatically detect anomalies, inconsistencies, and outdated information, significantly improving the efficiency of maintaining high-quality KGs (Hogan et al., 2021).

Moreover, integrating KGs with other advanced technologies, such as blockchain[3] for data provenance and graph analytics[4] for better data relationships, could offer new ways to ensure the ongoing quality of KGs in dynamic and rapidly evolving domains (Chen et al., 2021).

5. CORRECTING ASSERTIONS AND ALIGNMENTS IN KNOWLEDGE GRAPHS

As KGs evolve and grow, errors and inconsistencies inevitably arise, often due to the complex processes involved in data integration and enrichment. These issues can significantly impact the quality and reliability of the KG, making correction techniques crucial for maintaining its integrity. This section focuses on methods for correcting erroneous assertions and alignments within KGs, with an emphasis on techniques for identifying and addressing inconsistencies, improving data quality, and ensuring the accuracy of relationships between entities.

5.1 Erroneous Assertions in Knowledge Graphs

An assertion in a KG is a statement that links two or more entities through a specific relationship, such as "*Person X is the author of Book Y*". Over time, data integration from multiple sources, schema changes, and updates can introduce errors, leading to incorrect assertions. These errors can arise from several causes, including lexical ambiguity, semantic confusion, or data conflicts.

To identify and correct erroneous assertions, several techniques can be employed:

- **Related Entity Estimation**: This method involves identifying potential candidates for correcting erroneous assertions by estimating related entities based on similarity measures. For example, if an assertion about a person's birthplace is incorrectly linked, related entity estimation can identify other potential entities (e.g., alternative cities or countries) based on contextual information (Chen et al., 2021).
- **Assertion Prediction**: Once related entities are estimated, assertion prediction techniques predict the most likely correction by assigning a likelihood score to each candidate entity. These predictions are based on learned patterns or predefined rules in the KG. For example, if an incorrect assertion claims that "*Person X is a member of organization Z*", assertion prediction

can estimate the likelihood of this being true based on past data and relationships (Chen et al., 2021).

5.2 Alignment Issues in Knowledge Graphs

Alignment refers to the process of mapping or linking equivalent entities or concepts across different KGs or datasets. This is essential when integrating data from multiple sources, but alignment errors can introduce inconsistencies and contradictions in the graph.

- **Lexical and Semantic Confusion**: Errors in alignment often arise from lexical ambiguity (where different terms refer to the same entity) or semantic confusion (where two distinct entities are incorrectly mapped to one another). For example, in sports KGs, the terms "*Manchester United*" and "*Manchester City*" may be confused due to similar names, resulting in the misattribution of facts (e.g., players or championships) between the two football clubs (Chen et al., 2021).
- **Constraint-based Validation**: To address alignment issues, it is critical to apply constraint-based validation, which uses logical rules and schema constraints to verify the correctness of alignments. This includes ensuring that relationships between entities are valid under predefined constraints, such as property cardinality or entity type constraints. For example, if two entities are aligned as "actors" but have inconsistent attributes (e.g., a "director" being mistakenly aligned as an "actor"), the alignment can be flagged for correction (Töpper et al., 2012).

5.3 Correction Frameworks for KGs

A robust correction framework typically involves a multi-step process that combines several techniques to effectively detect and correct erroneous assertions and alignments within a KG. One prominent approach, described by Chen et al. (2021), integrates four key techniques. First, related entity estimation identifies potential candidates for correction by measuring the similarity between entities within the KG. Then, assertion prediction estimates the most likely correction for an erroneous assertion based on contextual patterns observed in the graph. Next, constraint-based validation uses predefined logical constraints to ensure the correctness of both assertions and alignments. Finally, correction decision-making combines the results from the previous steps to decide whether an assertion or alignment should be corrected, utilizing a weighted decision-making model. This comprehensive framework allows for effective error correction, ensuring the integrity and accuracy of the KG.

This correction framework is effective in mitigating the impact of erroneous data in large-scale KGs, but it also faces challenges such as scalability and accuracy. As KGs grow in size, the computational complexity of these techniques can increase, making it necessary to optimize them for efficiency (Töpper et al., 2012).

5.4 Challenges and Limitations of Correction Techniques

While current correction techniques show promise, several challenges remain:

- **Scalability**: As KGs expand, the sheer volume of data can make the correction process computationally expensive. This is particularly true for large-scale KGs that contain millions of entities and relationships (Hogan et al., 2021). Efficient algorithms that can handle vast amounts of data without compromising performance are crucial for ensuring the scalability of correction frameworks.
- **Deep Semantic Complexity**: Some alignment and assertion errors may involve complex semantic relationships that are difficult to identify and correct using automated techniques. For example, in specialized domains like law or healthcare, contextual understanding and domain expertise are often required to ensure the accuracy of corrections (Chen et al., 2021).
- **Data Quality Dependence**: The effectiveness of correction techniques relies heavily on the quality of the data used for training models and making predictions. Inaccurate or incomplete training data can lead to erroneous corrections, undermining the reliability of the KG (Chen et al., 2021).

5.5 Future Directions for Knowledge Graph Correction

The correction of erroneous assertions and alignments is an area of active research. Several future directions hold promise for improving the correction process:

- **Integration with Machine Learning**: Incorporating machine learning techniques, such as deep learning models, can enhance the ability of correction frameworks to predict and correct errors, particularly for complex, nuanced data. For example, deep learning models can be trained to detect subtle inconsistencies in entity relationships that are difficult to identify through traditional rule-based methods (Chen et al., 2021).
- **Human-in-the-Loop Approaches**: Combining automated correction techniques with human expertise can significantly improve the accuracy of cor-

rections. In certain cases, experts may be required to validate corrections, particularly when dealing with highly specialized domains or ambiguous data (Sequeda et al., 2019).

- **Contextual and Temporal Considerations**: Future correction frameworks could integrate temporal and contextual information to enhance their decision-making process. For example, aligning entities based on their historical relationships or considering how temporal changes affect the validity of assertions could improve the accuracy of corrections (Atig et al., 2022).

6. TIME ASPECT IN KNOWLEDGE GRAPH EVOLUTION

As the dynamic nature of knowledge and data continues to grow, the management of time within KGs has become a crucial factor in ensuring the accuracy and relevance of the data they contain. The time aspect in Knowledge Graph evolution refers to the challenges and strategies for integrating and managing temporal information within KGs. This involves addressing how KGs evolve over time, including the changes in their underlying data sources, the detection of anomalies that arise from these changes, and the cost of repairing any errors or inconsistencies introduced during the evolution process (Chen et al., 2021). Understanding how to manage time effectively in KGs is critical for maintaining their usefulness, particularly in applications that rely on up-to-date and accurate data.

6.1 Knowledge Graph Evolution

Knowledge Graphs evolve in response to the continuous influx of new data and the updating of existing information. This evolution can occur in several forms, such as the addition of new entities, the modification of existing relationships, or the deletion of outdated data. The impact of these changes on the quality of the KG is profound, as the evolving nature of data sources can lead to inconsistencies and inaccuracies in the graph structure (Baclawski et al., 2021). The change impact of each update must be carefully evaluated to determine whether the change is necessary or if it introduces errors into the KG.

Understanding the types of changes that affect a KG is vital for ensuring that the graph remains accurate and consistent. Some changes may be trivial and have little to no impact on the overall structure, while others may introduce significant disruptions that require careful management. For instance, a change in the structure of a source dataset, such as the introduction of new attributes or relationships, may necessitate updates to the KG's schema, potentially affecting existing data representations (Atig et al., 2022). Additionally, temporal alignment quality, which refers to the consistency of the alignment between different versions of the KG over time, plays a critical role in maintaining the graph's integrity (Chen et al., 2021).

6.2 Anomaly Detection

As KGs evolve, they are susceptible to anomalies that can arise from errors in data integration, updates, or modifications. These anomalies can take various forms, such as data inconsistencies, logical contradictions, or missing values. Detecting anomalies is essential to maintaining the accuracy of the KG, as these issues can negatively impact its usability in applications that require high levels of trust and reliability.

Various techniques are employed to detect anomalies within KGs. Consistency checking algorithms are commonly used to identify logical contradictions in the graph, such as conflicting relationships or invalid assertions. For example, if a KG asserts that "*Person X is both the parent and child of Person Y*", it would flag this as an anomaly. Similarly, semantic anomaly detection methods examine whether the relationships and attributes between entities are consistent with their expected semantic meanings (Töpper et al., 2012). These anomaly detection methods help ensure that the KG remains accurate and reliable as it evolves.

6.3 Repair Costs

When errors or anomalies are detected in a KG, the next step is to evaluate the repair costs associated with correcting these issues. The cost of repairing a KG can vary depending on the nature of the error and the complexity of the changes required. Repairing minor inaccuracies might involve simple updates to individual assertions, while more significant errors may require extensive changes to the graph's structure, schema, or alignment, leading to higher costs in terms of time and resources (Baclawski et al., 2021).

Determining when it is appropriate to repair versus when a reconstruction is necessary is a key consideration in KG evolution. For example, if a significant portion of the KG is corrupted or outdated, it might be more efficient to rebuild the graph from scratch rather than attempting to repair each individual error. On the other hand, minor inconsistencies may be more easily corrected by updating specific entities or relationships without requiring a complete overhaul of the KG (Atig et al., 2022). The decision to adopt an adaptive repair strategy or a full reconstruction approach depends on the balance between minimizing changes and maintaining consistency in the KG.

6.4 Temporal Knowledge Graphs

The representation of time in KGs is particularly challenging due to the need to accurately capture the evolution of knowledge over time. Temporal Knowledge Graphs (TKGs) are a specialized class of KGs that are explicitly designed to handle time-dependent information. These graphs incorporate temporal data in such a way that the history of entities and their relationships can be tracked over time, enabling more dynamic and comprehensive analyses (Atig et al., 2023).

TKGs are particularly useful in applications where understanding how entities and relationships change over time is crucial. For example, in the context of business intelligence, TKGs can help track changes in market trends, customer behavior, and product performance. By incorporating time into the KG, businesses can make more informed decisions based on historical data, as well as forecast future trends (Hogan et al., 2021). Temporal reasoning, which allows systems to make inferences about past and future events, is another important aspect of TKGs, as it enables more sophisticated analyses and decision-making processes. These features of Temporal Knowledge Graphs (TKGs) are especially valuable for practitioners in domains such as supply chain management, e-health, and smart cities, where understanding the evolution of data can significantly influence operational decisions.

6.5 Dataset for Experimentation

One of the major obstacles to advancing research on TKGs is the lack of readily available datasets that incorporate temporal information. To facilitate further research and experimentation, it is essential to develop and maintain datasets that reflect the evolution of knowledge over time. Several existing datasets, such as DBpedia, Wikidata, and other large-scale KGs, provide a foundation for creating TKGs, but their temporal aspects are often not fully utilized (Baclawski et al., 2021).

Experimenting with TKGs requires datasets that can accurately capture temporal changes, such as multiple versions of the same KG over time or datasets that change dynamically in real-time. By leveraging these temporal datasets, researchers can explore methods for improving the accuracy of time-based inferences, enhancing anomaly detection, and optimizing the repair process for KGs that evolve over time.

6.6 Future Directions

The future of temporal aspects in KG evolution is promising, with ongoing research focusing on improving how time is represented and managed within KGs. Key areas of future work include the development of scalable temporal reasoning techniques, the integration of TKGs with machine learning models to predict future changes in the graph, and the exploration of adaptive repair strategies that can handle evolving data sources more efficiently (Chen et al., 2021). Furthermore, advancements in distributed computing and blockchain technologies could offer new ways to manage temporal changes in KGs, ensuring that they remain accurate and consistent as they evolve. These directions require a clear understanding of the specific temporal challenges that arise in dynamic KG environments. Table 1 consolidates the key challenges discussed throughout this chapter, alongside the corresponding approaches and relevant literature. This summary serves as a reference framework for ongoing and future research aimed at enhancing the quality, consistency, and temporal robustness of Knowledge Graphs.

Table 1. Temporal challenges in knowledge graph evolution and their corresponding approaches

Temporal Challenge	Description	Proposed Approach
KG Evolution Tracking	Managing continuous updates to entities, relations, and schema.	Change impact analysis and schema adaptation strategies are used to assess the structural consequences of updates (Baclawski et al., 2021; Atig et al., 2022).
Anomaly Detection	Detecting contradictions or inconsistencies due to temporal updates.	Consistency checking and semantic anomaly detection help identify conflicting assertions as KGs evolve (Töpper et al., 2012; Chen et al., 2021).
Repair Cost Estimation	Deciding between localized repair and full KG reconstruction.	Cost models guide adaptive repair strategies based on the scope and impact of detected inconsistencies (Atig et al., 2022; Baclawski et al., 2021).
Temporal Alignment Quality	Ensuring consistency across temporal snapshots or KG versions.	Techniques include version-aware alignment metrics and entity tracking across time (Chen et al., 2021; Atig et al., 2022).
Temporal Reasoning	Inferring knowledge from temporal sequences or dependencies.	Time-annotated triples and reasoning models support the inference of time-sensitive knowledge (Davis, 2020; Atig et al., 2023).
Dataset Limitations	Lack of benchmark datasets that reflect temporal evolution.	Researchers are addressing this through synthetic temporal data generation and multi-version datasets like evolving Wikidata (Baclawski et al., 2021; Atig et al., 2023).
Scalability of Temporal Techniques	Ensuring methods scale with large and dynamic KGs.	Scalable anomaly detection and distributed frameworks are required to manage high-volume temporal data (Hogan et al., 2021; Chen et al., 2021).
Temporal Correction Strategies	Adapting error correction to temporal contexts and data histories.	Integrating historical data, contextual inference, and time-aware ML models enhances correction accuracy (Chen et al., 2021; Atig et al., 2022, 2023).

7. CONCLUSION AND FUTURE RESEARCH DIRECTIONS

Knowledge Graphs are rapidly emerging as essential tools for organizing and representing vast amounts of data across diverse domains. As they evolve over time, KGs face numerous challenges, particularly regarding the integration of new data, the correction of erroneous assertions, and the maintenance of consistency and accuracy. This chapter has explored the temporal aspects of KG evolution, emphasizing the importance of managing time in maintaining the integrity and relevance of these knowledge structures. From detecting anomalies and addressing data inconsistencies to integrating temporal data within the graph, effective management of time is crucial for ensuring that KGs remain up-to-date and reliable.

In addition to their theoretical and technical relevance, TKGs offer clear value for practical and managerial applications. In smart cities, TKGs support the planning of urban services by analyzing historical usage patterns and integrating real-time sensor data. In the healthcare sector, they enable the traceability of treatment protocols over time and help maintain up-to-date clinical knowledge. In finance, temporal modeling assists with detecting anomalies and risks in dynamic market data. Meanwhile, digital governance initiatives can leverage TKGs to ensure transparency and track changes across evolving public datasets. These practical use cases demonstrate how temporal aspects of KG evolution directly contribute to informed decision-making and operational efficiency across diverse domains.

The quality of KGs is deeply impacted by various factors, including the accuracy, completeness, coherency, and succinctness of the data they represent. Ensuring the quality of KGs requires not only ongoing efforts in data curation and enrichment but also robust correction frameworks to address errors and inconsistencies that naturally arise as KGs evolve. The correction frameworks, integrating techniques such as related entity estimation, assertion prediction, and constraint-based validation, provide a systematic approach to identifying and fixing errors, ensuring the reliability of KGs for their intended applications.

As KGs grow in scale and complexity, the temporal dimension becomes increasingly important. Temporal Knowledge Graphs allow for the tracking and representation of changes over time, enabling more dynamic and accurate analysis. However, the introduction of temporal elements into KGs raises several challenges, including the need for advanced temporal reasoning techniques, efficient anomaly detection, and cost-effective repair strategies. The growing need for real-time updates and the integration of continuously changing data sources further complicates the task of maintaining high-quality KGs.

Looking forward, several avenues for future research in the field of Knowledge Graph evolution are particularly promising. Machine learning techniques offer great potential for enhancing the accuracy of anomaly detection and error correction processes, especially as KGs grow larger and more complex. Deep learning models, for example, could be leveraged to improve the prediction of relationships and the identification of subtle inconsistencies that might otherwise go unnoticed. Another promising direction is the integration of blockchain technology to manage temporal changes in KGs, offering a decentralized and secure way to track the evolution of knowledge over time, ensuring data provenance, and preventing unauthorized changes (Baclawski et al., 2021).

Furthermore, the development of scalable temporal reasoning models is essential for improving the ability to infer changes in a KG over time. By enabling more efficient temporal reasoning, these models could support applications such as predictive analytics, where understanding the future state of knowledge is as important as maintaining its current accuracy. Additionally, research into adaptive repair strategies that can dynamically respond to the evolving nature of KGs will be key to reducing repair costs while maintaining the integrity of the graph (Hogan et al., 2021).

Finally, the ongoing standardization of methods for evaluating the quality of temporal aspects in KGs will be crucial for advancing research and ensuring that KGs remain reliable in real-world applications. The creation of open, temporal datasets for experimentation will provide valuable resources for developing and testing new techniques for managing time in KGs, facilitating the continued evolution of KGs in a more structured and reliable manner.

In conclusion, the management of temporal aspects within Knowledge Graphs is a rapidly evolving field that holds the key to improving the utility and reliability of KGs in a wide range of applications. By addressing the challenges of data consistency, quality control, and anomaly detection, and by leveraging advanced technologies such as machine learning and blockchain, future research will play a critical role in shaping the next generation of intelligent, adaptable, and high-quality Knowledge Graphs.

REFERENCES

Angles, R., & Gutierrez, C. (2008). Survey of Graph Database Models. *ACM Computing Surveys*, *40*(1), 1–39. DOI: 10.1145/1322432.1322433

Atig, Y., Zahaf, A., Bouchiha, D., & Malki, M. (2022). Alignment conservativity under the ontology change. [JITR]. *Journal of Information Technology Research*, *15*(1), 1–19. DOI: 10.4018/JITR.299923

Atig, Y., Zahaf, A., & Khiati, N. (2023). Temporal dimensions of quality in knowledge graph evolution: A comprehensive review. *Ingénierie des Systèmes d'Information*, *28*(4), 1081–1090. DOI: 10.18280/isi.280428

Baclawski, K., Bennett, M., Berg-Cross, G., Schneider, T., Sharma, R., Singer, J., & Sriram, R. D. (2021). Ontology summit 2020 communiqué: Knowledge graphs. *Applied Ontology*, *16*(2), 229–247. DOI: 10.3233/AO-210249

Baeza-Yates, R. (2018). Bias on the web. *Communications of the ACM*, *61*(6), 54–61. DOI: 10.1145/3209581

Bakker, R. R. (1987). Knowledge Graphs: Representation and structuring of scientific knowledge. Ph.D. Dissertation. University of Twente.

Batini, C., Rula, A., Scannapieco, M., & Viscusi, G. (2015). From data quality to big data quality. [JDM]. *Journal of Database Management*, *26*(1), 60–82. DOI: 10.4018/JDM.2015010103

Blumauer, A. (2014). From Taxonomies over Ontologies to Knowledge Graphs. Retrieved February 2023 from: https://blog.semantic-web.at/2014/07/15/from-taxonomies-over-ontologies-to-knowledgegraphs

Chen, J. Y., Jiménez-Ruiz, E., Horrocks, I., Chen, X., & Myklebust, E. B. (2021). Correcting assertions and alignments of large scale knowledge bases. *Semantic Web Journal*, *14*(3), 1–25. DOI: 10.3233/SW-210448

Davis, E. (2020). Time and space in knowledge graphs. Retrieved February 2023 from: https://go.aws/2SxOVZ9

Grishman, R. (2012). Information extraction: Capabilities and challenges. *Technical Report, NYU Dept. CS.*

Hepp, M. (2008). Ontologies: State of the art, business potential, and grand challenges. In *Ontology Management: Semantic Web, Semantic Web Services, and Business Applications* (pp. 3-22). Springer. DOI: 10.1007/978-0-387-69900-4_1

Hogan, A., Blomqvist, E., Cochez, M., d'Amato, C., Melo, G. D., Gutierrez, C., Kirrane, S., Gayo, J. E. L., Navigli, R., Neumaier, S., Ngomo, A. N., Polleres, A., Rashid, S. M., Rula, A., Schmelzeisen, L., Sequeda, J., Staab, S., & Zimmermann, A. (2021). Knowledge graphs. *ACM Computing Surveys*, *54*(4), 1–37. DOI: 10.1145/3447772

Hunt, A., & Thomas, D. (2003). The Trip-Packing Dilemma. *IEEE Software*, *20*(3), 106–107. DOI: 10.1109/MS.2003.1196331

Kontokostas, D., Westphal, P., Auer, S., Hellmann, S., Lehmann, J., Cornelissen, R., & Zaveri, A. (2014). Test-driven Evaluation of Linked Data Quality. In *Proceedings of the 23rd International Conference on World Wide Web*. ACM, 747–758.

Liu, S., d'Aquin, M., & Motta, E. (2017). Measuring accuracy of triples in knowledge graphs. In *Language, Data, and Knowledge: First International Conference, LDK 2017, Galway, Ireland* (pp. 343-357). DOI: 10.1007/978-3-319-59888-8_29

Lu, C. L., Bing, L. D., Lam, W., Chan, K., & Gu, Y. (2013). Web entity detection for semi-structured text data records with unlabeled data. *International Journal of Computational Linguistics and Applications*, *4*(2), 135–150.

Nakamoto, S. (2008). Bitcoin: A Peer-to-Peer Electronic Cash System. Retrieved from: https://bitcoin.org/bitcoin.pdf

Paulheim, H. (2017). Knowledge graph refinement: A survey of approaches and evaluation methods. *Semantic Web*, *8*(3), 489–508. DOI: 10.3233/SW-160218

Rada, R. (1986). Gradualness eases refinement of medical knowledge. *Medical Informatics*, *11*(1), 59–73. DOI: 10.3109/14639238608994975 PMID: 3515072

Rospocher, M., Van Erp, M., Vossen, P., Fokkens, A., Aldabe, I., Rigau, G., Soroa, A., Ploeger, T., & Bogaard, T. (2016). Building event-centric knowledge graphs from news. *Journal of Web Semantics*, *37*, 132–151. DOI: 10.1016/j.websem.2015.12.004

Sequeda, J. F., Briggs, W. J., Miranker, D. P., & Heideman, W. P. (2019). A pay-as-you-go methodology to design and build enterprise knowledge graphs from relational databases. In *The Semantic Web-ISWC 2019: 18th International Semantic Web Conference* (pp. 526-545). Springer International Publishing. DOI: 10.1007/978-3-030-30796-7_32

Töpper, G., Knuth, M., & Sack, H. (2012). DBpedia ontology enrichment for inconsistency detection. In *Proceedings of the 8th International Conference on Semantic Systems*, 33-40. DOI: 10.1145/2362499.2362505

ENDNOTES

1 https://apple.com/siri/

2 https://assistant.google.com/

3 A decentralized digital ledger that securely records transactions across multiple computers in such a way that the registered transactions cannot be altered retroactively without the alteration of all subsequent blocks and the consensus of the network (Nakamoto, 2008).

4 A set of techniques used to analyze and extract insights from graph-structured data by studying relationships and connections between nodes (entities) and edges (relationships) to uncover patterns, trends, and insights in various networks (Angles & Gutierrez, 2008).

Chapter 9
Accelerating AI-Driven Innovation: Effective Information Systems Project Management

Munir Ahmad
https://orcid.org/0000-0003-4836-6151
Survey of Pakistan, Pakistan

ABSTRACT

As digital transformation accelerates, the convergence of artificial intelligence (AI) and information systems (IS) project management is reshaping how projects are designed, executed, and assessed. This chapter examines how AI technologies, such as machine learning, predictive analytics, and intelligent automation, enhance decision-making, risk management, and operational efficiency across the project lifecycle. It also explores the impact on team collaboration, governance, and ethical considerations, including algorithmic bias and human oversight. By highlighting emerging best practices and future directions, the chapter offers insights into leveraging AI to drive adaptive, scalable, and innovative IS project outcomes.

INTRODUCTION

Artificial intelligence (AI) and information systems (IS) project management is one of the dynamic domains of innovation that has become a particularly crucial topic in the modern age of digital transformation. With a growing complexity as well as the need to be agile, "conventional project management methodologies" cannot usually keep up. AI, as a tool in data analysis, pattern recognition, and decision

DOI: 10.4018/979-8-3373-2352-7.ch009

support, can provide potent means to meet these challenges and bring the project outcomes to new heights.

Project managers are shifting away from making reactive decisions with the help of key technologies, including machine learning, predictive analytics, and intelligent automation (Mahfuzul & Shamim, 2024; Nenni et al., 2024; Shoushtari Bu-Ali et al., 2024). The tools give real-time information, automate routine work, and identify probable threats before they occur, thus increasing accuracy, efficiency, and strategic fit (Rahman et al., 2024; Uddin et al., 2024). An example would be analyzing the previous projects through machine learning models that would forecast cost overruns (Coffie & Cudjoe, 2024; Sohrabi & Noorzai, 2024) or schedule slips (Chimunhu et al., 2024), or using the natural language processing tools to analyze the stakeholder sentiment (Shen et al., 2024), or even automating the documentation (Conway et al., 2025; Leong et al., 2024).

This chapter critically analyzes the convergence of AI and IS project management by describing technology enablers, practical use, and emerging best practices. It touches upon the role of AI in project lifecycle changes of initiation and planning, implementation, monitoring, and closure, and challenges that project teams face concerning the use of AI in terms of team dynamics, governance, and stakeholder involvement. Also, it addresses ethical and organizational issues, such as data privacy, bias in algorithms, and the changing nature of human supervision. By placing the discussion in the larger scope of the event of digital transformation, the chapter highlights the increased importance of AI in the need to ensure that the IS projects are agile, scalable, and value-oriented. Finally, the aim is to keep an eye on the future and how to use AI to offer not only operational efficiency but also to use it as a vehicle in IS project management.

FOUNDATIONS OF INFORMATION SYSTEMS PROJECT MANAGEMENT

IS project management is a field that exists on the basis of systematic approaches set to help organizations in the development, implementation, and maintenance of highly complex technological solutions. This section discusses the basis of approaches that have been traditionally used in the management of IS projects, providing a general understanding of the linear and adaptive frameworks.

Waterfall Model

The waterfall model is one of the well-known and old methodologies in IS project management (Demirag et al., 2023; Saravanos & Curinga, 2023; Yahya & Maidin,

2022). It is a linear and sequential methodology, which implies that one stage of project development should be finished after another, and there could hardly be any overlapping. In the Waterfall model, the normal stages are the collection of the requirements, system design, implementation (coding), testing, deployment, and lastly, maintenance. One stage leads to another like a building block, and all the stages are structured in what can be called a cascade of activities, hence the name Waterfall. Figure 1 shows a glimpse of the waterfall model.

This process commences with requirements-gathering, which involves the collection of functional and technical requirements details from the stakeholders. These are supposed to be all-inclusive and constant during the project. After requirements are agreed upon, a project enters the system design phase, during which architects and engineers design blueprints on how the system should be developed. This is followed by the implementation stage, where the designers create code and start to code according to the design details. After the coding process is completed, the project is ready to pass into the testing phase, where the bugs should be found and eliminated, and the adherence to the requirements should be checked, as well as the performance of the entire system. Upon testing, the system goes to a live environment where it can be accessed by the end users. The last maintenance cycle is down-line maintenance and repairs, which is done at the end of the life cycle due to the usage of the system.

The strengths of the Waterfall model are based on its clarity, documentation, and control. The deliverables and review structures of the different stages are well established, and this makes it simpler to track down developments and control risks as well as assign resources. It is particularly appropriate for projects in which the scope is reasonably well-known and requirements are relatively well understood in advance, e.g., deploying infrastructure, or having to meet regulatory requirements. Moreover, being structured, it is easy to have formal control and audit, which is advantageous in such spheres as government, medical, or military, where traceability and documentation are required.

Nevertheless, the Waterfall model does present its fair share of drawbacks, especially when applied to the current iterative and dynamic digital setting. Its major weakness is rigidity, that is, once a phase has been completed, it may be time and money-consuming as well as disruptive to revert and rework the phase. In case of a change in user needs or market situation during the project, it is hard to be able to change as the rigid sequence does not allow it. Moreover, it is also normal to have delayed feedback loops in which the users only respond to the system when it is almost finished, and thus, the chances of not being pleased by the product do arise. The resulting lack of agility has the potential to contribute to inefficiencies, rework, or complete failure of a project should the initial assumptions be wrong.

Consequently, although the Waterfall model is still applicable to specific kinds of projects, this model has been seen as, to a significant extent, replaced (or supplemented) by more flexible and cyclical approaches to performing a similar task, namely, Agile frameworks the context of contemporary IS development. However, it is also important to understand its form and limitations to speak more contextually on how the AI technologies can bring more dynamism, real-time information support, and continual refinement to the otherwise planned project systems.

Figure 1. A Waterfall model

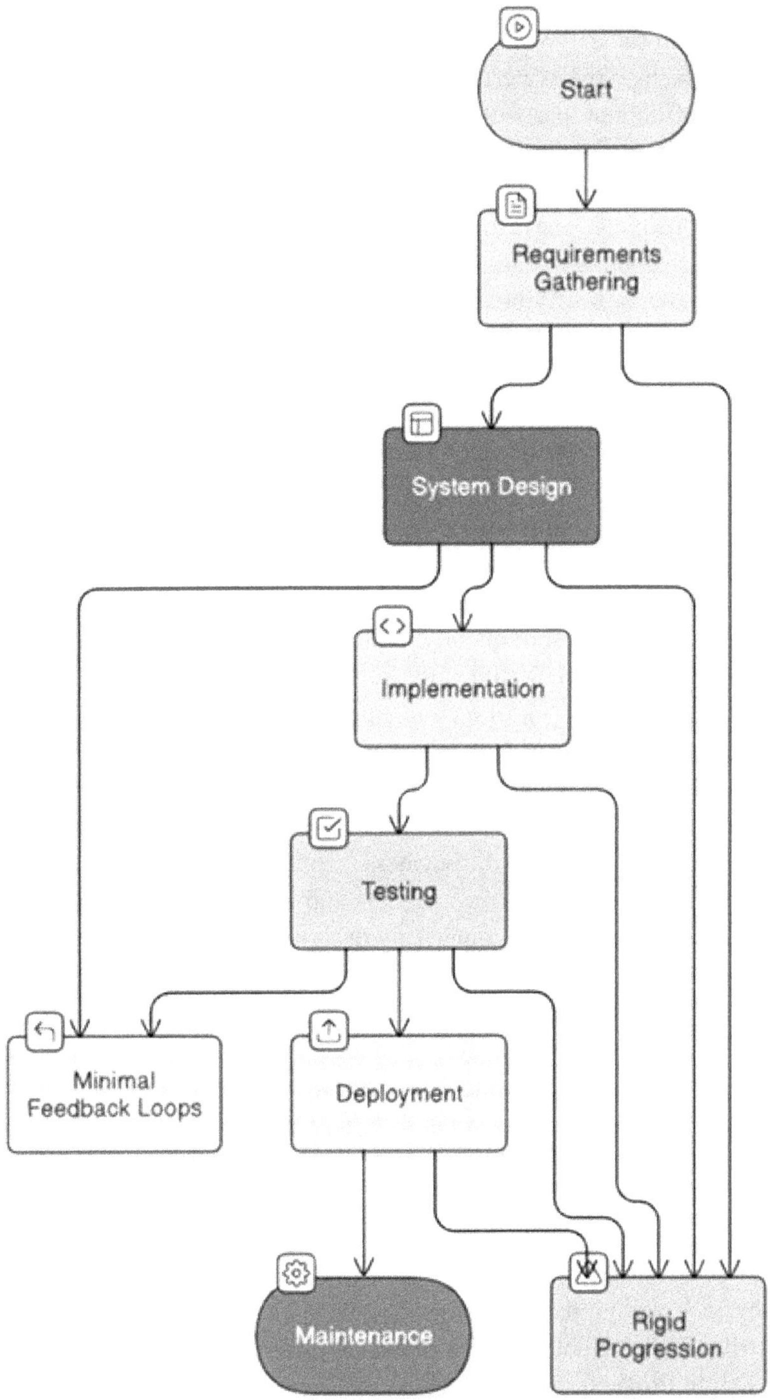

Agile Model

As opposed to the extreme and echelon forms of traditional models of Project management, such as the Waterfall, Agile forms of project management have become highly influential, particularly within the Information Systems (IS) project management sector (Gupta et al., 2022; Lano et al., 2024). Most notable agile approaches include Scrum and Kanban, where the key to success lies in iteration, teamwork, and responsiveness towards changes (Arun Sathe et al., 2023; Ozkan et al., 2022). These approaches are intended to flourish in volatile and unpredictable states, in which the needs of the users are shifting and immediate feedback is a key to the success of the project.

The concept of incremental delivery lies at the core of the Agile approach, and the work is broken down into small portions that can be deployed and inspected within a short period. It enables teams to re-evaluate priorities and change the course of operation in response to the input of stakeholders or a change in business thought. Agile is unlike Waterfall in that requirements are bound to change. This elasticity is quite useful in IS projects, in which the technological progress and expectations among users may alter mid-stream.

Scrum is one of the most frequently used Agile frameworks (Endres et al., 2022; Hron & Obwegeser, 2022). Scrum works in a framework of sprints, usually of two-four weeks, through the work of a cross-functional team, to produce a potentially shippable product increment. One of the most important aspects of Scrum is the designation of well-defined roles that will help to improve collaboration and responsibility. The role of the Product Owner is to establish the system features and prioritize the work according to the business significance. The Scrum Master is also a facilitator, so he or she eliminates barriers and makes sure that Agile values are followed. Development Team, comprising designers, programmers, and testers, is completely self-governing and shares common accountability in producing the work.

Scrum also has a list of ceremonies that are allegedly designed to promote transparency, feedback, and constant improvement, e.g., daily standing-up meetings, sprint planning, sprint reviews, and retrospectives. These frequent meetings enable teams to stay on track, review their operation, and quickly respond to a new problem.

Kanban is another common Agile methodology, though, unlike Scrum, it does not dictate the use of sprints and does not define the roles of the involved stakeholders (Ahmed et al., 2024; Strickroth et al., 2023). Rather, it is concerned with picturing work, restricting work in progress (WIP), and maximizing the workflow. Either physical or digital, kanban boards allow visualizing tasks in the form of cards distributed along columns that represent different stages of their completion (e.g., To Do, In Progress, Done). Such a visual method will improve transparency, collaboration, and allow for finding bottlenecks on the fly. Kanban can be applied especially in teams that have a constant flow of work or are involved in operational support duties whose priorities change too frequently.

Both Scrum and Kanban take Agile values but orient them to other team dynamics and project conditions. All these combined methodologies help IS project teams to become more responsive, user-centric, and innovative. Agile encourages organizations to stay lean by prioritizing changes in stakeholder interactions, continuous delivery, and responsive planning to reduce risk and increase value delivery. Complementary culture of accountability and trust promoted by the focus on collaboration and transparency is also critical in the complex IS environment that might involve a broad range of stakeholders and interdependence of systems. Table 1 shows the comparison between Scrum and Kanban, whereas Table 2 depicts the comparison of Waterfall and Agile models.

Table 1. Comparison table between Scrum and Kanban

Feature / Aspect	Scrum	Kanban
Approach	Iterative and time-boxed (Sprints)	Continuous flow
Structure	Defined roles, artifacts, and ceremonies	Flexible structure with minimal prescribed roles or events
Team Roles	Product Owner, Scrum Master, Development Team	No mandatory roles; can work with existing team roles
Work Planning	Sprint backlog defined at the start of each sprint	Work items pulled into workflow continuously
Work Visibility	Burndown charts, sprint boards	Visual Kanban boards (e.g., To Do, In Progress, Done)
WIP (Work-in-Progress) Limit	Not emphasized by default	Core principle—explicit WIP limits per column
Change Management	No changes allowed during the sprint	Changes can be made anytime, making it more flexible
Cadence	Fixed-length sprints (typically 2–4 weeks)	No fixed length; work is delivered as soon as it's ready
Feedback Loops	Sprint review and retrospective at the end of each sprint	Continuous feedback and optimization
Best Suited For	Projects with evolving but relatively structured goals	Service-based tasks, maintenance work, or teams needing high flexibility

Table 2. Comparison table between Waterfall and Agile

Feature / Aspect	Waterfall	Agile
Project Structure	Linear and sequential	Iterative and cyclical (often in short sprints)
Requirement Flexibility	Fixed and fully defined at the beginning	Evolving; re-prioritized throughout the project
Development Approach	One phase must finish before the next begins	Continuous development and integration
Customer Involvement	Minimal after initial requirements phase	Ongoing collaboration and feedback
Change Responsiveness	Difficult and costly to accommodate changes	Designed to adapt to changing requirements quickly
Deliverables	Delivered at the end of the project	Delivered incrementally in small, usable units
Feedback Loops	Delayed (usually post-deployment)	Continuous (after each sprint or iteration)
Testing Approach	Testing occurs after build phase is complete	Testing is continuous, integrated within development cycle
Project Visibility	Low visibility during execution; outcomes shown at the end	High visibility with frequent progress demonstrations
Risk Management	Risks identified and addressed in early stages	Risks surfaced and mitigated iteratively throughout
Team Structure	Structured and hierarchical	Cross-functional and self-organizing
Best Suited For	Projects with well-defined, stable requirements	Projects with uncertain, rapidly changing requirements

Even the selection of the methodology, whether the traditional (such as Waterfall) or adaptive (such as Agile) one, most IS project follows a well-established lifecycle that has five essential steps, including initiation, planning, execution, monitoring and controlling, and closure. All these stages are essential in making sure the project is well organized, has few risks, and achieves its goals.

The project starts with the initiation phase. It is a procedure that constitutes specification of the problem/opportunity to be tackled or exploited by means of the creation of an information system. The stage involves a statement of project aims, stakeholder identification, and feasibility reviews, which are technical, financial, and operational, to determine the project's viability. An initial business case and project charter are usually developed at this point, reaching a common ground with regard to the purpose and scope of the project.

Feasibility being established, the project takes the form of planning, whose framework is an ingredient to a successful project execution. At this phase, we will be dealing with realistic schedules, work breakdown structure, cost estimate, parting of operations, and risk identification. Gantt charts, project plans, communication guidelines, and contingency measures are developed to give a guide to the team as well as synchronize the expectations of stakeholders. This stage is particularly relevant in IS projects where there are hardware, software, and user interdependencies that must be handled with a lot of coordination. The implementation stage presupposes the real building and delivery of the system. These are coding, configuration, system integration, as well as legacy interface systems. It usually also includes testing, prototyping, and user training. Execution involves controlled team coordination, frequent cooperation with cross-functional teams to correlate with project objectives continuously.

Along with the execution, there is the monitoring and controlling that routes parallel to it and help keep the project on track. This includes monitoring the progress towards main performance indicators (KPIs), controlling budgets and plans, and reacting to new risks. Performance is measured with the help of tools like dashboards, variance reports, and quality audits, which help in taking appropriate corrective measures. Poor control at this phase may result in a scope creep, cost overruns, or missed defects.

The last step, project closure, helps to tie up loose ends by making project deliverables complete and accepted by the stakeholders formally. The test final phase encompasses testing of the final system, user acceptance, knowledge transfer, and handover of the system to fully operational or support staff. Notably, closure has to do with the recording of lessons, post-implementation review, and update of knowledge bases in organizations to enhance the performance of future projects. Nevertheless, in spite of these phased steps, IS projects are quite often hit by repeated and important difficulties that potentially tend to undermine success. Probably the most common is scope creep, which is the progressive growth of project deliverables without time, cost, or resource modifications. Scope creep frequently occurs due to ambiguous requirements, changing business demands, or the expectation of stakeholders that are not managed well. Otherwise, the budgets could go haywire; it could topple the schedules.

Despite the fact that the formulation of technical solutions is not necessarily a technical debt, one of the most serious concerns to be aware of is often the side effects of sub-optimal technical solutions being chosen, possibly because of time constraints or short-sightedness. This debt will appear as a softly coded system, ineffective system design, or lack of documentation, which raises the cost of maintenance of the system and lowers its flexibility in the long run. Technical debt is common in fast-moving IS situations where teams are concentrated on speed of delivery over sustainable development.

The next important problem that will influence the IS project's success is the stakeholders' misalignment. Several stakeholder groups are generally involved in the project; i.e. IT staff, end-users, executives, and vendors, and they all have their interests and expectations. Poor communication or inability to connect with the most important parties may result in the clash of priorities, change aversion, or the unwillingness of users to use the final product. In addition to this, the limitation of resources, be it time, budget, or skilled manpower, is a recurrent issue that requires teams to make trade-offs by the teams. The shortage of resources can result in premature development, inadequate testing, or limited functionality, which will lower the quality of the system and the satisfaction of its users. The constraints may even lead to abandonment of the projects and failure to achieve the desired benefits in some instances.

It is against this complicated backdrop of hierarchical segmentation of the project progress and project operative issues that the potential of transforming the field of IS project management through the utilization of artificial intelligence (AI) is being considered. AI technologies provide a new set of tools to solve most of these problems, as it is possible to base all decisions on data, automate repetitive tasks, and receive predictive information. To put example, machine learning can assist in early signs of cost increases in a project, whereas natural language processing can pick out important specifications in the communication of stakeholders. With the help of AI-driven analytics, we may be able to optimize and align the resources with past achievements, and smart bots can be effective when it comes to documentation or testing. It is notable that AI cannot substitute classic project approaches but complements their functions. It introduces intelligence, adaptability, as well as foresight into all steps of the project lifecycle. AI tools could provide support to project teams on activities ranging from refining their initial feasibility studies to closure reviews, steering through uncertainty and taming complexity, and eventually raising the probability of developing successful and user-centered IS solutions.

INTEGRATING AI INTO PROJECT WORKFLOWS

With the expansion and complexity of IS undertakings, organizations are increasingly relying on AI to reduce the costs of the project and improve efficiency, precision, and decision-making processes through the project lifecycle (Karim Zadeh Bu-Ali et al., 2024; Pan & Zhang, 2022; Sravanthi et al., 2023). The incorporation of AI into the processes of IS project work cannot be seen as a technological improvement, but rather a strategic change to the development of planning, implementation, and assessment of projects. In this section, we will discuss the particular spheres in which AI technologies change the project workflow and ensure better results.

Task automation is one of the actions of AI in project management that is the most direct and concrete. Monotone applications of administration, like a schedule of meetings, tracking of progress, reporting of status, logging issues, among others, can be taken by AI-based bots and virtual assistants. Such tools work 24/7 and make sure that periodic updates and reminders are automatically created so that project managers and staff can use their precious time to work on high-value activities. As an example, AI assistants may be integrated with tools such as Microsoft Teams or Slack and automatically assign tasks, send follow-ups, and update timelines on the basis of team outputs. Not only does this cut down on possible human error, but it also increases responsiveness and visibility of projects.

A third important spot is risk management and resource allocation via predictive analytics. Upon investigating past project information, AI systems are able to distinguish trends as well as connections that might be inaccessible ahead of time. Such insights assist project managers in forecasting the possible delays, cost overruns, or deficiency of resources before they materialize. To illustrate, with such algorithms as machine learning, high-risk tasks may be identified from historical performance data, and as a proactive measure, corrective measures may be prescribed. On the same note, AI-powered models can make the work of source allocation more effective by predicting team capacity, workload, and potential bottlenecks, hence making better use of human and material resources in the project lifecycle.

In the case of managing stakeholders and analyzing the communication process, Natural Language Processing (NLP) is also proving to be useful. IS projects are usually associated with different stakeholders whose expectations and communication patterns differ. NLP tools can provide summaries of themes, sentiment, and raise concerns or issues based upon emails, chat logs, meeting notes, and survey responses. Sentiment analysis can be used as an example of knowing that dissatisfaction exists among end-users at an earlier stage of development and taking timely measures. Also, NLP can assist with requirements drafting: formalizing the inputs of the stakeholders in the form of use cases or user stories, making project documentation more accurate and easily understood.

Another development of major importance that has happened due to AI is decision-support systems and intelligent dashboards. These systems summarize enormous data about project work to gain valuable knowledge in real-time visual forms. Smart dashboards can show/express KPIs, compare planned vs. actual performance, and possible scenarios of the project, in order to direct the decisions. In contrast to the static reports, AI-enhanced dashboards have dynamic design patterns such that when more information is available, it is accommodated in this dashboard in real-time, and this enables the project manager to make informed decisions within a short period. Other systems go so far as to give prescriptive advice, which might include reallocation of work and change of deadlines, given the state of the project health indicators.

In order to make these capabilities down-to-earth, practical examples and mini case studies about the benefits of the integration of AI introduce measurable values. To give an example, a worldwide consulting company has deployed AI-based resource planning software throughout the IS projects and decreased the incidence of project delays by 20 percent in less than one year. The other instance was when a public organization applied NLP in analyzing user feedback on its newly developed citizen services portal. The learned lessons resulted in quick iterations of the user interface and a 30 percent increase in the satisfaction of the users. These examples can also illustrate the strategic importance of AI integration, in addition to its technical feasibility, over and above the fact that it can be used to boost the effectiveness of projects in terms of speed, precision, and stakeholder involvement.

To conclude, AI technologies represent not just an automation and optimization of existing workflows but an addition of more predictive, adaptive, and user-entered solutions to IS project management. With these tools evolving, organizations with strategies to incorporate AI into their project environments will be better able to work with complexity and lower risk, and high-impact digital answers. Table 3 portrays the tools across the IS project lifecycle phases.

Table 3. AI tools across the IS project lifecycle phases

Project Phase	AI Tools/Technologies	Purpose/Functionality
Initiation	• NLP-based requirement extractors • Chatbots for stakeholder interviews	• Extract and analyze requirements from text/ email • Automate initial stakeholder Q&A
Planning	• Predictive analytics • AI-powered project estimators	• Forecast timelines, budgets, and resource needs • Identify high-risk areas
Execution	• RPA (Robotic Process Automation) • AI-powered scheduling bots	• Automate repetitive tasks (data entry, reporting) • Adjust schedules dynamically
Monitoring & Control	• Intelligent dashboards • Anomaly detection algorithms	• Real-time tracking of KPIs and milestones • Spot deviations in performance or budget
Closure	• NLP for documentation • Sentiment analysis tools	• Automate post-project reports and evaluations • Analyze feedback for lessons learned

MANAGING CHANGE AND INNOVATION WITH AI

Insertion of AI into the management of IS projects is not a mere technical task, but a change management issue. Achieving effective implementation of AI is determined by the organization traversing structural, cultural, and behavioral change amongst teams and departments. This part will investigate how strategic change management could be utilized in coping with these dynamics by including the aspect of human resistance, innovation culture, and empowering leaders to achieve sustainable performance outcomes.

Change Management Strategies

Using AI in IS projects can bring about changes in the workflow, new tools and decision-making process, and will change the practice of things that can be of major change. In that regard, effective plans on managing change are vital in order to facilitate a transition and minimize disruption. One of the most popular models, like the 8-Step Change Model by Kotter, can become an example of how to do it framework-wise: start with the sense of urgency in relation to adopting AI, form a guiding coalition of champions, state a change requirement clearly, and so forth.

Stakeholder mapping and impact assessments are also good strategies to use so that the effects on the different roles occupied can be known using AI tools. As an example, the implementation of a predictive analytics tool can alter the way project risks are estimated and prioritized, and this change, in its turn, might impact the project managers, analysts, and executives in different ways. Communication strategies, training opportunities, and pilot trials (such as sandbox environments) may facilitate the process and make the users feel confident. Also, organizations are advised to take the implementation of AI as a change process as opposed to a single implementation. It will entail the establishment of workable schedules and flexibility to implement changes, and construct feedback processes to enable duties learnt at early phases to guide subsequent deployments.

Overcoming Resistance

It is no surprise that when humans feel that AI represents a danger to their job, independence, or competence, they engage in resistance. This opposition needs to be managed with sympathy, openness, and active communication. Effective communication concerning the aim and advantages of AI adoption by communicating the intention to augment, rather than cannibalize, is also paramount to avoid fear and instead cultivate trust. Apart from good design in the first place, it can be used to co-design solutions with end-users, as this makes them feel a sense of ownership and, thus, more likely to remember and follow an AI-assisted way of doing things. As an example, entrusting the field technicians with the process of building a predictive maintenance dashboard can enhance the work tool and adoption.

Selecting and involving the so-called AI ambassadors or early adopters on teams where people are willing to experiment and can help influence others should also be a part of organizational identification and empowerment. Such champions will be capable of sharing success stories, mentoring other people, and making the use of

AI normalized throughout the organization. Notably, resistance does not appear only among the front-line employees. Other reasons that executives and senior stakeholders might be wary of doing AI are that it is new, or they are worried about responsibilities. In this case, executive development courses, peer benchmarking, and presentation of ROI will help eliminate concerns and build follow-through at leadership levels.

Culture of Innovation and Continuous Learning

To achieve breakthroughs in AI integration outside of a few localized applications, companies should avoid conducting trials that only prove validity in individual cases and instead develop a culture of experimentation, learning, and flexibility. This culture is established by establishing policies, incentives, and practices to explore new tools, analyze results, and disseminate experience between projects. Among the underlying factors is the investment in AI literacy at any level of the organization. The workshops, online courses, and practical training need not be restricted to data scientists, but they should be directed towards project managers, analysts, and support employees as well. Deconstructing AI concepts gives people a reason to stop being scared and allows them to engage in AI-enabled processes more constructively.

It can be effective to encourage cross-disciplinary innovation labs or hackathons. They provide an opportunity to have all levels of skills working on the same project, since it is necessary to quickly develop and test AI apps in a low-risk environment. Wins as a result of such efforts can be improved, amplified, and made an institution. In addition to that, failure should be re-interpreted as a learning opportunity. Through writing and discussing such practices, it is possible to form a common body of knowledge and enhance subsequent practices when AI models fail or automation fails.

Role of Leadership and Cross-Functional Collaboration

Leadership is an important factor that influences the vision, pace, and tone of AI adoption during the IS projects. Transformational leaders need to promote the concept of AI as a change in the technological equipment and, at the same time, as an innovation facilitator, efficiency, and quality of services. It entails aligning AI programs to organizational objectives, obtaining the prerequisite resources, and role-modeling an attitude of flexibility and lifelong learning.

Cross- functional collaboration should also be encouraged by the leaders and the silo that exists among the IT, operation, analytics, human resource and end user departments need to be broken. The nature of AI projects implies the use of interdisciplinary collaboration, as data engineers will have to collaborate with domain experts, UX designers have to closely collaborate with end-users, and compliance officers have to work closely with those who develop an AI. Such collaboration can be institutionalized via structures (i.e., for AI governance boards or project innovation councils) where decisions are made while various points of view inform the design and deployment of procedures and protocols.

Lastly, ethics and responsibility should also be incorporated into leadership. Since the vital choices regarding projects will be made with the use of AI tools, such as resource allocation, hiring algorithms, leaders should strive to be transparent, fair, and meet ethical expectations. Such dedication not only guarantees a successful completion of a project but also creates trust and credibility of longevity with the stakeholders.

Subsequently, slow but deliberate change and innovation management in an IS project setting involves a tactical, human-based approach when using AI. It requires strong change management, strategic resistance management, a culture of constant learning, and visionary leadership, which encourages teamwork and ethical management. With these factors adequately in place, organizations are in a position to realize the full potential of AI to bring structural transformation in the envisaging, implementation, and sustenance of IS projects.

Figure 2. Managing change and innovation with AI

RISKS, ETHICS, AND GOVERNANCE IN AI-ENABLED IS PROJECTS

Although AI presents capabilities in the IS project streamlining that have never been seen before, it comes with a very complicated set of risks, ethical and governance needs. Unaddressed, these challenges have the potential to damage relationships based on trust, cause failure of projects, or attract regulatory fines. This part unravels the most significant risk areas, including algorithmic bias, data privacy, and the necessity of strong governance, and provides realistic approaches to the implementation of responsible artificial intelligence.

Algorithmic Bias and Fairness

The removal of bias in AI systems is limited only to the data and assumptions they are founded. Algorithmic bias, which is a phenomenon in which AI models display preferences or treatment in favor of or against particular groups of people, based on gender, race, age, etc., is the most urgent ethical issue when it comes to AI-enhanced IS projects. It may happen even during training when the dataset gets a reflection of historical disparities or inadequate representation.

To illustrate, an AI system to be used in shortlisting candidates after applying to a job may be used discriminately against women or minorities, depending on how it is trained on the data training/samples consisting of candidates dominated by men as applicants or on a pattern of exotic hiring habits. In the same manner, an AI loan approval system can refuse credit to people based on their zip codes when the historic lending data shows the tendency of redlining.

Slight, but still influential, algorithmic bias can emerge in IS project settings too, e.g., in automated resource allocations that systematically favor some departments, risk designations that reveal historical injustices, or decision-support systems, which regularly make biased decisions. Such biases, when left unchecked, may poison trust, waste resources, and exacerbate systemic disadvantage. In that regard, active prevention is necessary during the AI development cycle.

Firstly, during its development, as well as following its implementation, bias audits ought to be performed by project teams. Workloads. These audits consist of subjecting AI models to different demographic and operationally concentrated sets to determine whether results are fair. They assist in pointing out uncoded biases that may be embedded in the training data or arise in the course of the algorithm's behavior as it is passed through time. To ensure constant checks in fairness, audits may be initiated at checkpoints; before implementation, during pilot vehicle periods, and at regular intervals following implementation.

Moreover, the concept of Explainable AI (XAI) is vital in picture visualization and the manner of AI systems' decision-making. Such tools (SHAP; SHapley Additive exPlanations or LIME; Local Interpretable Model-agnostic Explanations) can help understand the impact of which features have on which outputs. This visibility will give the developers and stakeholders a chance to identify the patterns that may indicate bias, say overuse of the ZIP code, income level, or job title- features that may be in correlation with the race, classes, or gender.

The structure of the teams developing these systems is just as crucial. Varied, cross-functional project teams and inclusive testing datasets are more critical to the interception and correction of bias early before it becomes scaled. The diversity in background and purpose of people in the system design and assessment bridge the technical specialist perspective, domain specialist perspective, and those who are the end-users of the system, and often provide a blind spot perspective. Meanwhile, inclusive datasets guarantee that the models tested by AI are put into all possible user scenarios and profiles and are less likely to become discriminatory in their work.

Finally, it has to be said that organizations do not need to reinvent the wheel; consistency already exists in terms of standards and checklists to develop ethical AI. Organizers like the Organization for Economic Co-operation and Development (OECD) and the Institute of Electrical and Electronics Engineers (IEEE) have released guidelines, frameworks, and fairness evaluation services. The identified resources offer real-life measures to ensure the incorporation of equity, accountability, and transparency of AI systems to ensure that IS projects can be consistent with global best practices and the expectations of society.

Data Privacy and Security

The AI systems usually utilize intensive sensitive data volumes, namely personal, behavioral, and transactional data, which generates certain cybersecurity and data privacy threats. Any errors in the handling of this data in an IS project that traverses the sectors of healthcare, finance, or the sector of government services may result in a legal breach, popular uproar, or even an ethical breach.

Specifically, lack of proper anonymization of medical data in the AI-based patient management system of a specific hospital may lead to disclosure of patients' diagnosis or treatment history, violating the HIPAA or GDPR laws. On the same note, an e-government portal with a back-end infrastructure, which is meant to serve people based on AI in automating service provisions, may jeopardize the data of citizens.

Addressing the risk of data privacy and security concerns in the upcoming integration of AI in Information Systems (IS) initiatives should be done in a multi-layered and proactive manner. Given that AI systems tend to deal with really large quantities of sensitive data, such as personal identifiers, behavioral patterns, and operational information, it is of paramount importance to make sure that such data is being handled responsibly, to retain user confidence as well as to adhere to the requirements of the regulator.

Among the cornerstone practices can be mentioned the adherence to data minimization principles that are there to make sure that the only amount of data that needs to be gathered and stored is that needed in the context of the intended purpose of the AI model. Having refrained from stockpiling unnecessary or irrelevant data elements, organizations minimize the risk of privacy violations and make the process of complying with such laws as the GDPR much easier. As an illustration, imagine there is an application of AI to predict staff performance, in which case there should be no need to process sensitive personal information like family background or biometrics without a justified reason and consent. In addition to restricting the possible abuse, this principle will foster data discipline within the company.

The other, having found utility, is the use of differential privacy, which enables the training of AI models on datasets without revealing the identity of the individuals. This is a technique that adds statistical noise to the data or query returns, thus inhibiting the reproducibility of results to any particular individual. It is especially in a public health/government IS project where aggregate information interest prevails, and privacy protection is essential. Giant companies such as Apple and Google already apply differential privacy, and it has become a de facto gold standard regarding privacy-preserving AI.

Security also should be integrated or made into the architecture through bottom-up technology. Billions of users should be shielded with strong access controls, end-to-end encryption, and role-based security policies that have to be built in, not an afterthought. This prevents unauthorized users from viewing sensitive data or performing certain functions in the system, which also greatly minimizes internal leakages or external attacks on the system. To illustrate this, we could say that in a hospital-based IS system, doctors could be granted access to complete an individual's record, whereas administration staff could only have access to scheduling data or billing data only restricting access to only what is needed to perform duties.

Lastly, periodic penetration tests and review of compliance procedures are necessary to identify the vulnerabilities before they can be exploited. Penetration tests mimic cyberattacks to identify the vulnerability of system defenses, whereas compliance reviews determine whether system practices meet legal and regulatory standards. The practices assist organizations in remaining ahead of the emerging threats and ensuring constant security assurance. These reviews are usually required in highly-regulated industries like banking or e-government, but are nonetheless a best practice in other industries in terms of risk management.

Transparency, Accountability, and Compliance

AI governance can answer a set of critically important inquiries that prescribe integrity, reliability, and accountability of AI-supported decision-making systems in the IS projects. The most important question is, who makes AI decisions? This addresses the necessity of visible ownership of the strategy of AI design, implementation, and performance. In the absence of accountability, any malfunctions or ethical failures in AI-ï¿ tended decisions could end in the gray zone where it is hard to blame and take corrective measures. AI product owners or data stewards are appointed to maintain the accuracy and fairness, and performance of the model in the long run, with accountability.

The other important point to consider is: How is AI decisions observed or questioned? Since AI systems are increasingly making critical decisions, including prioritization of projects, budget distribution, or priority classification of stakeholders, organizations should be able to provide mechanisms of redress and governance. This includes constant monitoring of performance, alert thresholds on anomaly detection as well as avenues that can be utilized by end-users or stakeholders to dispute AI-based results. As an example, in the case of a citizen-service-request prioritization use case of an IS implemented in the public sector based on AI, citizens must know what decisions are made and should have the opportunity to challenge them, as they affect their access to services.

Raising the question: Can AI models be audited and explained? Also becomes relevant. With AI governance, models must be not only effective at what they do but also explainable in what they do. Trust depends crucially on explainability, often in a high-stakes situation, such as in the case of public administration, healthcare, or finance. Explainable AI implies being able to trace back the decision to data entered into the system, feature weights, and logic of the algorithm to validate the decision and locate and possible sources of error and bias. Such tools as SHAP or LIME, together with adequate documentation, are important to meet this requirement.

A workable AI governance system would have to be built into the environment of the IS project to resolve such questions. To start with, such a framework involves well-elaborated roles and responsibilities in every level of AI development, implementation, and monitoring. Each developer, data scientist, domain expert and operational lead should know his or her role in the AI lifecycle to provide coherent coordination and accountability.

Second, companies ought to consider a few ethics committees or AI governance boards to approve high-risk AI applications the most notably where such projects can affect the rights, access, or welfare of users. Such committees assist in determining the relevance of AI tools with ethical considerations, values in society, and official requirements. As an example, a health department that utilizes an AI tool to prioritize patients to undergo remote consultations may apply an ethics board to guarantee that such a model damage either older individuals or individuals living in remote areas.

Third, governing must also involve standardized tools of documenting models, e.g. Model Cards, Datasets Datasheets. Such tools explain what the model is supposed to do, how exactly it was trained, which data was applied, the known limitations, and which ethical aspects can be applied. These artifacts facilitate transparency, auditability, and cross-team communication because assumptions and constraints are documented; when re-used or updated, models, assumptions, and constraints are documented.

Last but not least, a robust governance model will be aligned with the emergent international practices, including the EU AI Act, the NIST AI Risk Management Framework, and ISO/IEC 42001 on AI management systems. The standards provide the best practice guidelines in the classification of risks, philosophy of data governance, human supervision, and ongoing monitoring. By complying with them, companies demonstrate much more than legal compliance, but also the intention to become more responsible when it comes to innovation.

In another example, a European-based insurance firm introduced a three-level system of AI governance consisting of an operational AI team, an AI ethics board, and a compliance oversight unit. This organization allowed a more rapid pace of innovation, but still under the oversight of fairness, explainability, and risk exposure. Good governance also creates confidence among people. Transparency measures, such as the publication of algorithms or recourse options to the users, play a critical part in securing the legitimacy of the public in a public sector IS project like an AI welfare eligibility system, and in avoiding impairment.

Responsible integration of AI into IS projects requires a forward-looking, interdisciplinary strategy that focuses on risks and ethical ethos and needs open governance. Responsible AI by design should start with ethical evaluations and data privacy protection in place at the early stages of the AI lifecycle to make responsible systems. Simultaneously, there is a need to provide a superstructure of governance to establish accountability, regulatory compliance, and impacts that must be monitored continuously. This practice of involving a wide variety of stakeholders, such as legal specialists, technical builders, subject matter professionals, and impacted populations, not only predicts unintended effects but also aids equity in the results of AI. In case of the alignment of these elements, organizations will be able to realize the full potential of AI in transformation without reputational, legal, and operational losses. Responsible AI, as such, in this context, cannot merely be regarded as a compliance issue but represents a strategic requirement towards sustainable, inclusive innovation within the IS environments.

Moving towards the action phase, these principles can be transformed into a practice, where the Figure 3 shows the consolidated checklist on responsible AI deployment in public health IS projects. This checklist is a practical tool to help an organization consider the essentials when it comes to fairness, privacy, transparency, governance, and continuous monitoring.

Figure 3. Consolidated checklist for responsible AI deployment in public health IS projects

Bias & Equity in Health Outcomes

- Have datasets been reviewed for representation across genders, ethnicities, regions, and socioeconomic groups?
- Has fairness testing been conducted to avoid discriminatory risk scores or treatment recommendations?
- Are sensitive attributes (e.g., race, disability status) used responsibly and transparently?
- Is there clinical or ethical oversight on AI outputs affecting patient care decisions?

Health Data Privacy & Security

- Are personally identifiable health data anonymized or pseudonymized?
- Have patients been informed about how their data is used in AI models?
- Is data handled in accordance with HIPAA, GDPR, or local health data laws?
- Are robust cybersecurity protocols in place (encryption, access logs, multi-factor authentication)?

Transparency & Patient Trust

- Can clinicians and public health officials interpret AI recommendations or scores?
- Are AI-generated decisions accompanied by explanations or confidence levels?
- Are users (e.g., patients or clinicians) aware when an AI system is involved?
- Are there clear communication strategies to inform the public of AI use in services (e.g., triage bots)?

Governance, Ethics, and Compliance

- Has the AI system been reviewed by a health ethics board or digital health governance unit?
- Is there a named clinical or technical steward accountable for the system's outputs?
- Does the deployment comply with public health policy, consent, and safety standards?
- Is there a process for audit trails, reporting harm, and halting AI use if necessary?

Monitoring, Feedback, and Learning

- Is real-time monitoring set up to track performance, errors, and outcome disparities?
- Can frontline health workers report anomalies or suggest improvements?
- Are models retrained periodically using updated epidemiological and demographic data?
- Is there a feedback mechanism for affected patients or users?

CONCLUSION

With organizations straddling a much more complex environment of digital transformation, the potential incorporation of Artificial Intelligence (AI) into Information Systems (IS) project management is swiftly changing the very means in which initiatives are both envisioned and delivered, as well as maintained. This chapter has presented the background, opportunities, and challenges in AI-driven innovations in IS project contexts with a focus on the technical benefits as well as on the human side of the equation that is required to achieve success. We will end this book with a look into the future of project work, with some strategic advice to the practitioner, and at the types of skills that will be needed by leaders practicing in AI-augmented project environments.

There are a number of prominent trends that already indicate a radical change to the project management paradigm. Namely, the emergence of AI-driven project management software that can automate schedules, intelligently allocate resources, and offer real-time recommendations. Since such tools as Microsoft Project with AI add-ons, ClickUp AI, or Wrike with Work Intelligence are cutting down on manual overhead and improving the ability to make decisions.

Simultaneously, the introduction of independent planning systems of projects (where artificial intelligence (AI) is simulating various project scenarios and dynamically adapting their plans) is starting to challenge the conventional way of planning. They educate themselves on learning past data, industry standards, as well as project inputs, to make preventive changes to the scope, schedules, or staffing. Furthermore, AI-supported dashboards with real-time performance analytics are allowing project managers to monitor the delivery and track KPIs, anomalies, and react to arising risks much faster than they would have in the past. These systems are capable of signaling when there is early evidence of bottlenecks or budget mismatches, or resource conflicts, and agile responses can be made to keep projects back on track.

In a bid to maximize such opportunities, project managers should consider a list of top practices that are specific to AI-increased contexts. To start with, AI tools must be aligned with specific project objectives and objectives of stakeholders: not all the processes and not all the insights need automation and machine learning. The business value, feasibility, and user readiness should be used to decide what AI to include and how. Second, project managers should incorporate morals, justice, and openness in each stage of the project life cycle. This comprises running audits of bias, implementing bias-aware AI algorithms, and the presence of accountability mechanisms for AI-informed decisions. Such practices are further enhanced by involving the varied teams in the design and review activity.

Third, there must be a union between technical and non-technical teams. The project leaders need to make connections between data scientists, software engineers, domain experts, and the end-users by empowering effective communication and alignment of goals and feedback loops. Interdisciplinary fluency is a major leadership skill in AI-related projects. Last but not least, one should be dedicated to constant learning and flexibility. The AI tools rapidly change, and it is essential to keep up with new technologies, structures, and applications to remain competitive and trustworthy in the project.

With the constant growth of the paradigm in the domain of Information Systems (IS) project management with the inclusion of Artificial Intelligence (AI), the position of the project manager is facing a considerable transformation. The project leader of today is no longer a person who performs solely traditional planning and coordinating functions but is an IT-loving orchestrator, strategic planner, and ethical custodian, who is in a position to oversee large digital platforms without losing control of resulting responsible innovation. A predictive skill in this new context is data literacy. The project managers should be prepared to explore data-driven expert opinions, be literate in comprehending the reasoning behind AI systems, and raise questions and concerns regarding algorithmic results and performance statistics. Such fluidity gives them an opportunity to interpret automated recommendations, identify inconsistencies, and inform decision-making with a stronger confidence.

Change management expertise is also significant. The introduction of AI in work can turn upside down the established workflow upside down, change the role of the team, and offer new tools that require a behavior change. Project managers have to be future-ready, which is managing the transition of their teams, and that includes managing resistance, gaining buy-in, and adhering to a long span because resistance and forgetfulness can be quite likely on the part of the team members. A critical part of this transformation will be AI fluency, that is, familiarity with the concepts of machine learning, AI tools, ethical pitfalls, and how they are applied in various project application instances. Data scientists are not required in the work of project managers, though they should be familiar with the ways of integrating AI into various workflows, including automation, prediction, and decision-making assistance.

In addition, ethical judgment must be good. When AI systems start influencing decisions made about people, services, and outcomes, it is necessary to make sure that the project managers can forecast the unintended consequences, identify biases, certify transparency, and ensure accountability. Promoting justice, aligning the application of AI with organizational values, and ensuring that use remains within the expectations of society will become the characteristic of responsible leaders within the field. Last but not least, digital collaborative skills are obligatory. The future of project work is more and more hybrid and distributed and demands the ability to work effectively with cloud-based tools, collaborative dashboards, and virtual communications interfaces. A key capacity of project leadership in the modern environment is remote team management, real-time feedback synchronization, and collaboration across online working environments.

REFERENCES

Ahmed, I., Munir, F., Nafees, F., Mahmood, J., Chaudhry, S. A., Javaid, M., & Batool, K. (2024). The Influence of Kanban Agile Methodology on Software Project Management: A Survey Method. *International Conference on Engineering and Emerging Technologies, ICEET, 2024*. DOI: 10.1109/ICEET65156.2024.10913653

Arun Sathe, C., Panse, C., Nascimento, D., Tortorella, G., Goyannes Gusmão Caiado, R., & Manuel Maqueira, J. (2023). An Empirical Study on Impact of Project Management Constraints in Agile Software Development. *Brazilian Journal of Operations & Production Management*, *20*(3), 1796–1796. DOI: 10.14488/BJOPM.1796.2023

Chimunhu, P., Topal, E., Ajak, A. D., & Asad, M. W. A. (2024). Underground mine planning and scheduling optimization: Opportunities for embracing machine learning augmented capabilities. *Applications of Artificial Intelligence in Mining, Geotechnical and Geoengineering*, 183–195. DOI: 10.1016/B978-0-443-18764-3.00013-8

Coffie, G. H., & Cudjoe, S. K. F. (2024). Using extreme gradient boosting (XGBoost) machine learning to predict construction cost overruns. *International Journal of Construction Management*, *24*(16), 1742–1750. DOI: 10.1080/15623599.2023.2289754

Conway, A., Li, J., Rad, M. G., Mafeld, S., & Taati, B. (2025). Automating sedation state assessments using natural language processing. *Journal of Nursing Scholarship*, *57*(1), 17–27. DOI: 10.1111/jnu.12968 PMID: 38532639

Demirag, A., Öztürk, E. N. D., & Ünal, C. (2023). Analysis and Comparision of Waterfall Model and Agile Approach in Software Projects. *AJIT-e: Online Academic Journal of Information Technology*, *14*(54), 183–203. DOI: 10.5824/ajite.2023.03.002.x

Endres, M., Bican, P. M., & Wöllner, T. (2022). Sustainability meets agile: Using Scrum to develop frugal innovations. *Journal of Cleaner Production*, *347*, 130871. DOI: 10.1016/j.jclepro.2022.130871

Gupta, A., Poels, G., & Bera, P. (2022). Using Conceptual Models in Agile Software Development: A Possible Solution to Requirements Engineering Challenges in Agile Projects. *IEEE Access : Practical Innovations, Open Solutions*, *10*, 119745–119766. DOI: 10.1109/ACCESS.2022.3221428

Hron, M., & Obwegeser, N. (2022). Why and how is Scrum being adapted in practice: A systematic review. *Journal of Systems and Software*, *183*, 111110. DOI: 10.1016/j.jss.2021.111110

Lano, K., Haughton, H., Yuan, Z., & Alfraihi, H. (2024). Agile model-driven re-engineering. *Innovations in Systems and Software Engineering*, *20*(4), 559–584. DOI: 10.1007/s11334-024-00568-z

Leong, H., Gao, Y., Ji, S., Zhang, Y., & Pamuksuz, U. (2024). Efficient Fine-Tuning of Large Language Models for Automated Medical Documentation. *2024 4th International Conference on Digital Society and Intelligent Systems (DSInS)*, 204–209. DOI: 10.1109/DSInS64146.2024.10992195

Mahfuzul, M., & Shamim, I. (2024). Artificial Intelligence in Project Management: Enhancing Efficiency and Decision-Making. *International Journal of Management Information Systems and Data Science*, *1*(1), 1–6. DOI: 10.62304/ijmisds.v1i1.107

Nenni, M. E., De Felice, F., De Luca, C., & Forcina, A. (2024). How artificial intelligence will transform project management in the age of digitization: A systematic literature review. *Management Review Quarterly*, *75*(2), 1669–1716. DOI: 10.1007/s11301-024-00418-z

Ozkan, N., Bal, S., Erdogan, T. G., & Gok, M. S. (2022). Scrum, Kanban or a Mix of Both? A Systematic Literature Review. *Proceedings of the 17th Conference on Computer Science and Intelligence Systems, FedCSIS 2022*, 883–893. DOI: 10.15439/2022F143

Pan, Y., & Zhang, L. (2022). Integrating BIM and AI for Smart Construction Management: Current Status and Future Directions. *Archives of Computational Methods in Engineering 2022 30:2*, *30*(2), 1081–1110. DOI: 10.1007/s11831-022-09830-8

Rahman, M., Sarwar, H., Kader, A., Goncalves, T., & Tin, T. T. (2024). Review and Empirical Analysis of Machine Learning-Based Software Effort Estimation. *IEEE Access : Practical Innovations, Open Solutions*, *12*, 85661–85680. DOI: 10.1109/ACCESS.2024.3404879

Saravanos, A., & Curinga, M. X. (2023). Simulating the Software Development Lifecycle: The Waterfall Model. *Applied System Innovation 2023, Vol. 6, Page 108*, *6*(6), 108. DOI: 10.3390/asi6060108

Shen, Y., Yang, L., & Deng, B. (2024). NLP-Driven Sentiment Analysis for Stakeholder Feedback in Sustainable Projects. *2024 6th International Conference on Frontier Technologies of Information and Computer, ICFTIC 2024*, 713–716. DOI: 10.1109/ICFTIC64248.2024.10913250

Shoushtari Bu-Ali, F., Daghighi, A., Ghafourian, E., & Shoushtari, F. (2024). Application of Artificial Intelligence in Project Management. *International Journal of Industrial Engineering and Operational Research*. http://ijieor.ir

Sohrabi, H., & Noorzai, E. (2024). Risk-supported case-based reasoning approach for cost overrun estimation of water-related projects using machine learning. *Engineering, Construction, and Architectural Management, 31*(2), 544–570. DOI: 10.1108/ECAM-05-2022-0450

Sravanthi, J., Sobti, R., Semwal, A., Shravan, M., Al-Hilali, A. A., & Bader Alazzam, M. (2023). AI-Assisted Resource Allocation in Project Management. *2023 3rd International Conference on Advance Computing and Innovative Technologies in Engineering, ICACITE 2023*, 70–74. DOI: 10.1109/ICACITE57410.2023.10182760

Strickroth, S., Kreidenweis, M., & Wurm, Z. (2023). Learning from Agile Methods: Using a Kanban Board for Classroom Orchestration. *Lecture Notes in Networks and Systems, 633 LNNS*, 68–79. DOI: 10.1007/978-3-031-26876-2_7

Uddin, S., Yan, S., & Lu, H. (2024). Machine learning and deep learning in project analytics: Methods, applications and research trends. *Production Planning and Control*. DOI: 10.1080/09537287.2024.2320790;PAGE:STRING:ARTICLE/CHAPTER

Yahya, N., & Maidin, S. S. (2022). The Waterfall Model with Agile Scrum as the Hybrid Agile Model for the Software Engineering Team. *2022 10th International Conference on Cyber and IT Service Management, CITSM 2022*. DOI: 10.1109/CITSM56380.2022.9936036

Compilation of References

Abd Majid, M., & Zainol Ariffin, K. A. (2021). Model for successful development and implementation of Cyber Security Operations Centre (SOC). *PLoS One*, *16*(11), e0260157. DOI: 10.1371/journal.pone.0260157 PMID: 34797896

Abdelkader, S., Amissah, J., Kinga, S., Mugerwa, G., Emmanuel, E., Mansour, D.-E. A., Bajaj, M., Blazek, V., & Prokop, L. (2024). Securing Modern Power Systems: Implementing Comprehensive Strategies to Enhance Resilience and Reliability Against Cyber-Attacks. *Results in Engineering*, *23*, 102647–102647. DOI: 10.1016/j.rineng.2024.102647

Aggarwal, C. C. (2018). *Machine Learning for Text*. Springer. DOI: 10.1007/978-3-319-73531-3

Ahlert, A. (2022). The Future of Vehicle Development Using Virtual Prototypes and an Interconnected Software Infrastructure. *Proceedings*, 229–243. DOI: 10.1007/978-3-658-37009-1_16

Ahmad, A., Maynard, S. B., Desouza, K. C., Kotsias, J., Whitty, M. T., & Baskerville, R. L. (2021). How can organizations develop situation awareness for incident response: A case study of management practice. *Computers & Security*, *101*(1), 102122. DOI: 10.1016/j.cose.2020.102122

Ahmed, I., Munir, F., Nafees, F., Mahmood, J., Chaudhry, S. A., Javaid, M., & Batool, K. (2024). The Influence of Kanban Agile Methodology on Software Project Management: A Survey Method. *International Conference on Engineering and Emerging Technologies, ICEET, 2024*. DOI: 10.1109/ICEET65156.2024.10913653

Akinsola, A., & Akinde, A. (2024). Enhancing Software Supply Chain Resilience: Strategy For Mitigating Software Supply Chain Security Risks And Ensuring Security Continuity In Development Lifecycle. *International Journal on Soft Computing*, *15*(1/2), 01-18. DOI: 10.5121/ijsc.2024.15201

Ali, M., Khan, S. U., & Vasilakos, A. V. (2018). Security in cloud computing: Opportunities and challenges. *Information Sciences, 305*(1), 357–383. DOI: 10.1016/j.ins.2015.01.025

Alvarez Tech. (2024, August 14). *Crowdstrike Outage: What We Now Know – Alvarez Tech.* (2024, August 14). Alvarez Technology Group. https://www.alvareztg.com/crowdstrike-outage-what-we-now-know/

Amft, S., Höltervennhoff, S., Huaman, N., Krause, A., Simko, L., Acar, Y., & Fahl, S. (2023). "We've Disabled MFA for You": An Evaluation of the Security and Usability of Multi-Factor Authentication Recovery Deployments. In *CCS 2023 - Proceedings of the 2023 ACM SIGSAC Conference on Computer and Communications Security* (pp. 3138–3152). DOI: 10.1145/3576915.3623180

Ammar, M., Haleem, A., Javaid, M., Walia, R., & Bahl, S. (2021). Improving material quality management and manufacturing organization systems through Industry 4.0 technologies. *Materials Today: Proceedings, 45*, 5089–5096. DOI: 10.1016/j.matpr.2021.01.585

Andrews, D. (2015). The circular economy, design thinking, and education for sustainability. *Local Economy, 30*(3), 305–315. DOI: 10.1177/0269094215578226

Angles, R., & Gutierrez, C. (2008). Survey of Graph Database Models. *ACM Computing Surveys, 40*(1), 1–39. DOI: 10.1145/1322432.1322433

Arnold, C., Kiel, D., & Voigt, K.-I. (2016). How the Industrial Internet of Things changes business models in different manufacturing industries. *International Journal of Innovation Management, 20*(8), 1640015. DOI: 10.1142/S1363919616400156

Arun Sathe, C., Panse, C., Nascimento, D., Tortorella, G., Goyannes Gusmão Caiado, R., & Manuel Maqueira, J. (2023). An Empirical Study on Impact of Project Management Constraints in Agile Software Development. *Brazilian Journal of Operations & Production Management, 20*(3), 1796–1796. DOI: 10.14488/BJOPM.1796.2023

Ashare, M. (2024, July 25). *American Airlines credits IT teams with quick recovery from CrowdStrike disruption.* CIO Dive. https://www.ciodive.com/news/american-airlines-crowdstrike-outage-operatioins-recovery/722428/

Atig, Y., Zahaf, A., Bouchiha, D., & Malki, M. (2022). Alignment conservativity under the ontology change. [JITR]. *Journal of Information Technology Research, 15*(1), 1–19. DOI: 10.4018/JITR.299923

Atig, Y., Zahaf, A., & Khiati, N. (2023). Temporal dimensions of quality in knowledge graph evolution: A comprehensive review. *Ingénierie des Systèmes d'Information, 28*(4), 1081–1090. DOI: 10.18280/isi.280428

Atlas, M., & Florida, R. (1998). Green manufacturing. In Handbook of Technology Management, 1385–1393.

Aukker, T., De Koning, A., & Wood, R., (2013). EXIOPOL–development and illustrative analyses of a detailed global MR EE SUT/IOT. *Economic Systems Research*, *25*(1), 50–70. DOI: 10.1080/09535314.2012.761952

Ayyaswamy, K. (2024e). Enhancing Digital Technology Planning, Leadership, and Management to Transform Education. In Bhatia, M., & Mushtaq, M. T. (Eds.), *Navigating Innovative Technologies and Intelligent Systems in Modern Education* (pp. 1–9). IGI Global., DOI: 10.4018/979-8-3693-5370-7.ch001

Azad, M. A., Abdullah, S., Arshad, J., Lallie, H., & Ahmed, Y. H. (2024). Verify and trust: A multidimensional survey of zero-trust security in the age of IoT. *Internet of Things: Engineering Cyber Physical Human Systems*, *27*, 101227. DOI: 10.1016/j.iot.2024.101227

Azzeh, M., & Bou Nassif, A. (2016). A hybrid model for estimating software project effort from use case points. *Applied Soft Computing*, *49*, 981–989. DOI: 10.1016/j.asoc.2016.05.008

Baclawski, K., Bennett, M., Berg-Cross, G., Schneider, T., Sharma, R., Singer, J., & Sriram, R. D. (2021). Ontology summit 2020 communiqué: Knowledge graphs. *Applied Ontology*, *16*(2), 229–247. DOI: 10.3233/AO-210249

Baeza-Yates, R. (2018). Bias on the web. *Communications of the ACM*, *61*(6), 54–61. DOI: 10.1145/3209581

Bag, S., & Pretorius, J. H. C. (2022). Relationships between industry 4.0, sustainable manufacturing and circular economy: Proposal of a research framework. *The International Journal of Organizational Analysis*, *30*(4), 864–898. DOI: 10.1108/IJOA-04-2020-2120

Bahi, J., Contassot-Vivier, S., & Couturier, R. (2005). Dynamic load balancing and efficient load estimators for asynchronous iterative algorithms. *IEEE Transactions on Parallel and Distributed Systems*, *16*(4), 289–299. DOI: 10.1109/TPDS.2005.45

Bakker, R. R. (1987). Knowledge Graphs: Representation and structuring of scientific knowledge. Ph.D. Dissertation. University of Twente.

Barbin, J. P., & Rashidi, H. (2015). A decision support system for estimating cost of software projects using a hybrid of multi-layer artificial neural network and decision tree. *International Journal in Foundations of Computer Science & Technology*. DOI: 10.5121/ijfcst.2015.5603

Batini, C., Rula, A., Scannapieco, M., & Viscusi, G. (2015). From data quality to big data quality. [JDM]. *Journal of Database Management, 26*(1), 60–82. DOI: 10.4018/JDM.2015010103

Beers, S. Z. (2011). *21st century skills: Preparing students for THEIR future*. National Education Association.

Behrendt, A., Odenwälder, P., Müller, N., & Schmitz, C. (n.d.). Industry 4.0 Demystified—Lean's Next Level. McKinsey, McKinsey Co. Retrieved January 9, 2020, from https://www.mckinsey.com/business-functions/operations/our-insights/industry-4-0-demystified-leans-next-level

Beynon-Davies, S. P. (2025). IS failure and risk assessment: The case of the London Ambulance Service computer-aided dispatch system. *European Conference on Information Systems*. https://www.semanticscholar.org/paper/IS-failure-and-risk-assessment%3A-The-case-of-the-Beynon-Davies/b638329883751f68452bf5dcc177b4d46bae7734

Bhamra, T. (2016). *Design for Sustainability*. Informa UK Limited. DOI: 10.4324/9781315576664

Bhatt, S., Pham, T. K., Gupta, M., Benson, J., Park, J., & Sandhu, R. (2021). Attribute-Based Access Control for AWS Internet of Things and Secure Industries of the Future. *IEEE Access : Practical Innovations, Open Solutions, 9*, 107200–107223. DOI: 10.1109/ACCESS.2021.3101218

Bird, S., Klein, E., & Loper, E. (2009). *Natural Language Processing with Python*. O'Reilly Media.

Blei, D. M., Ng, A. Y., & Jordan, M. I. (2003). Latent Dirichlet Allocation. *Journal of Machine Learning Research, 3*, 993–1022.

Blumauer, A. (2014). From Taxonomies over Ontologies to Knowledge Graphs. Retrieved February 2023 from: https://blog.semantic-web.at/2014/07/15/from-taxonomies-over-ontologies-to-knowledgegraphs

Boehm, B. W. (1989). *Software engineering economics*. Prentice-Hall.

Boehm, B. W., & Abts, C. (2000). Software risk management: Principles and practices. *IEEE Software, 17*(4), 38–44.

Braccini, A. M., & Margherita, E. G. (2018). Exploring Organizational Sustainability of Industry 4.0 under the Triple Bottom Line: The Case of a Manufacturing Company. *Sustainability (Basel), 11*(1), 36. DOI: 10.3390/su11010036

Breque, M., De Nul, L., & Petridis, A. (2021). *Industry 5.0: Towards a sustainable, human-centric, and resilient European industry*. European Commission, Directorate-General for Research and Innovation.

Broder, M., & Charlton, J. (2025). Design to cost methodology saves estimated $1.2 billion on AIM-9X missile program.

Burnstein, I. (2025). *Practical Software Testing*. Springer Professional Computing.

Bu, S.-J., & Cho, S.-B. (2020). A convolutional neural-based learning classifier system for detecting database intrusion via insider attack. *Information Sciences*, *512*, 123–136. DOI: 10.1016/j.ins.2019.09.055

Call for papers - Journal of Cleaner Production I ScienceDirect.com by Elsevier. (n.d.). https://www.sciencedirect.com/journal/journal-of-cleaner-production/about/call-for-papers#supply-chain-management-innovation-practices-for-sustainability-achievement-under-carbon-trading-era

Campbell, T., Williams, C., & Ivanova, O., (2011). *Could 3D printing change the world? Technologies, Potential, and Implications of Additive Manufacturing*. Atlantic Council.

Cavoukian, A. (2012). *Privacy by design: The 7 foundational principles*. Information and Privacy Commissioner of Ontario.

Chakraborty, R., Alam, M., & Rustam, F. (2022). A Comprehensive Survey on Fake News Detection: Data, Methods, and Future Directions. *IEEE Access : Practical Innovations, Open Solutions*, *10*, 26824–26844.

Chang, V., Golightly, L., Modesti, P., Xu, Q. A., Doan, L. M. T., Hall, K., Boddu, S., & Kobusińska, A. (2022). A Survey on Intrusion Detection Systems for Fog and Cloud Computing. *Future Internet*, *14*(3), 89. DOI: 10.3390/fi14030089

Chen, B., Jiang, X., Yang, X., & Gao, X. (Eds.). (2023). Global Cleaner Production Conference (GCPC) 2023. Journal of Cleaner Production https://www.sciencedirect.com/journal/journal-of-cleaner-production/special-issues

Chen, J. Y., Jiménez-Ruiz, E., Horrocks, I., Chen, X., & Myklebust, E. B. (2021). Correcting assertions and alignments of large scale knowledge bases. *Semantic Web Journal*, *14*(3), 1–25. DOI: 10.3233/SW-210448

Chimunhu, P., Topal, E., Ajak, A. D., & Asad, M. W. A. (2024). Underground mine planning and scheduling optimization: Opportunities for embracing machine learning augmented capabilities. *Applications of Artificial Intelligence in Mining, Geotechnical and Geoengineering*, 183–195. DOI: 10.1016/B978-0-443-18764-3.00013-8

Chin, T., Li, G., Jiao, H., Addo, F., & Jawahar, I. (2019). Career sustainability during manufacturing innovation. *Career Development International, 24*(6), 509–528. DOI: 10.1108/CDI-02-2019-0034

Chong, S., Pan, G. T., Chin, J., Show, P. L., Yang, T. C. K., & Huang, C. M. (2018). Integration of 3D printing and Industry 4.0 into engineering teaching. *Sustainability (Basel), 10*(11), 3960. DOI: 10.3390/su10113960

ClimateWatch. (2020). Historical GHG Emissions. Retrieved June 24, 2021, from https://www.climatewatchdata.org/ghg-emissions?end_year=2018&start_year=1990

COCOMO II model – Software Engineering Institute. (n.d.). https://resources.sei.cmu.edu/library/asset-view.cfm?assetid=50804

Coffie, G. H., & Cudjoe, S. K. F. (2024). Using extreme gradient boosting (XGBoost) machine learning to predict construction cost overruns. *International Journal of Construction Management, 24*(16), 1742–1750. DOI: 10.1080/15623599.2023.2289754

Conway, A., Li, J., Rad, M. G., Mafeld, S., & Taati, B. (2025). Automating sedation state assessments using natural language processing. *Journal of Nursing Scholarship, 57*(1), 17–27. DOI: 10.1111/jnu.12968 PMID: 38532639

Cook, R. (2000). 8.6.4 Denver International Airport: How could system engineering principles have prevented disaster? *INCOSE International Symposium, 10*(1), 849–854. DOI: 10.1002/j.2334-5837.2000.tb00464.x

Culot, G., Nassimbeni, G., Podrecca, M., & Sartor, M. (2021). The ISO/IEC 27001 information security management standard: Literature review and theory-based research agenda. *The TQM Journal, 33*(7), 76–105. DOI: 10.1108/TQM-09-2020-0202

Cundiff, J., McCallum, T., Rich, A., Truax, M., Ward, T., & Havelka, D. (2018). Healthcare.gov: Opportunity out of disaster. *The Journal of Information and Systems in Education*. https://www.semanticscholar.org/paper/Healthcare.gov%3A-Opportunity-out-of-Disaster-Cundiff-McCallum/479e5ca280497d9150839631f5785b4c46067737

Daah, C., Qureshi, A., Awan, I., & Konur, S. (2024). Enhancing Zero Trust Models in the Financial Industry through Blockchain Integration: A Proposed Framework. *Electronics (Basel), 13*(5), 865. DOI: 10.3390/electronics13050865

Dam, S., Mandal, G., Dasgupta, K., & Dutta, P. (2021). An ant-colony-Based meta-heuristic approach for load balancing in cloud computing. *Research Anthology on Architectures, Frameworks, and Integration Strategies for Distributed and Cloud Computing*, 873-903. DOI: 10.4018/978-1-7998-5339-8.ch041

Dasgupta, K., Mandal, B., Dutta, P., Mandal, J. K., & Dam, S. (2013). A genetic algorithm (GA) based load balancing strategy for cloud computing. *Procedia Technology, 10*, 340–347. DOI: 10.1016/j.protcy.2013.12.369

DataCouch. (2024, September 3). *The Falcon's great Fall: The 2024 Update That Shook CrowdStrike's Legacy*. Medium; Medium. https://datacouch.medium.com/the-falcons-great-fall-the-2024-update-that-shook-crowdstrike-s-legacy-1d55c89e1ac1

Davis, E. (2020). Time and space in knowledge graphs. Retrieved February 2023 from: https://go.aws/2SxOVZ9

De Zoysa. (2024, July 27). *Microsoft global outages caused by CrowdStrike software glitch*. https://www.researchgate.net/publication/382625564_Microsoft_global_outages_caused_by_CrowdStrike_software_glitch

Deif, A. M. (2011). A system model for green manufacturing. *Journal of Cleaner Production, 19*(14), 1553–1559. DOI: 10.1016/j.jclepro.2011.05.022

Demirag, A., Öztürk, E. N. D., & Ünal, C. (2023). Analysis and Comparision of Waterfall Model and Agile Approach in Software Projects. *AJIT-e: Online Academic Journal of Information Technology, 14*(54), 183–203. DOI: 10.5824/ajite.2023.03.002.x

Devlin, J., Chang, M. W., Lee, K., & Toutanova, K. (2019). BERT: Pre-training of Deep Bidirectional Transformers for Language Understanding. *Proceedings of NAACL-HLT, 2019*, 4171–4186.

Dey, D., Majumder, A., Agrawal, Y., Tewari, S., & Mohapatra, H. (2024). Smart mobility revolution. *Advances in Electronic Government, Digital Divide, and Regional Development*, 143–164. DOI: 10.4018/979-8-3693-6740-7.ch006

Dincer, I., & Acar, C. (2015). A review on clean energy solutions for better sustainability. *International Journal of Energy Research, 39*(5), 585–606. DOI: 10.1002/er.3329

Dissanayake, N., Zahedi, M., Jayatilaka, A., & Babar, M. A. (2022). Why, How and Where of Delays in Software Security Patch Management: An Empirical Investigation in the Healthcare Sector. *Proceedings of the ACM on Human-Computer Interaction, 6*(CSCW2), 1–29. DOI: 10.1145/3555087

Duan, W., Khurshid, A., Khan, K., & Călin, A. C. (2024). Transforming industry: Investigating 4.0 technologies for sustainable product evolution in China through a novel fuzzy three-way decision-making process. *Technological Forecasting and Social Change, 200*, 123125. DOI: 10.1016/j.techfore.2023.123125

Elliott, R. N. (2016). Energy efficiency and industry: The national trend. Washington DC: American Council for an Energy-Efficient Economy. Retrieved from http://aceee.org/blog/2015/12/energy-efficiency-and-industry

Endres, M., Bican, P. M., & Wöllner, T. (2022). Sustainability meets agile: Using Scrum to develop frugal innovations. *Journal of Cleaner Production*, *347*, 130871. DOI: 10.1016/j.jclepro.2022.130871

Engemann, K. J., & Miller, H. E. (2024). Toward revealing concealed risks for agile IT service management practices. *Information Systems and e-Business Management*. DOI: 10.1007/s10257-023-00666-8

Epureanu, B. I., Li, X., Nassehi, A., & Koren, Y. (2020). Self-repair of intelligent manufacturing systems by deep reinforcement learning. *CIRP Annals*, *69*(1), 421–424. DOI: 10.1016/j.cirp.2020.04.008

Everett, G. D., & McLeod, R. (2025). *Software Testing*. John Wiley & Sons Inc. Google Books. https://books.google.com/books?hl=en&lr=&id=z8UdPmvkBHEC&oi=fnd&pg=PR7&dq=Everett

Feldman, R., & Sanger, J. (2007). *The Text Mining Handbook: Advanced Approaches in Analyzing Unstructured Data*. Cambridge University Press.

Ferragina, P., & Scaiella, U. (2010). TAGME: On-the-fly Annotation of Short Text Fragments. *Proceedings of the 19th ACM Conference on Information and Knowledge Management (CIKM'10)*, 1625–1628. DOI: 10.1145/1871437.1871689

Finkelstein, A. (1993). *Report of the inquiry into the London Ambulance Service*. https://www.semanticscholar.org/paper/Report-of-the-Inquiry-into-the-London-Ambulance-Finkelstein/5c22db59e0e008589750c1470ffdf628ea6747f5

Fitzgerald, B., & Stol, K.-J. (2017). Continuous software engineering: A roadmap and agenda. *Journal of Systems and Software*, *123*, 176–189. DOI: 10.1016/j.jss.2015.06.063

Fountain, J. (2025). The difficulties of Healthcare.gov need to be seen in the context of an acrimonious political climate and the poor record of large and complex IT projects. https://www.semanticscholar.org/paper/The-difficulties-of-Healthcare.gov-need-to-be-seen-Fountain/21574e69475d44398e9e1a81cba7355436408178

Fung, B. (2024, July 24). We finally know what caused the global tech outage - and how much it cost. CNN. https://edition.cnn.com/2024/07/24/tech/crowdstrike-outage-cost-cause/index.html

Garetti, M., & Taisch, M. (2011). Sustainable manufacturing: Trends and research challenges. *Production Planning and Control*, *23*(2-3), 83–104. DOI: 10.1080/09537287.2011.591619

Garousi, V., & Mäntylä, M. V. (2016). When and what to automate in software testing? A multi-vocal literature review. *Information and Software Technology*, *76*, 92–117. DOI: 10.1016/j.infsof.2016.04.015

Geissdoerfer, M., Savaget, P., Bocken, N. M., & Hultink, E. J. (2017). The Circular Economy–A New Sustainability Paradigm? *Journal of Cleaner Production*, *143*, 757–768. DOI: 10.1016/j.jclepro.2016.12.048

George, A. S. (2024). When Trust Fails: Examining Systemic Risk in the Digital Economy from the 2024 CrowdStrike Outage. *Partners Universal Multidisciplinary Research Journal, 1*(2), 134–152. DOI: 10.5281/zenodo.12828222

Ge, X. (2025). Analysis of legal framework solutions to protect retail consumers. *International Journal of Retail & Distribution Management*, *53*(2), 1–16. DOI: 10.1108/IJRDM-02-2023-0055

Ghayoomi, H., Laskey, K., Miller-Hooks, E., Hooks, C., & Tariverdi, M. (2021). Assessing resilience of hospitals to cyberattack. *Digital Health*, *7*, 20552076211059366. DOI: 10.1177/20552076211059366 PMID: 34868621

Giuffrida, C., Kuijsten, A., & Tanenbaum, A. S. (2013). Safe and automatic live update for operating systems. *SIGPLAN Notices*, *48*(4), 279–292. DOI: 10.1145/2499368.2451147

Gobinath, V. M., Kathirvel, A., Rajesh Kanna, S. K., & Annamalai, K. (2024). "Chapter 5: Smart Technology in Management Industries: A Useful Perspective", Artificial Intelligence Applied to Industry 4.0, Wiley Publiser, USA, 1st Edition, July 2024, pp.93-106, DOI: 10.1002/9781394216147.ch5

González-Granadillo, G., González-Zarzosa, S., & Diaz, R. (2021). Security information and event management (SIEM): Analysis, trends, and usage in critical infrastructures. *Sensors (Basel)*, *21*(14), 4759. DOI: 10.3390/s21144759 PMID: 34300500

Grishman, R. (2012). Information extraction: Capabilities and challenges. *Technical Report, NYU Dept. CS.*

Grus, J. (2019). *Data Science from Scratch: First Principles with Python.* O'Reilly Media.

Gulbaz, R., Siddiqui, A. B., Anjum, N., Alotaibi, A. A., Althobaiti, T., & Ramzan, N. (2021). Balancer genetic algorithm—A novel task scheduling optimization approach in cloud computing. *Applied Sciences (Basel, Switzerland), 11*(14), 6244. DOI: 10.3390/app11146244

Gupta, A., Poels, G., & Bera, P. (2022). Using Conceptual Models in Agile Software Development: A Possible Solution to Requirements Engineering Challenges in Agile Projects. *IEEE Access : Practical Innovations, Open Solutions, 10*, 119745–119766. DOI: 10.1109/ACCESS.2022.3221428

Haapamäki, E., & Sihvonen, J. (2022). Cybersecurity in Accounting Research. *Routledge EBooks*, 182–214. DOI: 10.4324/9781003198123-10

Habib, M. K., & Chimsom, C. (2019). Industry 4.0: Sustainability and design principles. In 2019 20th International Conference on Research and Education in Mechatronics (REM) (pp. 1–8). IEEE.

Hale, B., van Bossuyt, D. L., Papakonstantinou, N., & O'Halloran, B. (2021). A zero-trust methodology for security of complex systems with machine learning components. In *Proceedings of the ASME Design Engineering Technical Conference* (Vol. 2). DOI: 10.1115/DETC2021-70442

Han, J., Kamber, M., & Pei, J. (2011). *Data Mining: Concepts and Techniques*. Morgan Kaufmann.

Hanmer, R. S. (2025). *Patterns for Fault Tolerant Software*. Wiley. Google Books. https://books.google.com/books?hl=en&lr=&id=jZgSAAAAQBAJ&oi=fnd&pg=PP12&dq=Hanmer

Heller, T. C., & Shukla, P. R. (2003). Development and climate: Engaging developing countries. In Beyond Kyoto: Advancing the international effort against climate change, 111-140.

Hepp, M. (2008). Ontologies: State of the art, business potential, and grand challenges. In *Ontology Management: Semantic Web, Semantic Web Services, and Business Applications* (pp. 3-22). Springer. DOI: 10.1007/978-0-387-69900-4_1

Highsmith, J. (2013). Adaptive Software Development: A Collaborative Approach to Managing Complex Systems. In *Google Books*. Addison-Wesley., https://books.google.com/books?hl=en&lr=&id=CVcUAAAAQBAJ&oi=fnd&pg=PR7&dq=Highsmith

Hijazi, H., (2012). A review of risk management in different software development methodologies. *International Journal of Computer Applications, 45*(7), 975–8887.

Hoch, D. J., Kunz, D., & Kauffman, S. (2000). *The evolution of software project management and software engineering economics*. Springer.

Hogan, A., Blomqvist, E., Cochez, M., d'Amato, C., Melo, G. D., Gutierrez, C., Kirrane, S., Gayo, J. E. L., Navigli, R., Neumaier, S., Ngomo, A. N., Polleres, A., Rashid, S. M., Rula, A., Schmelzeisen, L., Sequeda, J., Staab, S., & Zimmermann, A. (2021). Knowledge graphs. *ACM Computing Surveys, 54*(4), 1–37. DOI: 10.1145/3447772

Holmes, W., Bialik, M., & Fadel, C. (2019). *Artificial intelligence in education: Promises and implications for teaching and learning*. Center for Curriculum Redesign.

Hougham, M. (1996). London Ambulance Service computer-aided despatch system. *International Journal of Project Management, 14*(2), 103–110. DOI: 10.1016/0263-7863(95)00067-4

Hron, M., & Obwegeser, N. (2022). Why and how is Scrum being adapted in practice: A systematic review. *Journal of Systems and Software, 183*, 111110. DOI: 10.1016/j.jss.2021.111110

Hunt, A., & Thomas, D. (2003). The Trip-Packing Dilemma. *IEEE Software, 20*(3), 106–107. DOI: 10.1109/MS.2003.1196331

ISO/IEC. (2013). *Information technology – Security techniques – Information security management systems – Requirements (ISO/IEC 27001:2013)*. International Organization for Standardization.

Jabbour, A., Jabbour, C.J.C., Foropon, C., & Filho, MG (2018). When titans meet—Can Industry 4.0 revolutionize the environmentally sustainable manufacturing wave? The role of critical success factors. Technol. Soc. Chang., pp. 132, 18–25.

Joachims, T. (1998). Text Categorization with Support Vector Machines: Learning with Many Relevant Features. *European Conference on Machine Learning*, 137-142. DOI: 10.1007/BFb0026683

Johnson, R. (2024, August 9). *Lessons from Crowdstrike outage and incident response plan*. Cybersecurity and Cloud Services. Www.cai.iohttps://www.cai.io/resources/thought-leadership/cybersecurity-insights-and-prevention-strategies-from-the-crowdstrike-incident

Jolin, J. S., Theophilus, A., and Kathirvel, A. (2025). Two factor mutual authentication with fingerprint and MAC Address Validation, International Journal of Communication Networks and Information Security, Vol. 16, No. 6, 2024, pp. 56 – 68. Publisher:Institute of Information Technology, Kohat University of Science and Technology, ISSN:2076-0930 E-ISSN:2073-607X, DoI:DOI: 10.5815/ijcnis.2024.06.05

Jones, D. (2024, July 25). *CrowdStrike disruption direct losses to reach $5.4B for Fortune 500, study finds*. Cybersecurity Dive. https://www.cybersecuritydive.com/news/crowdstrike-cost-fortune-500-losses-cyber-insurance/722396/

Jones, C. (2007). *Estimating software costs: Bringing realism to estimating* (2nd ed.). McGraw-Hill.

Jovane, F., Yoshikawa, H., Alting, L., Boër, C., Westkamper, E., Williams, D., Tseng, M., Seliger, G., & Paci, A. (2008). The incoming global technological and industrial revolution towards competitive, sustainable manufacturing. *CIRP Annals*, *57*(2), 641–659. DOI: 10.1016/j.cirp.2008.09.010

Junior, J. A. G., Busso, C. M., Gobbo, S. C. O., & Carreão, H. (2018). Making the links between environmental protection, process safety, and Industry 4.0. *Process Safety and Environmental Protection*, *117*, 372–382. DOI: 10.1016/j.psep.2018.05.017

Jurczuk, M., & Suprynowicz, M. (2024). Consent in Data Privacy: A General Comparison of GDPR and HIPAA. *Adam Mickiewicz University Law Review*, *16*, 173–194. DOI: 10.14746/ppuam.2024.16.07

Kanagasundaram, H. and Kathirvel, A. (2019), EIMO-ESOLSR: energy efficient and security-based model for OLSR routing protocol in mobile ad-hoc network. IET Communications, 13: 553-559. https://doi.org/10.1049/iet-com.2018.5564DOI: 10.1049/iet-com.2018.5564

Kathirvel, A., & Maheswaran, C. P. (2023), “Chapter 8: Enhanced AI-Based Intrusion Detection and Response System for WSN”, Artificial Intelligence for Intrusion Detection Systems, CRC Publiser/Chapman and Hall, New York, 1st Edition. DOI: 10.1201/9781003346340-8

Kathirvel, A., Subramaniam, M., Navaneethan, S., & Sabarinath, C. (2021), “Improved IDR Response System for Sensor Network”, Journal of Web Engineering, Vol. 20 1, 53–88, DOI: 10.13052/jwe1540-9589.2013

Kathirvel, A. (2024d). Applications of Serverless Computing: Systematic Overview. In Aluvalu, R., & Maheswari, U. (Eds.), *Serverless Computing Concepts, Technology and Architecture* (Vol. 221-233). IGI Global., DOI: 10.4018/979-8-3693-1682-5.ch014

Kathirvel, A. (2024f). Innovation and Industry Application: IoT-Based Robotics Frontier of Automation in Industry Application. In Satishkumar, D., & Sivaraja, M. (Eds.), *Internet of Things and AI for Natural Disaster Management and Prediction* (pp. 83–105). IGI Global., DOI: 10.4018/979-8-3693-4284-8.ch004

Kathirvel, A., Gobinath, V. M., Naren, A. K., & Maheswaran, C. P. (2025). AI-based automated disease detection based on symptoms healthcare for pets and birds. In *AI and the Revival of Big Data* (pp. 311–345). IGI Global., DOI: 10.4018/979-8-3693-8472-5.ch014

Kathirvel, A., & Naren, A. K. (2024e). Diabetes and Pre-Diabetes Prediction by AI Using Tuned XGB Classifier. In Khang, A. (Ed.), *Medical Robotics and AI-Assisted Diagnostics for a High-Tech Healthcare Industry* (pp. 52–64). IGI Global., DOI: 10.4018/979-8-3693-2105-8.ch004

Kathirvel, A., Naren, A. K., & Santhoshi, B. (2024b). Business Intelligent and Blockchain in Entrepreneurship. In *Entrepreneurship Innovation and Education for Performance Improvement*. IGI Global., DOI: 10.4018/979-8-3693-7903-5.ch015

Kathirvel, A., Naren, A. K., & Subramanian, C. (2024a). Intelligent Serverless Computing Technology and Recent Trends: A Review. In *Driving Transformative Technology Trends with Cloud Computing*. IGI Global., DOI: 10.4018/979-8-3693-2869-9.ch002

Kathirvel, N., Ayyaswamy, K., Saravanan, N., & Kaliappan, P. (2025). Mathematical approach. *Advances in Electronic Government, Digital Divide, and Regional Development*, 253–280. DOI: 10.4018/979-8-3693-7205-0.ch012

Kaur, R., Gabrijelčič, D., & Klobučar, T. (2023). Artificial intelligence for cybersecurity: Literature review and future research directions. *Information Fusion*, *97*, 101804. DOI: 10.1016/j.inffus.2023.101804

Kendall, K. E., & Kendall, J. E. (2009). *Systems analysis and design* (8th ed.). Pearson Education.

Kerner, S. M. (2024, October 29). *CrowdStrike outage explained: What caused it and what's next*. TechTarget. https://www.techtarget.com/whatis/feature/Explaining-the-largest-IT-outage-in-history-and-whats-next

Kerr, W., & Ryan, C. (2001). Eco-efficiency gains from remanufacturing: A case study of photocopier remanufacturing at Fuji Xerox Australia. *Journal of Cleaner Production*, *9*(1), 75–81. DOI: 10.1016/S0959-6526(00)00032-9

Khezri, A., Benderbal, H. H., & Benyoucef, L. (2019). A sustainable reconfigurable manufacturing system design focusing on environmentally hazardous wastes, in 2019 24th IEEE International Conference on Emerging Technologies and Factory Automation (ETFA), September, 317–324.

Kloppenborg, T. J., & Anantatmula, V. (2013). *Project management: A system approach to planning, scheduling, and controlling* (10th ed.). Pearson Prentice Hall.

Kontokostas, D., Westphal, P., Auer, S., Hellmann, S., Lehmann, J., Cornelissen, R., & Zaveri, A. (2014). Test-driven Evaluation of Linked Data Quality. In *Proceedings of the 23rd International Conference on World Wide Web*. ACM, 747–758.

Kopetz, H., & Steiner, W. (2022). *Real-Time Systems*. (2022). Real-time systems: design principles for distributed embedded applications. Springer Nature. https://tinyurl.com/2u62suk9

Kukreja, S., & Dalal, S. (2018). Modified drosophila optimization algorithm for managing re-sources in cloud environment. *International Journal of Engineering & Technology, 7*(2.4), 165. DOI: 10.14419/ijet.v7i2.4.13031

Kumar Singh Sandeep, A. (2014). Scheduling algorithm with load balancing in cloud computing. *International Journal of Scientific and Engineering Research, 2*(1), 38–43. DOI: 10.70729/J201391

Kumar, S., Mohapatra, H., & Dalai, A. K. (2024). Enhancing energy efficiency in wireless sensor networks via clustering approach. *2024 4th International Conference on Artificial Intelligence and Signal Processing (AISP)*, 1-6. DOI: 10.1109/AISP61711.2024.10870799

Kumar, R., & Rao, P. (2018). Green manufacturing technology - solution for environmental impact and waste. *Sustainable Development*, *4*(12), 532–535.

Landry, J. R. (2009). Analyzing the London Ambulance Service's computer-aided despatch (LASCAD) failure as a case of administrative evil. *Proceedings of the Special Interest Group on Management Information System's 47th Annual Conference on Computer Personnel Research – SIGMIS-CPR'09*. DOI: 10.1145/1542130.1542163

Lano, K., Haughton, H., Yuan, Z., & Alfraihi, H. (2024). Agile model-driven re-engineering. *Innovations in Systems and Software Engineering*, *20*(4), 559–584. DOI: 10.1007/s11334-024-00568-z

Leong, H., Gao, Y., Ji, S., Zhang, Y., & Pamuksuz, U. (2024). Efficient Fine-Tuning of Large Language Models for Automated Medical Documentation. *2024 4th International Conference on Digital Society and Intelligent Systems (DSInS)*, 204–209. DOI: 10.1109/DSInS64146.2024.10992195

Leong, W. D., Lam, H. L., Ng, W. P. Q., Lim, C. H., Tan, C. P., & Ponnambalam, S. G. (2019). Lean and green manufacturing—A review of its applications and impacts. *Process Integration and Optimization for Sustainability*, *3*(1), 5–23. DOI: 10.1007/s41660-019-00082-x

Leveson, N. G., & Turner, C. S. (1993). An investigation of the Therac-25 accidents. *Computer*, *26*(7), 18–41. DOI: 10.1109/MC.1993.274940

Li, B. H., Zhang, L., & Wang, S. L., (2010). Cloud manufacturing: A new service-oriented networked manufacturing model. *Jisuanji Jicheng Zhizao Xitong*, *16*(1), 1–7.

Lim, F. J., & Sian, T. B. (2025). Overview of software re-engineering concepts, models and approaches. *JOIV: International Journal on Informatics Visualization*, *9*(1), 46–56. DOI: 10.62527/joiv.9.1.3034

Lin, Z., Liu, Y., Sun, M., & Liu, Y. (2021). Pre-trained Transformers for Text Ranking: BERT and Beyond. *arXiv preprint arXiv:2105.08362*.

Lindh, M., & Nolin, J. (2016). Information We Collect: Surveillance and Privacy in the Implementation of Google Apps for Education. *European Educational Research Journal*, *15*(6), 644–663. DOI: 10.1177/1474904116654917

Lin, W., Liang, C., Wang, J. Z., & Buyya, R. (2012). Bandwidth-aware divisible task scheduling for cloud computing. *Software, Practice & Experience*, *44*(2), 163–174. DOI: 10.1002/spe.2163

Lipner, S. (2018). The Trustworthy Computing Security Development Lifecycle. *20th Annual Computer Security Applications Conference*. DOI: 10.1109/CSAC.2004.41

Liu, S., d'Aquin, M., & Motta, E. (2017). Measuring accuracy of triples in knowledge graphs. In *Language, Data, and Knowledge: First International Conference, LDK 2017, Galway, Ireland* (pp. 343-357). DOI: 10.1007/978-3-319-59888-8_29

Liu, Y., Ott, M., Goyal, N., Du, J., Joshi, M., Chen, D., . . . Stoyanov, V. (2019). RoBERTa: A Robustly Optimized BERT Pretraining Approach. *arXiv preprint arXiv:1907.11692*.

Liu, Y., & Wang, Y. (2015). A study on software development month effort. *Journal of Software*, 798–804. DOI: 10.17706/jsw.10.7.798-804

Li, X., Bayrak, A. E., Epureanu, B. I., & Koren, Y. (2018). Real-time teaming of multiple reconfigurable manufacturing systems. *CIRP Annals*, *67*(1), 437–440. DOI: 10.1016/j.cirp.2018.04.051

Li, X., Li, N., Kolmanovsky, I., & Epureanu, B. I. (2021). Stochastic model predictive control for remanufacturing system management. *Journal of Manufacturing Systems*, *59*, 355–366. DOI: 10.1016/j.jmsy.2021.02.002

Lu, C. L., Bing, L. D., Lam, W., Chan, K., & Gu, Y. (2013). Web entity detection for semi-structured text data records with unlabeled data. *International Journal of Computational Linguistics and Applications*, *4*(2), 135–150.

Mahfuzul, M., & Shamim, I. (2024). Artificial Intelligence in Project Management: Enhancing Efficiency and Decision-Making. *International Journal of Management Information Systems and Data Science, 1*(1), 1–6. DOI: 10.62304/ijmisds.v1i1.107

Makasarwala, H. A., & Hazari, P. (2016). Using genetic algorithm for load balancing in cloud computing. *2016 8th International Conference on Electronics, Computers and Artificial Intelligence (ECAI)*, 1-6. DOI: 10.1109/ECAI.2016.7861166

Malatji, M., Marnewick, A. L., & Von Solms, S. (2022). Cybersecurity capabilities for critical infrastructure resilience. *Information and Computer Security, 30*(2), 255–279. DOI: 10.1108/ICS-06-2021-0091

Manning, C. D., Raghavan, P., & Schütze, H. (2008). *Introduction to Information Retrieval*. Cambridge University Press. DOI: 10.1017/CBO9780511809071

Mao, J., & Feng, S. (2018). Condition-based load balancing algorithm in distributed rendering. *2018 IEEE 3rd Advanced Information Technology, Electronic and Automation Control Conference (IAEAC)*, 1133-1139. DOI: 10.1109/IAEAC.2018.8577231

McGrath, K. (2024). The Golden Circle: A case study of organizational change at the London Ambulance Service. *AIS Electronic Library (AISeL)*. https://aisel.aisnet.org/ecis2001/52/

Mikolov, T., Sutskever, I., Chen, K., Corrado, G. S., & Dean, J. (2013). Distributed Representations of Words and Phrases and Their Compositionality. *Advances in Neural Information Processing Systems (NeurIPS'13)*, 3111–3119.

Mircoserve. (2024, August 21). *CrowdStrike Incident: What Happened And What Did We Learn? | Microserve Canada*. Microserve Canada. https://www.microserve.ca/blog/crowdstrike-incident-summary-and-lessons/

Mishra, A., Alzoubi, Y. I., Gill, A. Q., & Anwar, M. J. (2022). Cybersecurity Enterprises Policies: A Comparative Study. *Sensors (Basel), 22*(2), 1–35. DOI: 10.3390/s22020538 PMID: 35062504

Misra, N. N., Dixit, Y., Al-Mallahi, A., Bhullar, M. S., Upadhyay, R., & Martynenko, A. (2022). IoT, Big Data, and Artificial Intelligence in Agriculture and Food Industry. *IEEE Internet of Things Journal, 9*(9), 6305–6324. DOI: 10.1109/JIOT.2020.2998584

Mohapatra, H. (2025). The role of 6G in empowering smart cities enabling ubiquitous connectivity and intelligent infrastructure. *Advances in Wireless Technologies and Telecommunication*, 231–254. DOI: 10.4018/979-8-3693-8799-3.ch008

Mohapatra, H., & Mishra, S. R. (2024). Analysis of sector-specific responses of AI generative. In Generative, A. I. (Ed.), *Current Trends and Applications* (pp. 167–184). Springer Nature Singapore. DOI: 10.1007/978-981-97-8460-8_9

Mohapatra, H., & Mishra, S. R. (2024). Unlocking insights: Exploring data analytics and AI tool performance across industries. In *Data analytics and machine learning: Navigating the big data landscape* (pp. 265–288). Springer Nature Singapore. DOI: 10.1007/978-981-97-0448-4_13

Molyneaux, I. (2014). *The Art of Application Performance Testing*. O'Reilly. Google Books. https://books.google.com/books?hl=en&lr=&id=187UBQAAQBAJ&oi=fnd&pg=PR3&dq=Molyneaux

Montealegre, R., & Keil, M. (2000). Deescalating information technology projects: Lessons from the Denver International Airport. *Management Information Systems Quarterly*, *24*(3), 417–447. DOI: 10.2307/3250968

Moradbeiky, A., (2020). *Open hybrid model: A new ensemble model for software development cost estimation*. Computing and Informatics., DOI: 10.31577/cai_2020_6_1148

Müller, J. M., Kiel, D., & Voigt, K. I. (2018). What drives the implementation of Industry 4.0? The role of opportunities and challenges in the context of sustainability. *Sustainability (Basel)*, *10*(1), 247. DOI: 10.3390/su10010247

Munir, S., Kollnig, K., Shuba, A., & Shafiq, Z. (2024, April 4). *Google's Chrome Antitrust Paradox*. ArXiv.org. https://arxiv.org/abs/2406.11856

Murthi, S. (2002, September). Preventive risk management software for software projects. *IT Professional*, *4*(5), 9–15. DOI: 10.1109/MITP.2002.1041172

Nahavandi, S. (2019). Industry 5.0—A Human-Centric Solution. *Sustainability (Basel)*, *11*(16), 4371. DOI: 10.3390/su11164371

Nakamoto, S. (2008). Bitcoin: A Peer-to-Peer Electronic Cash System. Retrieved from: https://bitcoin.org/bitcoin.pdf

Naren, A. K., Kathirvel, A., & Santhoshi, B. (2024). Chapter 5: Critical Approaches to Data Engineering Systems Innovation and Industry Application Using IoT. In Critical Approaches to Data Engineering Systems and Analysis, Hershey, PA: IGI Global, 2024.DoI: DOI: 10.4018/979-8-3693-2260-4.ch005

Naseer, N. I. (2024). The crowdstrike incident: Analysis and unveiling the intricacies of modern cybersecurity breaches. *World Journal of Advanced Engineering Technology and Sciences*, *13*(1), 728–733. DOI: 10.30574/wjaets.2024.13.1.0473

Nega, A. T. (2019). The trend of software cost estimation in Ethiopia case study: Addis Ababa. *International Journal of Engineering and Computer Science*. DOI: 10.18535/ijecs/v8i12.4413

Nenni, M. E., De Felice, F., De Luca, C., & Forcina, A. (2024). How artificial intelligence will transform project management in the age of digitization: A systematic literature review. *Management Review Quarterly*, *75*(2), 1669–1716. DOI: 10.1007/s11301-024-00418-z

Neumann, P. G. (2000). Practical architectures for survivable systems and networks. Prepared by SRI International for the US Army Research Laboratory. https://shorturl.at/l6vOg

Nimbalkar, S., Guo, W., & Petri, C., (2017). *Innovative manufacturing technologies and data analytics for improving energy efficiency in industrial energy systems*. Oak Ridge National Laboratory.

NIST. (2012). *Computer security incident handling guide (Special Publication 800-61 Revision 2)*. National Institute of Standards and Technology.

NIST. (2018). *Framework for improving critical infrastructure cybersecurity (Version 1.1)*. National Institute of Standards and Technology.

NIST. (2018). *Risk management framework for information systems and organizations: A system life cycle approach for security and privacy (Special Publication 800-37 Revision 2)*. National Institute of Standards and Technology.

NIST. (2020). *Zero trust architecture (SP 800-207)*. National Institute of Standards and Technology.

Nolan, L. (2024, July 29). *Consequences of Compliance: The CrowdStrike Outage of 19 July 2024*. USENIX. https://www.usenix.org/publications/loginonline/consequences-compliance-crowdstrike-outage-19-july-2024

Nordhaus, W. (2017). Integrated assessment models of climate change. NBER Reporter, pp. 16, 16–20.

Nordli, E. T., Haugeland, S. G., Nguyen, P. H., Song, H., & Chauvel, F. (2023). Migrating monoliths to cloud-native microservices for customizable SaaS. *Information and Software Technology*, *160*, 107230. https://doi.org/https://doi.org/10.1016/j.infsof.2023.107230. DOI: 10.1016/j.infsof.2023.107230

Nurdiani, I., (2011, August). Risk identification and risk mitigation instruments for global software development: Systematic review and survey results. *2011 IEEE Sixth International Conference on Global Software Engineering Workshop*, 36–41. DOI: 10.1109/ICGSE-W.2011.16

Office of Government Commerce (OGC). (2011). *ITIL Service Design* (2nd ed.). The Stationery Office.

Office of Government Commerce (OGC). (2011). *ITIL Service Operation* (2nd ed.). The Stationery Office.

Office of Government Commerce (OGC). (2011). *ITIL Service Strategy* (2nd ed.). The Stationery Office.

Ogbanufe, O. M., & Baham, C. (2023). Using Multi-Factor Authentication for Online Account Security: Examining the Influence of Anticipated Regret. *Information Systems Frontiers*, *25*(2), 897–916. DOI: 10.1007/s10796-022-10278-1

Olszewski, L., & Wingreen, S. C. (2011). The FBI Sentinel Project. *Journal of Cases on Information Technology*, *13*(3), 84–102. DOI: 10.4018/jcit.2011070105

Ozkan, N., Bal, S., Erdogan, T. G., & Gok, M. S. (2022). Scrum, Kanban or a Mix of Both? A Systematic Literature Review. *Proceedings of the 17th Conference on Computer Science and Intelligence Systems, FedCSIS 2022*, 883–893. DOI: 10.15439/2022F143

Padmaja, K., & Seshadri, R. (2021). Analytics on real time security attacks in healthcare, retail and banking applications in the cloud. *Evolutionary Intelligence*, *14*(2), 595–605. DOI: 10.1007/s12065-019-00337-z

Pallavi, G. B., & Jayarekha, P. (2022). Secure and efficient multi-tenant database management system for cloud computing environment. *International Journal of Information Technology : an Official Journal of Bharati Vidyapeeth's Institute of Computer Applications and Management*, *14*(2), 703–711. DOI: 10.1007/s41870-019-00416-5

Pan, Y., & Zhang, L. (2022). Integrating BIM and AI for Smart Construction Management: Current Status and Future Directions. *Archives of Computational Methods in Engineering 2022 30:2*, *30*(2), 1081–1110. DOI: 10.1007/s11831-022-09830-8

Parkinson, C. N. (1957). *Parkinson's law: The pursuit of progress*. John Murray.

Park, J., Kim, U., Yun, D., & Yeom, K. (2020). Approach for Selecting and Integrating Cloud Services to Construct Hybrid Cloud. *Journal of Grid Computing*, *18*(3), 441–469. DOI: 10.1007/s10723-020-09519-x

Paulheim, H. (2017). Knowledge graph refinement: A survey of approaches and evaluation methods. *Semantic Web*, *8*(3), 489–508. DOI: 10.3233/SW-160218

Pennington, J., Socher, R., & Manning, C. (2014). GloVe: Global Vectors for Word Representation. *Proceedings of the 2014 Conference on Empirical Methods in Natural Language Processing (EMNLP)*, 1532–1543. DOI: 10.3115/v1/D14-1162

Pérez-Fortes, M., Moya, J. A., Vatopoulos, K., & Tzimas, E. (2014). CO2 capture and utilization in cement and iron and steel industries. *Energy Procedia*, *63*, 6534–6543. DOI: 10.1016/j.egypro.2014.11.689

Piccarozzi, M., Aquilani, B., & Gatti, C. (2018). Industry 4.0 in management studies: A systematic literature review. *Sustainability (Basel)*, *10*(10), 3821. DOI: 10.3390/su10103821

Plex Systems Inc. (n.d.). Plex manufacturing cloud. Retrieved from https://www.plex.com/

Poniszewska-Maranda, A., Matusiak, R., Kryvinska, N., & Yasar, A. U. H. (2020). A real-time service system in the cloud. *Journal of Ambient Intelligence and Humanized Computing*, *11*(3), 961–977. DOI: 10.1007/s12652-019-01203-7

Preston, W. C. (2007). Backup and Recovery: Inexpensive Backup Solutions for Open Systems. *Backup and Recovery*. (2025). O'Reilly. Google Books. https://books.google.com/books?hl=en&lr=&id=QgpIAgAAQBAJ&oi=fnd&pg=PR7&dq=Preston

Qiu, X., Sun, T., Xu, Y., Shao, Y., Dai, N., & Huang, X. (2020). Pre-trained Models for Natural Language Processing: A Survey. [JAIR]. *Journal of Artificial Intelligence Research*, *57*, 361–437.

Rada, R. (1986). Gradualness eases refinement of medical knowledge. *Medical Informatics*, *11*(1), 59–73. DOI: 10.3109/14639238608994975 PMID: 3515072

Radoglou-Grammatikis, P., Sarigiannidis, P., Iturbe, E., Rios, E., Martinez, S., Sarigiannidis, A., Eftathopoulos, G., Spyridis, Y., Sesis, A., Vakakis, N., Tzovaras, D., Kafetzakis, E., Giannoulakis, I., Tzifas, M., Giannakoulias, A., Angelopoulos, M., & Ramos, F. (2021). SPEAR SIEM: A Security Information and Event Management system for the Smart Grid. *Computer Networks*, *193*, 108008. DOI: 10.1016/j.comnet.2021.108008

Rahman, M., Sarwar, H., Kader, A., Goncalves, T., & Tin, T. T. (2024). Review and Empirical Analysis of Machine Learning-Based Software Effort Estimation. *IEEE Access : Practical Innovations, Open Solutions*, *12*, 85661–85680. DOI: 10.1109/ACCESS.2024.3404879

Raj, S., Sheel, S., Singh, R., Ashar, S., & Mohapatra, H. (2025). Securing smart cities. *New Horizons in Leadership*, 487-512. DOI: 10.4018/979-8-3693-6437-6.ch021

Rajput, S. S., & Kushwah, V. S. (2016). A genetic based improved load balanced MIN-MIN task scheduling algorithm for load balancing in cloud computing. *2016 8th International Conference on Computational Intelligence and Communication Networks (CICN)*, 677-681. DOI: 10.1109/CICN.2016.139

Ren, X., Zhang, Y., He, S., & Sun, M. (2021). Denoising Multi-source Distant Supervision for Relation Extraction. [TACL]. *Transactions of the Association for Computational Linguistics*, *9*, 1–16.

Ribeiro, M. T., Singh, S., & Guestrin, C. (2016). "Why Should I Trust You?" Explaining the Predictions of Any Classifier. *Proceedings of the 22nd ACM SIGKDD International Conference on Knowledge Discovery and Data Mining (KDD'16)*, 1135-1144.

Rimal, B. P., Choi, E., & Lumb, I. (2009). A taxonomy and survey of cloud computing systems. *2009 Fifth International Joint Conference on INC, IMS and IDC*, 44-51. DOI: 10.1109/NCM.2009.218

Rithik, G., Kathirvel, A., & Naren, A. K. (2024). The IoT of Robotics: The Frontier of Automation. In *Artificial Intelligence-Enabled Digital Twin for Smart Manufacturing, Wiley Publiser- Scrivener Publishing LLC, Online*. Print., DOI: 10.1002/9781394303601.ch13

Rittinghouse, J. W., & Hancock, W. M. (2025). *Cybersecurity Operations Handbook*. Elsevier Digital Press. Google Books. https://books.google.com/books?hl=en&lr=&id=BKYSfjEsi78C&oi=fnd&pg=PP1&dq=CISM

Rospocher, M., Van Erp, M., Vossen, P., Fokkens, A., Aldabe, I., Rigau, G., Soroa, A., Ploeger, T., & Bogaard, T. (2016). Building event-centric knowledge graphs from news. *Journal of Web Semantics*, *37*, 132–151. DOI: 10.1016/j.websem.2015.12.004

Rupprecht, L., Reiser, A., & Kemper, A. (2012). Dynamic load balancing in data grids by global load estimation. *2012 11th International Symposium on Parallel and Distributed Computing*, 243-250. DOI: 10.1109/ISPDC.2012.40

Russell, S. J., & Norvig, P. (2020). *Artificial Intelligence: A Modern Approach* (4th ed.). Pearson.

Saadat, A., & Masehian, E. (2019). Load balancing in cloud computing using genetic algorithm and fuzzy logic. *2019 International Conference on Computational Science and Computational Intelligence (CSCI)*, 1435-1440. DOI: 10.1109/CSCI49370.2019.00268

Sah, R. K., Singh, A. K., Yadav, A. K., & Mohapatra, H. (2024). Cloud-enabled platforms for social and civic engagement in smart urban environments. *Advances in Electronic Government, Digital Divide, and Regional Development*, 215–234. DOI: 10.4018/979-8-3693-6740-7.ch009

Salam, A. (2020). *Internet of Things in sustainable energy systems. In the Internet of Things for Sustainable Community Development*. Springer.

Salton, G., & McGill, M. J. (1983). *Introduction to Modern Information Retrieval*. McGraw-Hill.

Saravanos, A., & Curinga, M. X. (2023). Simulating the Software Development Lifecycle: The Waterfall Model. *Applied System Innovation 2023, Vol. 6, Page 108, 6*(6), 108. DOI: 10.3390/asi6060108

Sarmiento, J. R. R., Monroy, J., Moreno, F.-A., Galindo, C., Bonelo, J.-M., & González-Jiménez, J. (2020). *A predictive model for maintaining industrial machinery in the context of Sendler, U. (2017). The Internet Internets: IThingsie 4.0 unleashed*. Springer.

Sebastiani, F. (2002). Machine Learning in Automated Text Categorization. *ACM Computing Surveys*, *34*(1), 1–47. DOI: 10.1145/505282.505283

Sequeda, J. F., Briggs, W. J., Miranker, D. P., & Heideman, W. P. (2019). A pay-as-you-go methodology to design and build enterprise knowledge graphs from relational databases. In *The Semantic Web-ISWC 2019: 18th International Semantic Web Conference* (pp. 526-545). Springer International Publishing. DOI: 10.1007/978-3-030-30796-7_32

Serhiienko, O., Mashchenko, M., Samorodov, B., Babichev, A., & Klimenko, O. (2024). Simulation and Optimisation of Business Process Management: Case Study of IT Company. *Business Systems Research*, *15*(1), 67–90. DOI: 10.2478/bsrj-2024-0004

Shah, P. (2015, March 23). The pains of government technology: An investigation into the rollout of Healthcare.gov. *Duke.edu*. https://dukespace.lib.duke.edu/items/891d4d18-55cd-44a8-83a0-18bf2b79e108

Shekhar, S., & Kumar, U. (2016, May 17). Review of various software cost estimation techniques. *International Journal of Computer Applications*, *141*(11), 31–34. DOI: 10.5120/ijca2016909867

Shen, Y., Yang, L., & Deng, B. (2024). NLP-Driven Sentiment Analysis for Stakeholder Feedback in Sustainable Projects. *2024 6th International Conference on Frontier Technologies of Information and Computer, ICFTIC 2024*, 713–716. DOI: 10.1109/ICFTIC64248.2024.10913250

Sheridan, K., Clark, K., & Williams, A. (2021). Designing AI learning through empathy and creativity: A design thinking approach. *Journal of the Learning Sciences, 30*(3), 341–366. DOI: 10.1080/10508406.2021.1879935

Shoushtari Bu-Ali, F., Daghighi, A., Ghafourian, E., & Shoushtari, F. (2024). Application of Artificial Intelligence in Project Management. *International Journal of Industrial Engineering and Operational Research.* http://ijieor.ir

Sidana, S., Tiwari, N., Gupta, A., & Kushwaha, I. S. (2016). NBST algorithm: A load balancing algorithm in cloud computing. *2016 International Conference on Computing, Communication and Automation (ICCCA)*, 1178-1181. DOI: 10.1109/CCAA.2016.7813914

Silvis-Cividjian, N. (2024). Therac-25 accidents: We keep on learning from them. *Computer, 57*(12), 69–78. DOI: 10.1109/MC.2024.3450197

Singh, S., Sanwar Hosen, A. S. M., & Yoon, B. (2021). Blockchain Security Attacks, Challenges, and Solutions for the Future Distributed IoT Network. *IEEE Access : Practical Innovations, Open Solutions, 9*, 13938–13959. DOI: 10.1109/ACCESS.2021.3051602

Sivasankari, S., & Aneetha, A. (2024). Ant colony optimization-load balancing in cloud computing. *2024 Third International Conference on Distributed Computing and Electrical Circuits and Electronics (ICDCECE)*, 1-4. DOI: 10.1109/ICDCECE60827.2024.10549182

Sohrabi, H., & Noorzai, E. (2024). Risk-supported case-based reasoning approach for cost overrun estimation of water-related projects using machine learning. *Engineering, Construction, and Architectural Management, 31*(2), 544–570. DOI: 10.1108/ECAM-05-2022-0450

Sommerville, I. (2011). *Software engineering* (9th ed.). Addison-Wesley.

Sravanthi, J., Sobti, R., Semwal, A., Shravan, M., Al-Hilali, A. A., & Bader Alazzam, M. (2023). AI-Assisted Resource Allocation in Project Management. *2023 3rd International Conference on Advance Computing and Innovative Technologies in Engineering, ICACITE 2023*, 70–74. DOI: 10.1109/ICACITE57410.2023.10182760

Srinivas, M., & Patnaik, L. (1994). Adaptive probabilities of crossover and mutation in genetic algorithms. *IEEE Transactions on Systems, Man, and Cybernetics, 24*(4), 656–667. DOI: 10.1109/21.286385

Stanford Law School. (2019). *TTLF Working Paper Series | Stanford Law School.* Stanford Law School. https://law.stanford.edu/transatlantic-technology-law-forum/ttlfs-working-paper-series/

Strickroth, S., Kreidenweis, M., & Wurm, Z. (2023). Learning from Agile Methods: Using a Kanban Board for Classroom Orchestration. *Lecture Notes in Networks and Systems, 633 LNNS*, 68–79. DOI: 10.1007/978-3-031-26876-2_7

Subramaniam, M., Kathirvel, A., Sabitha, E., & Anwar Basha, H. (2021). "Modified Firefly Algorithm and Fuzzy C-Mean Clustering Based Semantic Information Retrieval", Journal of Web Engineering, Vol. 20 1, 33–52. DOI: 10.13052/jwe1540-9589.2012

Sundar, R. and Kathirvel, A. (2020a), "Aggressively delivered mechanism over variable length density using a simulated annealing algorithm in mobile ad hoc network", Transactions on Emerging Telecommunications Technologies, pp. 1 – 13. Wiley-Blackwell. DOI: 10.1002/ett.3863

Swartz, A. J. (1996). Airport 95. *Software Engineering Notes, 21*(2), 79–83. DOI: 10.1145/227531.227544

Tan, P. N., Steinbach, M., & Kumar, V. (2005). *Introduction to Data Mining*. Pearson.

Töpper, G., Knuth, M., & Sack, H. (2012). DBpedia ontology enrichment for inconsistency detection. In *Proceedings of the 8th International Conference on Semantic Systems*, 33-40. DOI: 10.1145/2362499.2362505

Tully, J., Selzer, J., Phillips, J. P., O'Connor, P., & Dameff, C. (2020). Healthcare Challenges in the Era of Cybersecurity. *Health Security, 18*(3), 228–231. DOI: 10.1089/hs.2019.0123 PMID: 32559153

Uchendu, B., Nurse, J. R. C., Bada, M., & Furnell, S. (2021). Developing a cyber security culture: Current practices and future needs. *Computers & Security, 109*(1), 102387. DOI: 10.1016/j.cose.2021.102387

Uddin, S., Yan, S., & Lu, H. (2024). Machine learning and deep learning in project analytics: Methods, applications and research trends. *Production Planning and Control*. DOI: 10.1080/09537287.2024.2320790;PAGE:STRING:ARTICLE/CHAPTER

Utting, M., & Legeard, B. (2010). Practical model-based testing: a tools approach. Elsevier. (2025). https://books.google.com/books?hl=en&lr=&id=8hAGtY4-oOoC&oi=fnd&pg=PP1&dq=Utting

Vaniea, K., & Rashidi, Y. (2016). Tales of Software Updates. *Proceedings of the 2016 CHI Conference on Human Factors in Computing Systems - CHI '16*, 3215–3226. DOI: 10.1145/2858036.2858303

Varga, S., Barreto, G., & Battaglin, P. D. (2020). A holistic IT infrastructure management framework. *International Journal on Computer Science and Engineering*, *21*(1), 1–9. DOI: 10.1504/IJCSE.2020.105222

Vasudev, R., Harini, N., & Neethu, M. R. (2023). Multi-Factor Authentication System With ID Card Credentials For Secure Transactions. In *2023 14th International Conference on Computing Communication and Networking Technologies, ICCCNT 2023*. DOI: 10.1109/ICCCNT56998.2023.10308252

Vaswani, A., Shazeer, N., Parmar, N., Uszkoreit, J., Jones, L., Gomez, A. N., Kaiser, Ł., & Polosukhin, I. (2017). Attention Is All You Need. *Advances in Neural Information Processing Systems (NeurIPS'17)*, 5998–6008.

Waibel, M., Steenkamp, L., Moloko, N., & Oosthuizen, G. (2017). Investigating the Effects of Smart Production Systems on Sustainability Elements. *Procedia Manufacturing*, *8*, 731–737. DOI: 10.1016/j.promfg.2017.02.094

Wang, S., Wan, J., Li, D., & Zhang, C. (2016). Implementing Smart Factory of Industrie 4.0: An Outlook. Int. J. Distrib. Sens. Netw., p. 12, 3159805–3159810.

Wang, T., Liu, Z., Chen, Y., Xu, Y., & Dai, X. (2014). Load balancing task scheduling based on genetic algorithm in cloud computing. *2014 IEEE 12th International Conference on Dependable, Autonomic and Secure Computing*, 146-152. DOI: 10.1109/DASC.2014.35

Wang, A. Z., Scherr, K. A., Wong, C. A., & Ubel, P. A. (2017). Poor consumer comprehension and plan selection inconsistencies under the 2016 HealthCare. gov choice architecture. *MDM Policy & Practice*, *2*(1), 238146831771644. DOI: 10.1177/2381468317716441 PMID: 29892710

Wara, M. (2007). Is the global carbon market working? *Nature*, *445*(7128), 595–596. DOI: 10.1038/445595a PMID: 17287794

WCED. (n,d). Our common future. Retrieved from https://sustainabledevelopment .un.org/content/documents/5987our-common-future.pdf

Wided, A., Çelebi, N., & Fatima, B. (2023). Effective cloudlet scheduling algorithm for load balancing in cloud computing using fuzzy logic. *Advances in Information Security, Privacy, and Ethics*, 226–243. DOI: 10.4018/979-8-3693-0593-5.ch010

Wilner, A. S., Luce, H., Ouellet, E., Williams, O., & Costa, N. (2021). From public health to cyber hygiene: Cybersecurity and Canada's healthcare sector. *International Journal (Toronto, Ont.)*, *76*(4), 522–543. DOI: 10.1177/00207020211067946

Wismann, S. T., Engbæk, J. S., Vendelbo, S. B., Bendixen, F. B., Eriksen, W. L., Aasberg-Petersen, K., Frandsen, C., Chorkendorff, I., & Mortensen, P. M. (2019). Electrified methane reforming: A compact approach to greener industrial hydrogen production. *Science*, *364*(6442), 756–759. DOI: 10.1126/science.aaw8775 PMID: 31123131

Witten, I. H., Frank, E., Hall, M. A., & Pal, C. J. (2016). *Data Mining: Practical Machine Learning Tools and Techniques* (4th ed.). Morgan Kaufmann.

Yahya, N., & Maidin, S. S. (2022). The Waterfall Model with Agile Scrum as the Hybrid Agile Model for the Software Engineering Team. *2022 10th International Conference on Cyber and IT Service Management, CITSM 2022*. DOI: 10.1109/CITSM56380.2022.9936036

Yang, Z., Dai, Z., Yang, Y., Carbonell, J., Salakhutdinov, R., & Le, Q. V. (2019). XLNet: Generalized Autoregressive Pretraining for Language Understanding. *Advances in Neural Information Processing Systems (NeurIPS'19)*, 5753–5763.

Yang, J., Ye, Y., Li, X., Lü, X., & Chen, R. (2018). Flexible, conductive, and highly pressure-sensitive graphene-polyimide foam for pressure sensor application. *Composites Science and Technology*, *164*, 187–194. DOI: 10.1016/j.compscitech.2018.05.044

Yang, P., Xiong, N., & Ren, J. (2020). Data Security and Privacy Protection for Cloud Storage: A Survey. *IEEE Access : Practical Innovations, Open Solutions*, *8*, 131723–131740. DOI: 10.1109/ACCESS.2020.3009876

Yin, W., Kann, K., Yu, M., & Schütze, H. (2017). Comparative Study of CNN and RNN for Natural Language Processing. *Proceedings of the 56th Annual Meeting of the Association for Computational Linguistics (ACL'17)*, 1543–1552.

Zahavy, T., Ben-Zrihem, N., & Mannor, S. (2016). Graying the black box: Understanding DQNs. *Proceedings of the International Conference on Machine Learning (ICML'16)*, 1899–1908.

Zakaria, N. A., et al. (2021). Optimized COCOMO parameters using hybrid particle swarm optimization. *International Journal of Advances in Intelligent Informatics*. DOI: 10.26555/ijain.v7i2.583

Zardari, S. (2009). Software risk management. *2009 International Conference on Information Management and Engineering*, 375–379. DOI: 10.1109/ICIME.2009.138

Zawacki-Richter, O., Marín, V. I., Bond, M., & Gouverneur, F. (2019). Systematic review of research on artificial intelligence applications in higher education. *International Journal of Educational Technology in Higher Education*, *16*(1), 1–27. DOI: 10.1186/s41239-019-0171-0

Zhai, C., & Massung, S. (2016). *Text Data Management and Analysis: A Practical Introduction to Information Retrieval and Text Mining*. ACM Books. McCallum, A., & Nigam, K. (1998). A Comparison of Event Models for Naive Bayes Text Classification. *AAAI-98 Workshop on Learning for Text Categorization*, 41-48. DOI: 10.1145/2915031

Zhang, X., Ao, X., Cai, W., et al. (2019). A sustainability evaluation method integrating the energy, economy, and environment in remanufacturing systems. Journal of Cleaner Production, p. 239, 118100.

Zhang, Y., & Wallace, B. C. (2017). A Sensitivity Analysis of (and Practitioners' Guide to) Convolutional Neural Networks for Sentence Classification. *Proceedings of the 8th International Joint Conference on Natural Language Processing (EMNLP'17)*, 253–263.

Zheng, M., Hong, Q., & Shoubao, Y. (2013). A flexible load-balancing traffic grooming algorithm in service overlay network. *2013 International Conference on Cloud Computing and Big Data*, 211-216. DOI: 10.1109/CLOUDCOM-ASIA.2013.19

Zhou, J., Zhou, Y., Wang, B., & Zang, J. (2019). Human–cyber–physical systems (HCPSs) in the context of new-generation intelligent manufacturing. *Engineering (Beijing)*, *5*(4), 624–636. DOI: 10.1016/j.eng.2019.07.015

Zhu, F. (2023). Cloud computing load balancing based on improved genetic algorithm. *International Journal of Global Energy Issues*, *1*(1), 1. DOI: 10.1504/IJGEI.2023.10054590

About the Contributors

Rahul Patel is a seasoned Educator, Author, and practitioner in Information Technology Management and Cyber Security with over 25 years of experience. Rahul Patel holds a PhD in Management of Information Systems from Northcentral University and professional cybersecurity certifications CISM and CISSP. Currently Rahul Patel is associated with Illinois Institute of Technology and University of Arizona Global Campus.

***

A. Mohan, Professor, Department of Computer Science and Engineering, SIMATS Engineering, Saveetha University, Chennai 602105.

Munir Ahmad is a seasoned professional in the realm of Spatial Data Infrastructure (SDI), Geo-Information Productions, Information Systems, and Information Governance, boasting over 25 years of dedicated experience in the field. With a PhD in Computer Science, Dr. Ahmad's expertise spans Spatial Data Production, Management, Processing, Analysis, Visualization, and Quality Control. Throughout his career, Dr. Ahmad has been deeply involved in the development and deployment of SDI systems specially in the context of Pakistan, leveraging his proficiency in Spatial Database Design, Web, Mobile & Desktop GIS, and Geo Web Services Architecture. His contributions to Volunteered Geographic Information (VGI) and Open Source Geoportal & Metadata Portal have significantly enriched the geospatial community. As a trainer and researcher, Dr. Ahmad has authored over 50 publications, advancing the industry's knowledge base and fostering innovation in Geo-Tech, Data Governance, and Information Infrastructure, and Emerging Technologies. His commitment to Research and Development (R&D) is evident in his role as a dedicated educator and mentor in the field.

Adnan Ibrahim Alrabea received the Dr. Eng. Degree in 2004 from the Electronic and Communication Department, Faculty of Engineering, Donetsk University, Ukraine. He is Visiting Associate Professor, Vice 0f Dean and assistant of dean at Prince Abdullah Bin Ghazi College of Communications and Information Technology at Al-Balqa Applied University, As-Salt, Jordan. His research interests cover: analyzing the various types of analytic and discrete event simulation techniques, performance evaluation of communication networks, application of intelligent techniques in managing computer communication network, and performing comparative studies between various policies and strategies of routing, congestion control, sub netting of computer communication networks. He published 30 articles in various refereed international journals and conferences covering: Computer Networks, Expert Systems, Software Agents, E-learning, Image processing, wireless sensor networks and Pattern Recognition. Also, in the current time, he is too interested in making a lot of scientific research in wireless sensor networks in view point of enhancing its algorithms of congestion control as well as routing protocols.

Anto Lourdu Xavier Raj Arockia Selvarathinam is a Healthcare and AI Researcher currently serving as a Research Assistant at Grand Valley State University, College of Computing, Department of Data Science and Analytics. His research focuses on predictive modeling, multimodal learning, and explainable AI techniques to advance patient outcomes in clinical settings. Anto has contributed as a peer reviewer and editorial member for Q1 journals including Scientific Reports, Frontiers, Elsevier, and Springer. He has published and reviewed works in areas such as Alzheimer's disease diagnosis, medical imaging, health informatics, and drug discovery using GANs and LLMs. A verified ORCID member and IEEE contributor, he is actively involved in global scientific publishing and peer review to support rigorous, interdisciplinary AI research in healthcare.

Yahia Atig pursued his higher studies in Computer Science, obtaining his Engineer degree from Saida University, Algeria, in 2009, followed by a Magister degree from ESI-Algiers in 2013. He later completed his Ph.D. in Computer Science at Sidi Bel Abbes University, Algeria, in 2022. Since then, he has been attached to the Institute of Sciences, Department of Computer Science, at the University Center of Naama as a Lecturer. His research expertise spans semantic web, linked data, ontology engineering, knowledge management, and information systems.

Kathirvel Ayyaswamy, acquired, B.E.(CSE), M.E. (CSE) from Crescent Engineering College affiliated to University of Madras and Ph. D (CSE.) from Anna University. He is currently working as Professor, Dept of Computer Science and

Engineering, Saveetha Engineering College, Chennai. In-charge for CSE Cyber Forensics Research Group. He is a studious researcher by himself, completed 18 sponsored research projects worth of Rs 103 lakhs and published more than 110 articles in journals and conferences. 6 research scholars have completed Ph. D and 7 under progress under his guidance. He is working as scientific and editorial board member of many journals. He has reviewed dozens of papers in many journals. He has author of 13 books. His research interests are protocol development for wireless ad hoc networks, security in ad hoc network, data communication and networks, mobile computing, wireless networks, WSN and DTN. He is a Life member of the ISTE (India), IACSIT (Singapore), Life Member IAENG (Hong Kong), Member ICST (Europe), IAES, etc. He has given a number of guest lecturers/expert talks and seminars, workshops and symposiums.

Çiğdem Bakır received the B.S. degree in computer engineering from the University of Sakarya, in 2010, and the M.S. and Ph.D. degrees in computer engineering from Yildiz Technical University, Istanbul. She is currently pursuing the doctorate degree in computer science with the University of Yildiz Technical, Istanbul. She has been an Assistant Professor with the Software Engineering Department, Dumlupinar University, since 2021. Her research interests include information security, distributed database, big data, blockchain technology, cloud computing, and computer networks.

A Prabhu Chakkaravarthy was born on 18th February 1985 in Tamilnadu, India. He received his Ph.D. in Computer Science and Engineering from Sathyabama Institute of Science and Technology, Chennai, India. He is graduated from Anna University, Chennai in 2007 with the Bachelor of Technology degree in Computer Science and Engineering. He received the Master of Technology degree in Computer Science and Engineering from Sathyabama University, Chennai in 2012 with Distinction. He is currently working as an Assistant Professor in Networking and Communications, SRM Institute of Science and Technology, Kattankulathur, Chennai, India. He has published more than 70 research papers in national, international conferences, journals including 8 in Science Citation Indexed journals with 120 citations. He has published 10 patents, 2 patents granted. His research interests include IoT, Artificial Intelligence, Deep Learning, Data Science, Signal Processing and Image Processing.

Maurice Dawson is an Assistant Professor of Information Technology and Management within the School of Applied Technology at Illinois Institute of Technology. Additionally, he serves as Director and Distinguished Member of the IIT Center for Cyber Security and Forensics Education (C2SAFE) and responsible for working with the faculty who are members of this center. He has a Doctor of Computer Science from Colorado Technical University and a Doctor of Philosophy in Cyber Security from the Intelligent Systems Research Centre at London Metropolitan University. Additionally, he is the co-editor of Developing Next-Generation Countermeasures for Homeland Security Threat Prevention, and New Threats and Countermeasures in Digital Crime and Cyber Terrorism, published by IGI Global in 2017, and 2015 respectively. Dawson has received a Fulbright Scholar Grant to the School of Electrical Engineering and Computer Science at South Ural State University in Russia in 2015 for Business Intelligence and more recently an award to the College of Computer & Information Science of Prince Sultan University in Saudi Arabia for cyber security for the period of 2017-2018.

J. Dhanalakshmi was born on 6 th September 1992 in Tamilnadu, India. She received the B.E. degree in Computer Science and Engineering and M.E. degree in Computer Science and Engineering from Anna University, Tamil Nadu, India. She was ranked 31st at Anna University for her Masters degree in Computer Science and Engineering. She was a software developer at Fermtronics Technology Solutions until 2018. She completed her Ph.D. degree at the School of Computer Science and Engineering in B.S. Abdur Rahman Crescent Institute of Science and Technology, located in Chennai, India. She is currently pursuing a postdoctoral fellowship at the National Kaohsiung University of Science and Technology, which is located in Kaohsiung, Taiwan. She is currently working as an Assistant Professor in Data Science and Business Systems, SRM Institute of Science and Technology, Kattankulathur, Chennai, India. She published more than 10 research papers in International, National Journals including Conferences and Book Chapter in SCI and Scopus Indexed. Her research interests include Energy Analytics, Artificial Intelligence, Deep Learning, Data Science, Internet of Things (IOT) and Machine Learning.

Nadri Khiati pursued his higher studies in Computer Science, obtaining his Engineer degree from the University Saida, Algeria, in 2010, followed by a Magister degree from the University of Sidi Bel Abbes in 2014. He is currently completing his Ph.D. in Computer Science at the University of Sidi Bel Abbes, Algeria. He is affiliated with the Department of Computer Science, at the University of Saida as an Assistant Prefessor. His research interests include the semantic web, linked data, software engineering, and information systems.

A.V.Senthil Kumar is working as a Professor and Director, PG and Research Department of Computer Applications, Hindusthan College of Arts & Science, Coimbatore, Tamilnadu. To his credit he has industrial experience for five years and teaching experience of 27 years. He has also received his Doctor of Science (D.Sc in Computer Science). He has to his credit 50 Book Chapters, 225 papers in International and National Journals 64 papers in International Conferences in International and National Conferences, and edited 14 books and 2 Text books. He is as Associate Editor of IEEE Access. He is an Editor-in-Chief for many journals and Key Member for India, Machine Intelligence Research Lab (MIR Labs). He is an Editorial Board Member and Reviewer for various International Journals. He is also a Committee member for various International Conferences.

Aparna Kumari is associated with the Department of Computer Science and Engineering at the Institute of Technology, Nirma University, Ahmedabad, India. With over 17 years of experience in research and academia, she has established herself as a leading expert in areas such as Artificial Intelligence, Blockchain, Quantum Computing, Smart Grid Systems, Healthcare 5.0, and Electric Vehicles. She holds a Ph.D. in Computer Science and Engineering from Nirma University, and completed her M.Tech. and MCA from reputed central university Jawaharlal Nehru University, New Delhi. Dr. Kumari has authored or co-authored more than 57 research publications, including 32 papers in SCI-indexed journals and 19 papers in IEEE ComSoc-sponsored international conferences. Her research, published in renowned journals such as IEEE Network, IEEE Internet of Things Journal, and Elsevier's leading publications, has earned her a total impact factor exceeding 209. Recognized as one of the world's top 2% researchers by Stanford University (2021–2024), she is also the recipient of several prestigious awards, including the EARG Award 2024 for Excellence in Research and Development and the Shri Pralhad P. Chhabria Award 2023 (Runner-Up in the Best Woman Professional – Early Career category). She has successfully completed multiple funded research and consultancy projects, edited SCOPUS-indexed books with leading publishers like Elsevier, IGI Global, and Springer, and holds multiple national and international patents. As a committed academician, she actively mentors Ph.D. and M.Tech. scholars, serves on technical program committees of reputed international conferences such as IEEE GLOBECOM and IEEE ICC, and is regularly invited as a speaker for expert lectures and workshops across the globe.

Hitesh Mohapatra is an Associate Professor at the School of Computer Engineering, KIIT Deemed to be University, in Odisha, India. He holds a Ph.D. in Computer Science & Engineering from Veer Surendra Sai University of Technology, with a focus on designing fault-tolerant models for wireless sensor networks integrated with smart city applications. His academic journey includes a Bachelor's degree in Information Technology from B.P.U.T and a Master's degree in Computer Science & Engineering from Odisha University of Technology and Research. Dr. Mohapatra has over 15 years of experience in both academia and industry, contributing significantly to research in areas such as IoT, wireless sensor networks, fault tolerance, and smart city applications. His research has been published in various high-impact journals and conferences, with citations noted in the thousands. He has authored and co-authored over 50 research articles indexed by SCI and Scopus databases, along with several books on topics including software engineering, IoT in smart cities, and programming.

Sudha Rajesh, received her Bachelor's degree in Computer Science and Engineering from Shri Angalamman College of Engineering and Technology affiliated to Anna University, Tamil Nadu, India and Master's degree in Computer Science and Engineering from Pavendhar Bharathidasan College of Engineering and Technology affiliated to Anna University, Tamil Nadu, India. She received her Doctor of Philosophy in Faculty of Computer Science and Engineering from Sathyabama Institute of Science and Technology, Tamil Nadu, India. She is currently working as Associate Professor in the Department of Computational Intelligence in SRM Institute of Science and Technology, Chennai. She has 18+ years of experience in teaching and research. Her area of interest includes Python, Machine Learning, Data Science, Software Engineering, Software Quality Attributes and Estimation of Design Patterns and Data Mining. She published 50+ research papers in various International Journals and Conferences. She published 9 Indian Patent. She received Best Teacher Award and Research Excellence Award in 2022 and 2023 respectively. She holds the position of a reviewer and an editorial board member in reputed International Journals. She is a Life Time Member in ISTE, ACM.

Binastya Anggara Sekti has been a Lecturer at the faculty of Computer Science, at Esa Unggul University, Jakarta since 2016 and is active in the Artificial Intelligence and Information Security Study Group. He is a graduate of Informatics Engineering from the Bandung Institute of Technology and achieved a Master's Degree from Trisakti University, Jakarta. Before as a Lecture, he was an IT practitioner at several companies in Jakarta for more than 25 years. Some of the projects that have been completed are building Data Centers at Internet Service Providers . He also finished many IT projects.

Index

A

C

D

E

F

G

I

T

V

www.ingramcontent.com/pod-product-compliance
Lightning Source LLC
LaVergne TN
LVHW081331300926
849161LV00008B/1947
9798337323527